In It to Win It

STEVEN J. LAWSON

HARVEST HOUSE PUBLISHERS
EUGENE, OREGON

Cover by Dugan Design Group, Bloomington, Minnesota

Published in association with the literary agency of Wolgemuth & Associates, Inc.

IN IT TO WIN IT
Copyright © 1992, 2013 by Steven J. Lawson
Published by Harvest House Publishers
Eugene, Oregon 97402
www.harvesthousepublishers.com

Library of Congress Cataloging-in-Publication Data
Lawson, Steven J.
In it to win it / Steven J. Lawson.
   p. cm.
ISBN 978-0-7369-5352-8 (pbk.)
ISBN 978-0-7369-5353-5 (eBook)
1. Success—Religious aspects—Christianity. 2. Sports—Religious aspects—Christianity. I. Title.
BV4598.3.L39 2013
650.1—dc23
                                                              2013005871

Printed in the United States of America

13 14 15 16 17 18 19 20 21 / VP-JH / 10 9 8 7 6 5 4 3 2 1

*This book is dedicated
to my three sons,
ANDREW, JAMES, and JOHN
who bring me much joy.*

*May you run your race strong and
may your lives significantly impact this world
with the gospel of Jesus Christ.*

*"I press on toward the goal for the prize
of the upward call of God in Christ Jesus."*
PHILIPPIANS 3:14

Acknowledgments

Pete Dye, one of the world's foremost golf architects, is known for his diabolical course designs. Among these legendary layouts are PGA West, Sawgrass TPC, Kiawah Ocean Course, and Crooked Stick. One day, Dye was asked about one of his prized projects, Harbour Town at Hilton Head. Officially, the name Jack Nicklaus appears as the coarchitect with Dye.

"How much did Jack actually contribute?" asked the interviewer.

"Jack certainly helped," answered Dye. "But the course is the result of more than Jack's help. Six or seven people contributed significant input about its design—people whose names do not officially appear on the scorecards."

This book is much like that Pete Dye golf course. Many people have made key contributions, people whose names do not officially appear on the scorecard. But the comparison between a Dye course and this book do not end there.

Golf courses mature over time. Trees grow. The grass deepens. The rough thickens. So do authors.

Since this book first appeared more than twenty years ago, originally titled *Men Who Win,* a newer version is now in order. That is what you are holding in your hands.

Responsible for this new edition, I want to thank the publishing team at Harvest House. I want to thank Steve Miller, my editor, for his polishing touch, and Bob Hawkins Jr., the publisher, for supporting this project.

Moreover, I want to thank Erik Wolgemuth for making the arrangements for this to be a smooth effort.

My wife, Anne, has been my loving encourager as God's chosen helpmate. She, along with our three sons—Andrew, James, and John—and daughter, Grace Anne, have supported me in God's call upon my life.

Contents

Foreword

*I*n *It to Win It* is an important reminder of just how big a race we are involved in as Christians. Steven Lawson's biblical teaching and practical applications remind all of us how to successfully compete for the ultimate prize—bringing glory to Christ.

As Christians, we have no higher calling than that of pursuing the prize of becoming more like Christ. When we pour maximum effort and focus into this pursuit, it brings great delight to God—and to us as well. In the same way a runner gets tremendous satisfaction from a race well run, we will experience true inner fulfillment as we are diligent to excel in the Christian life.

While winning this race requires great discipline, the rewards are incredible and will last forever. Sports lover or not, this book will help to bring you closer to our Lord and teach you to "run in such a way that you may win" (1 Corinthians 9:24).

—Allyson Felix,
triple gold medalist, 2012 London Olympics

1

Out of the Rat Race...
into the Right Race

There are only two kinds of people in this world—winners and losers.

Whether it be in the world of business and the bottom line, the world of sports and the final score, or whatever the competitive arena, people want to be winners. Everything in our culture is driven by this stark reality.

No one wants to be a loser.

Everyone wants to be a *winner*.

I want to talk to you about being a winner, but not in temporal or trivial things. This book is all about winning in those things that are truly important, those things are that of eternal significance and last forever. I am talking about being a winner where it really counts—with God.

But before we go any further, I want to dispel a deadly myth. It is the false notion that being a Christian means that you automatically become a loser. Many assume that following Jesus Christ requires that you lose your competitive drive, roll over, and play dead.

But nothing could be further from the truth. The fact is, you will never truly become a winner in life until you give yourself entirely to Christ. Only then are you positioned to be a winner.

Winning is running on a new track. It is running with new direction, according to new rules, pressing to a new finish line. It is running to receive a new prize—one that you are compelled to win with a new motivation.

The apostle Paul writes, "Do you not know that those who run in a race all run, but only one receives the prize? Run in such a way that you may win" (1 Corinthians 9:24). As Christians, we still run to win. But we compete not for mere earthly accolades. Instead, we now push ahead for the applause of heaven.

When you become a Christian, you do not stop competing. As a believer in Christ, you simply run an entirely new race. God does not remove your drive to win. To the contrary, He gives you a new will to win where it really matters.

As we run, our feet still leave a trail of dust, but with a new strength that God provides. Our legs still sprint in full stride, but with new aim on the narrow path that leads to life. Our hearts still pound as we near the finish line, but our prize is an eternal crown.

From the starting blocks to the finish line, God calls us to become a winner where it counts—that is, in His eternal kingdom. He urges us to pursue His new direction for our lives. He exhorts us to run with a holy passion to win the prize of the upward call.

My desire is that God will ignite a fire within you to live victoriously in what truly matters in this life. My goal is to help you chart your course, set your pace, and point you to the finish line. My stated aim is to help you design a game plan so that you may "run in such a way that you may win."

Are you ready?

Which Race Will You Run?

We are running one of two races. We are either running the rat race, or the right race. There are no other tracks on which to run. For this reason, we must be careful which race we run. The race we choose will determine the path we take in life, which, ultimately, determines which finish line we cross and where we will spend eternity.

Jesus identified these two races when He said, "Enter through the narrow gate; for the gate is wide and the way is broad that leads to destruction, and there are many who enter through it. For the gate is small and the way is narrow that leads to life, and there are few who find it" (Matthew 7:13-14).

There are not three races in which we may run in life. Not four, not ten—only two. There are two races, two crowds, two starting points, two tracks, two finish lines.

What does this have to do with winning? you may ask.

Everything.

To be a winner, you must enter the right race. You must run on the right track. And you must win the right prize. To win the wrong race is, tragically, to lose.

I want to begin by examining this wrong race. I call it the rat race.

In Lane Number One—the Rat Race

Jesus described the rat race this way: "The gate is wide, and the way is broad that leads to destruction, and there are many who enter through it." Here it is—a wide gate, a broad way, many racers, and a destructive end.

When Jesus spoke those words two thousand years ago, He was standing on a grassy hill overlooking the Sea of Galilee. His band of obscure followers surrounded Him along with the curious multitude. As our Lord concluded this heart-searching sermon, the Sermon on the Mount, He contrasted a broad path and a narrow path. All people, He stated, are traveling one of these two paths.

In those days, most roads were nothing more than paths of dirt worn down by the constant treading of travelers. If our Lord were addressing these words to our modern generation, He would proba- bly describe the rat race as an entirely different kind of thoroughfare. This broad path might be a busy, concrete-paved, multilane interstate— maybe a major artery running through a bustling metropolitan city. Here is the updated version of the broad path—the rat race.

Bumper-to-Bumper

It is Friday afternoon, straight up five-o'clock, and you are stuck in serious rush-hour traffic. Cars are stacked up bumper-to-bumper. All eight lanes are clogged. The traffic is creeping along at a snail's pace.

This interstate is now the world's largest parking lot. Funny, but today you are not laughing.

Impatient drivers jockey back and forth from one lane to the next, seeking to find any advantage. One car darts in front of you. You jam on your brakes. It seems all you do is ride your brakes. Red brake lights have been staring you in the eyes ever since you left the office.

Suddenly the cars in your lane come to a screeching halt. There is a wreck ahead. No one is going anywhere now.

You try to switch to the next lane, but there is zero room to do so. You think, *Please, will somebody let me over?* Fat chance. You just sit tight with your blinker going.

All the while, the sun is baking down, blinding you as its glare reflects off the glassed office towers.

As you approach a major interchange, the traffic clogs up yet more. "Where do all these people live?" you mutter. Worse, you have another forty minutes before you even arrive home.

It has been one long day at the office. You spent a month there this afternoon. A stack of unfinished papers are left on your desk, buried under a pile of unreturned phone calls. The whole mess will be waiting for you on Monday morning. So will the weekly sales meeting. And you still have not met your quota.

Billboards along the expressway entice you: "Come Fly with Us." You see glorious pictures of Bermuda and Hawaii. You agree. *That is what I need—a vacation. Get out of town. A break from the rat race.*

But right now, you cannot even get out of your lane. Another billboard boasts, "We Are Ready When You Are." Ready? I am *past* ready! I am done.

This is the rat race. The fast lane in life. But today, it could not be any slower. You are one of a million varmints in search of the elusive cheese. When Jesus talked about the broad path, He probably had something like this busy highway in mind.

What is the rat race all about? Who is on it? Where is it headed? Jesus said four things about it. This rodent race is wide open, crowded, deadly, and easily accessed.

A Wide-Open Thoroughfare

First, the rat race is *wide open.*

Jesus said it is a broad path. This means the rat race is an expansive thoroughfare. A spacious freeway. An immense superhighway. Being broad, it is not confining or restricting. There are few limitations. You can do your own thing, live by your own values, adopt your own priorities. In other words, anything goes.

The broad path is inclusive in its lifestyle. A person can set his own agenda and run his own life. He can be his own boss, make his own decisions, call his own shots. It all revolves around self. Not God, but self.

This broad path is self-centered, self-promoting, self-serving, self-absorbing. On the broad path, a person can do his own thing. There is constant movement ahead. This advance forward gives an adrenaline rush of accomplishment, achievement, and advancement.

There are few rules. Few boundaries. Few restrictions. There is tolerance of most everything. There are plenty of lanes for a person to try. He can live however he pleases. Just go with the flow—like a dead fish floating downstream.

This is the rat race, the broad path. It is the wide-open pursuit of this world to the exclusion of living for God. It is paved with the pursuit of money, knowledge, and popularity. Anything but God. It is built upon prestige, position, and possessions. It is living to make a living, but never living to make a life.

A while back, I was standing in a bookstore and the lingo of the rat race struck me. It is all about me, my, and mine. Its mantra is "What is in it for *me?*" "It's *my* life!" "Those are *mine.*" The world's smooth-talking gurus spew out a success-driven message for people with a craving to get ahead.

They preach things like "The Superachiever's Secret," "The Success Formula," "Take Charge Now," "Peak Productivity," "Wealth Unlimited," "Numero Uno," "Getting the Most," "Getting Set for Life," "How to Play the Tax Game and Win."

The advertisements read, "Nice Guys Finish Rich," "Success Achievement," and "The Neuropsychology of Achievement."

That is precisely the message of the rat race. One headline reads, "If the corporate ladder's wrung you out, give us a call." In other words, the upward push gives you everything except what you want—peace and fulfillment. The mice marathon overpromises and underdelivers.

Another corporate achiever put it this way: "I spent all my life climbing the corporate ladder, only to reach the top and discover it was leaning against the wrong wall."

Does that sound like winning?

The rat race is a treadmill. Those who are on it run, but never arrive. They strive, but never succeed. They reach, but never obtain. Sure, they may get ahead. But ahead of what? Ahead of others? Ahead of last month's performance? Ahead in position, prestige, and possessions?

Is this winning?

Other rat racers are literally running for their lives. They are running from paycheck to paycheck. They are running to make ends meet. They are running to stay just ahead of their creditors.

But for all their running, they never get ahead in what really counts. They never find satisfaction, joy, peace—the desires of the heart. The broad path never leads to personal fulfillment, only to futility. Why? It never leads to God.

It Is a Jam-Packed Rat Race

Second, Jesus said that the rat race is also *crowded*.

Jesus stated that "many" are on this path. It is jam-packed, full of frantic runners. We can call them the rat pack. Most people you know are on it. If you doubt that, just look around. Most of those with whom you rub shoulders are on it. Most of your peers are on it. Most of your neighbors are on it. Most of your family members are on it. Maybe even you.

Who are these rat racers? They are anyone who is under the dominant influence of the world system. Many are good upstanding people who push to get ahead. But in so doing, they push God to the back of their lives. Or worse, they push Him out entirely.

In this fast lane, there are two breeds of rats. One is those who have never committed their life to Christ. Many of these are good, hard-working people, those caught up in the race of life. But they have no time for God. They may acknowledge His existence, but they live independent of Him. They may even go to church, but their heart is not in it.

Jesus calls these rats "lost." They run without any divine direction. They live without any thought for eternity. They live only for the here and now. They could not be any more lost.

There is another breed of rat racers—a hybrid sort of rat. These are Christians who have committed their lives to Christ but have strayed off track. They have been lured back to the rat race. Though converted, they have allowed themselves to be momentarily squeezed back into the mold of the world. The lure of modern culture has pulled them back into pursuing the wrong priorities.

This second breed of rat tries to live in two worlds at the same time. They attempt to have one foot in heaven and one foot in the world. They are miserable when they sit in church. And they are miserable when they punch in at work. They are strangers and aliens in this world who have returned to friendship status with the world.

Could this describe you?

A Path that Seems Easy

Third, the rat race is *deadly*.

Jesus strongly warned that this race is headed to "destruction." This word *destruction* has a bone-chilling ring to it. It means the ruin of everything that is valuable, the complete loss of well-being. It is the loss of happiness, peace, and contentment. It is the loss of meaningful relationships, significance, and the true purpose in living. Ultimately, it is the loss of one's soul.

On the outside, rat racers look like they have it all together. Their smiling faces make them appear happy. Their attractive appearances make them look successful. Outwardly, their houses are beautiful, their lawns neatly manicured, their shrubs trimmed.

But inwardly, their lives have no eternal purpose. An empty feeling haunts them. Their path is strewn with bankrupt marriages, failed dreams, alienated children, and embittered relationships. Their lives are perishing.

Ultimately, the rat race empties into hell. A Christless eternity is their finish line. Solomon put it this way: "There is a way which seems right to a man, but its end is the way of death" (Proverbs 14:12).

This is the rat race. It is attractive, appealing, and crowded with travelers. It is easy to choose this broad path. You just go with the flow. You follow the crowd.

But no matter how you keep score, winning the rat race is losing. It is crossing the *wrong* finish line. The rat race is toxic to the soul. It leads to eternal destruction.

An Easy Entrance Ramp

Fourth, the rat race is *easily accessible*.

Jesus declared that the entrance into the rat race is a broad gate. In other words, it has a wide entrance ramp. It is easy to get into the rat race. It is easy to be lured in, sucked in, or pushed in. Many just slip into it. You can even stumble into it. No one is ever turned away. It is always easy access.

The entrance ramp is so broad that you can bring all your baggage with you. Nothing has to be left behind. You can bring your lifestyle of pursuing sin. You can bring your old priorities. Nothing changes in your life.

This broad gate requires no break with the past. It requires no renouncing of sin. No repentance. No turning from the world's values.

It looks so enticing. It promises much, but destroys all that is valuable. Like cancer, it eats away our very lives. In the end, it destroys our souls.

This is the rat race—wide open, crowded, deadly, easily accessible. No wonder Jesus warns us against it. Could this be the race you are running?

In Lane Number Two—the Right Race

Lying next to the wrong race is a totally different race. It begins at a different starting line. It is run on a different lane. It has a different crowd on its track. It arrives at a different finish line. Simply put, it is God's race for our lives. This race is the right race.

Jesus calls this track the narrow path. He says, "Enter through the narrow gate...For the gate is small and the way is narrow that leads to life, and there are few who find it" (Matthew 7:13-14).

Several years ago, I traveled to Israel for a month of study in the Holy Land. During my stay, I went to the Sea of Galilee and stood exactly where Jesus was when He spoke these words. Today, only one lonely tree stands on a grassy hill overlooking the sea.

As I walked back to the bus, I stumbled onto a worn, dusty foot-path. Where it was headed, I did not know. Who would be walking there, who could say. All I knew is it was a narrow path—just barely wide enough for one person to walk on it.

My professor pointed to the path, saying, "Now there is a picture for you to take. There is a narrow path just like the one Jesus referred to when He said, 'The way is narrow that leads to life.'" Such a path would have been taken by a few travelers in Jesus' day.

But today, businessmen are not walking to work on a narrow path through a grassy field. How would Jesus describe the narrow path today?

Here Is a Narrow Path!

Let me take you to the lonely back roads of North Carolina. My wife's parents have a house in the Smoky Mountains, where they wanted to be as far away from the congestion of the city as possible. They bought a remote mountain site and chose to live on top of it during the summer months.

To travel to their mountain home, we go from a four-lane inter-state, to a two-lane highway, to a side road, to a single-lane dirt road, to a squirrel trail. Trust me, this place is remote.

As we approach the base of this mountain, an iron gate stands as the only entrance. The brass sign reads "Private Drive." Behind the gate is an isolated, single-lane road—the *only* road, I might add—leading to the top. Once an old logging trail, it is now graded and paved.

When our children were younger, as we started the steep climb up this narrow path, they would instinctively lower the windows and hang out the sides. The scenery is breathtaking—lofty pines, towering birches, the greenest grass imaginable. You can hear the mountain brook flowing alongside the road. Surrounding mountains on both sides dwarf us.

Every time we take this road, we all enjoy the scenery—everyone, that is, except me. My eyes are glued to this narrow road—a tight, single lane. There are no guardrails. No curbs. No shoulders. One wrong turn, and we are back at the bottom.

No one else travels this private road. There is no traffic whatsoever. No approaching cars. No one jumping into our lane. It is just us and this narrow path. We can go nowhere except to the top. There is only one reason to be on this road—to get to the top.

As the road spirals upward, weaving through the thick trees, the air grows cooler. Each turn is sharp, angling hard. As we pass through a bank of floating clouds, we see the cows grazing on the mountainside. Then the foreman's cabin above the road. Then the red barn. Then rows of planted Christmas trees appear.

The road makes one last turn back into a dense forest. Our eyes adjust due to the dark shadows under the canopy of trees. At last, we are at the top.

The view from the summit is spectacular. It looks like we are on top of the world. We can see across the valley to the main ridge of the Smoky Mountains, painted in muted shades of purple and blue. Mount Pisgah looms across the horizon. Clouds dot the valley below.

Perched atop this pinnacle is the family house. There is a guest cabin on the top peak. No matter how hot the summer, it is cool here.

This lonely mountain road stands in stark contrast to the traffic-clogged interstate highway described earlier. This road is narrow, tight, secluded, lonely, hard to find. But it leads to an unforgettable experience at the top. This road is like the Christian life.

In what way does it resemble following Christ?

What Is the Narrow Path Like?

It Is Tight

First, the narrow path is *tight*.

This road, Jesus said, is narrow, meaning it is tight, confining, and restricting. It is a one-lane road. Its travelers are hemmed in by tight boundaries. The perimeter is carefully defined.

Stepping over its edge leads to certain danger. This path confines its travelers, but not in a stifling way. It limits only in a protective sense. The tightness of this road gives safety—and singleness of direction—to all on it.

Jesus Christ teaches that this narrow path is the Christian life—a life lived by faith in humble submission to Him. Those on it seek first the kingdom of God and His righteousness. It is narrow with no room for side pursuits. There is only room on this path for a person to walk with Christ. It only allows for following Him in an intimate, personal relationship.

Jesus said, "If any one wishes to come after Me, he must deny himself, and take up his cross and follow Me" (Matthew 16:24). To follow Him is to pursue Him on this narrow path. It mandates our exclusive loyalty and total allegiance to Him.

Christ also said, "If anyone comes to Me, and does not hate his own father and mother and wife and children and brothers and sisters, yes, and even his own life, he cannot be My disciple" (Luke 14:26). Pursuing Him means there can be no other first loves. This narrow path mandates that Jesus Christ is number one.

It Has Few Travelers, Often Alone

Second, the narrow path is *almost empty*.

Jesus said that "few" travel it. This road is not a clogged interstate. Instead, it is the road less traveled.

Jesus calls these travelers His "little flock" (Luke 12:32).

Most people we know are not on this path. Most of those with whom we went to school are probably not on this narrow path. Most people we sat next to on the airplane last week are more than likely not on this path. Few will find it.

Few.

To run the right race requires breaking from the many who are in the rat pack so you can run with the few who are in the right race. Sure, there are many running God's race. But compared to those on the broad path, those on the narrow way are few. That makes this often a lonely race. Many times we will find ourselves running alone.

You must break from the pack. You must leave behind the multitude in order to run with the few. You must turn from the crowd and be willing to stand with a small pack of runners.

It Leads to the Top

Third, the narrow path leads to *fullness of life*.

Let us hear Jesus' words again: "The gate is small and the way is narrow that leads to life, and there are few who find it" (Matthew 7:14). He is talking about living life to the fullest.

This road alone leads to life. This is the very opposite of spiritual death. It is contrary to a mere empty, hollow existence. It is one thing to be alive. It is something else to have life.

Jesus said, "I came that they may have life, and have it abundantly" (John 10:10). He also said, "I am the resurrection and the life; he who believes in Me will live even if he dies" (John 11:25). Further, "I am the way, and the truth, and the life" (John 14:6).

This is to say, all who are on "the way" are experiencing "the life"— eternal life, spiritual life, supernatural life, abundant life, everlasting life.

Then, beyond the grave, there are only two final destinies that await us—heaven and hell. Everyone will spend eternity in one of these two places. There are no exceptions. Jesus was saying that only one road leads to be with God forever.

Ultimately, this narrow path leads to heaven.

It Has a Hard-to-Find Gate

Fourth, the narrow path is *secluded*.

Jesus cautioned, "Enter through the narrow gate...the gate is small...and there are few who find it." The narrow gate that leads onto this narrow path is hard to find. That is why it requires searching for it with all our hearts. This small gate is off the beaten path, away from the noisy throng.

Finding this small gate requires the Holy Spirit to discover it. This gate is so narrow that entering it requires heart-searching repentance. No one just stumbles upon it. Nor does anyone trip through it.

Jesus said, "Strive to enter through the narrow door; for many, I tell you, will seek to enter and will not be able" (Luke 13:24). To "strive" signifies a great search and struggle to enter it. This small gate is entered by faith alone, apart from any works. But it is difficult because it is a faith that is marked by wholehearted commitment.

This narrow gate, in reality, is Jesus Christ Himself. He is the door for the sheep: "I am the door; if anyone enters through Me, he will be saved, and will go in and out and find pasture" (John 10:9). Entering this gate requires a decisive step of faith in Christ. It involves the unreserved surrender of our lives to Christ, entrusting our entire being to Him.

No amount of good works may gain admission into this race. Entering this narrow gate means coming to Christ. It is receiving Him as one's personal Lord and Savior. This resolute step of faith is the most important step anyone will ever make in life.

The Only Race Worth Winning

Let me be very clear at this point. The world says winning is getting ahead in the rat race. It says, "He who dies with the most toys wins the game." But winning the rat race is *not* winning.

God says winning is about something entirely different. The Bible asserts that winning is running a *different* race, by a *different* standard, with a *different* crowd, to win a *different* prize. Only winning the *right* race is winning.

The world says winning is living before you die. Jesus says winning is dying before you live. That is, winning requires dying to self and dying to the pursuit of this world. There must be a crucifixion of the old life before there can be the resurrection of the new life. Only in dying do we find life.

True winning is coming to know God. It is a personal relationship with Jesus Christ. It is committing your life to Christ. It is choosing to live not for self, but for Him. Winning is following Christ in willing obedience and seeking to do His will.

Winning is running the race He has set before you. It is serving Him and giving your life to advance His kingdom. It is running faithfully to the end. It is persevering to the finish line. It is winning Christ's incorruptible crown.

If you win God's race, it does not matter where else you may lose. But if you lose God's race, it matters not where else you may win.

Which Race Are You Running?

I have just described two totally different races. We are all running one of these two races. Either we are in the rat race, speeding down the broad path or we are in the right race, pressing on down the narrow path. Which race are you running?

There is the rat race—run on the crowded expressway of life. And there is the right race—run on a narrow, single-lane back road in life. One is a busy thoroughfare; the other is the road less traveled. One leads to destruction; the other to life. One is self-focused; the other is God-focused. One is easy to enter; the other is hard to find, much less enter. One leads to destruction; the other leads to life.

Which race are *you* running?

Because you are reading this book, there is a strong likelihood that you may be a genuine Christian. But if you are not, I will show you how to enter the right race through faith in Jesus Christ. More about that later.

If you have already entered the right race, you may feel yourself drifting back into the old rat race. If so, this book is especially for you. This is a temptation with which we all struggle. It is too easy for our focus to shift from the Lord to this world system. The apostle John warned us, "Do not love the world nor the things in the world" (1 John 2:15). The rat race is a fatal attraction that we must resist. I want to help us reject this lure so that we remain on track and run the right race.

A Struggle to Stay on Track

To this day, the enticement of the rat race is still a powerful temptation in my life. I can still be easily sucked back into it. It can still entice and hypnotize my heart. For each of us, our struggle with the lure of the world continues. Even after entering the right race, we must fight the seductive temptation of the rat race.

Years ago, I made the decision to go to seminary and enter the ministry. That was a major decision for me—to leave my career in finance and banking in order to pursue God's call upon my life.

To support myself through seminary, I decided to write and market my own sports magazine. I wrote a publication called *Gospel Gridiron,* in which I covered the Dallas Cowboys with a distinctively Christian agenda. Each week, I interviewed Christian coaches and players like Tom Landry, Mike Ditka, Dan Reeves, Roger Staubach, or other Cowboys who had a strong faith in the Lord.

Further, I wrote a Bible study called "The Game Plan." I also had a section titled "Pigskin Prophet," in which I predicted the scores of the upcoming games.

As you can imagine, this was a fun and rewarding enterprise. But something subtle began to occur to me.

Writing this magazine began to eat up an increasingly larger commitment of my time. It drained my physical energy. It sapped my spiritual vitality. My heart became so focused upon this business endeavor that my love for God began to wane.

The publication became so successful it paid my way through theological training. I then expanded into major league baseball publishing. I approached the Texas Rangers and received permission to create and write their official newsletter.

I named my publication *Pennant Fever.* Almost overnight, it became a smashing success. Not only was *Pennant Fever* sold in the Rangers' stadium, but also in many convenience stores in the Dallas-Fort Worth metropolis.

The momentum began to snowball. A bank in Fort Worth bought my publication's logo for its bumper stickers. Soon the Rangers offered to me the rights to their annual yearbook, a nice glossy volume. All this had major benefits for me.

Then an NBA team, the Dallas Mavericks, approached me to write and publish a similar magazine for them. Other ventures in other cities were in place. Before I knew it, I had a year-round, full-time business in place, ready to steamroll ahead.

Veering Off the Track

But wait a minute! I thought. *What am I doing?* The tail was now wagging the dog. I was suffering from pennant fever. School was on the back shelf, and this new business began to dominate me. A choice between memorizing Greek verb tenses or interviewing the New York Yankees was too seductive for me.

I was blinded by the stadium lights.

Without realizing it, I was being enticed back into a rat race that had little to do with God's calling on my life. It became so all-consuming that I realized I would have to make a major decision. Would it be seminary training or sportswriting? In reality, my choice was between God's will for my life or my own preferences.

Can you believe it? Here I was, pursuing a theological education, preparing my life to serve the Lord, but I was running an entirely different race. I had been lured by the rat race.

I must tell you that only through God's Word, and His indwelling Spirit convicting my heart, was I enabled to resist this temptation and get back in the right race.

Please do not misunderstand. You do not have to go to seminary to pursue God's will. I am not saying you must go into a vocationally Christian occupation. But you do have to follow God's plan for your life. None of us are free to run our own race.

The world system dangles its cheap trinkets before us in order to grab our hearts and lure us in a different direction. The world appeals to our competitive nature to get ahead and to push to the top. The rat race almost ate my lunch. It can happen to all of us, even to believers.

If you are living under the constant pull of the rat race, I want to help you get back on track and run the right race. I wish I could tell you that the struggle is over. I wish I could say that you will no longer be tempted by the world. But until we reach for the finish line, the rat race will contend for our loyalties.

Get Back in the Race!

Perhaps you are running the right race, but you have slowed down your pace. Maybe you are weary or tired from the demands of the race. Or maybe you have seated yourself along the side of the track and become a mere spectator. Or you have tripped and fallen into sin. Or your schedule has become so full that your focus is divided between God and the rat race.

It could be that you have picked up excess baggage that is slowing you down. This extra weight is draining your energy and impeding your speed.

If so, I want to help you remove those needless encumbrances. I want to encourage you so that you can run God's race and win.

We all experience times when our spiritual progress gets bogged down. It is critical that we learn how to push through such stagnant seasons and reassert ourselves to win the race. Wherever you are, it is important that you be alert and not miss out on winning God's race. Be in it to win it.

Wake Up and Get in the Race!

The year was 1968, my senior year in high school, and we were a good football team. Late in the season, we were undefeated and ready to play our archrival, who was also undefeated. Everything was in place for this to be the biggest game of the year. The stage was set for this schoolboy showdown, certainly one of the most important moments in our young lives.

It was Friday afternoon, and we entered our gym, a big, domed coliseum, to get dressed for the game. The routine was to put on our uniforms in the locker room and then go into the empty coliseum to get focused. In the quiet solitude of the gym, we would lie flat on our backs and stare at the ceiling. We would visualize executing our plays, anticipating how we were going to beat our opponent.

There were about sixty of us in the dark room. It was so quiet you could hear a pin drop. Suddenly our head coach came in and said, "All right, men, it is time to get on the bus and go to the game."

We grabbed our helmets and shoes and walked in our stocking feet across the hardwood gym floor to get into the bus. We were men on a mission.

That night, the stadium was electric. The whole community had turned out to see this collision between two undefeated powerhouses. I am glad to tell you that we blew our rivals out of the water. By half-time, the score was 35-0. We did not even have to punt. Five possessions, five touchdowns. If this had been a prize fight, they would have called it off. The final score was 41-6 in a blowout!

After the game, everyone was elated. The student body, the parents, the band, even the faculty were all ecstatic. As we loaded the bus for the jubilant ride home, our fans were excitedly cheering us.

By the time our bus pulled up at the gym, we had a large crowd waiting. As we got off, we had to fight our way through all the people. I remember the band was playing the school fight song. The cheerleaders were cheering.

Once inside the locker room, it was complete bedlam. We were boxing with each other. We were popping one other with towels. I think our roughhousing was more dangerous than the game itself!

As was my habit, I slipped into the empty coliseum to be alone. I began peeling off my jersey and pads and replaying the whole game in my mind, savoring every play.

As I was removing my jersey, I looked across the floor and saw the lone figure of a person. The red exit sign—the only light in the gym—was profiling the silhouette as this individual was walking toward me.

It was one of my teammates. He had his full football uniform on. And it was apparent to me that he was drowsy, as if he had just awakened.

As he approached me, he said, "Let's get on the bus and go to the game!"

I said, "The game's over. We won, 41-6! You missed the whole thing." My teammate had apparently stayed up late the night before and when he laid down in the gym before the game, he fell sound asleep—and never woke up until after the game.

Do not let this happen to you. Do not sleep through the biggest race of your life. Do not miss out on the opportunity to be a winner where it really counts. Do not be lulled to sleep by the seductive pull of the world. Stay on the narrow path that leads to life. Get out of the rat race, and into the right race.

Be in it to win it.

2

Heaven's
Heisman

The Master's green jacket. The Olympic gold medal. The Lombardi Trophy. A World Series ring. The Wimbledon Cup. An NBA championship. The Stanley Cup.

These are all coveted prizes from the world of sports. Hyped by the media, coveted by athletes, the dream of young boys and girls everywhere, these emblems of success mark out our champions for fame and immortality.

But there is one trophy, I dare say, that stands alone. There is one trophy that towers head and shoulders above the rest. The winner of this award vaults to the pinnacle of athletic stardom for decades to come. It is awarded each year by the Downtown Athletic Club of New York City to the most outstanding collegiate football player in America. I refer to the Heisman Trophy.

The list of past Heisman winners reads like a who's who of gridiron greats. Past winners include Hall of Famers like Doc Blanchard, Glenn Davis, Doak Walker, Paul Hornung, and Billy Cannon. To this list has been added Roger Staubach, Tony Dorsett, Earl Campbell, Herschel Walker, and Bo Jackson.

These are larger-than-life legends who dominated the collegiate game. Most went on to excel at the professional level. They were gridiron greats who ignited the fan base and packed stadiums. These Saturday afternoon heroes electrified the alumni and elevated the standard of excellence. They were shooting stars who rose above the competition.

The Most Coveted Prize in Sports

First awarded in 1935, the Heisman Trophy has become the most iconic prize in sports. The statue itself depicts a muscular football player, driving for yardage, straight-arming his way to a touchdown. Cast in bronze, the bust is unimposing in size—a little more than a foot long and high, mounted on a seventeen-and-one-half by five-and-one-half-inch base, set on a three-foot marble pedestal.

Though relatively small in size, this luminous award is towering in its significance, symbolic of the highest level of achievement. It is, simply, the most coveted award in American sports.

The mystical aura of the Heisman is further intensified by its dramatic presentation on live television. The four or five finalists are flown to New York to attend the award ceremony at the Downtown Athletic Club. There, on a Saturday in early December, before the watching eyes of the nation, the winner is announced in suspenseful fashion and presented the Heisman.

Imagine the built-up emotions of these finalists as they sit in the richly paneled, lavishly decorated trophy room, awaiting the name of the winner to be read. Portraits of past winners line the walls. The tension increases as each finalist contemplates the highly publicized accomplishments of the other all-Americans who are vying for the same cherished prize.

As the winner is announced, he steps to the podium. He fights back tears. His voice quivers. He humbly thanks his parents, who gave him the emotional support needed to excel. He thanks his coaches and teammates. He then holds up the trophy, triumphantly, for all to see. The quest for the Heisman is now complete. It has once again identified the best America has to offer.

The Heisman of Ancient Days

The esteem of winning such a prestigious trophy is nothing new. There was a similarly coveted award in the world of sports in the ancient world—the victor's crown. Capturing this laurelled wreath became the obsession of athletes. This ancient award became synonymous with the most popular figures of the day as it was bestowed on the winners of the Olympic and Isthmian athletic games. The victor's crown—a wreath of leaves—was the Heisman Trophy of the first century.

I want to turn back the calendar to the year AD 53. We are traveling with the apostle Paul from the city of Corinth, the most splendid city of ancient Greece, across the isthmus, the narrow strip of land that joins southern Greece with the mainland. We are en route to the famous Isthmian Games, second in importance only to the Olympics.

It is here on the shores of the Mediterranean Sea, near Corinth, that the Isthmian Games are held. These athletic games are a major event, hosted every two years.

As we arrive at the stadium, several sights attract our attention. We are immediately impressed with the massive throngs of people who are gathering from all corners of the Roman Empire. Thousands are descending upon Isthmus to witness this spectacle.

We notice the enormous sports coliseum with its precisely cut marble blocks. We are struck by its perfectly constructed symmetrical rows. Once inside, we see that the emperor's velvet box is filled with the political dignitaries of the day. These games are the place for the rich and famous to be seen.

We are inspired by the beautifully manicured track and field nestled in the center of the stadium. On the cinders, we see assembled the finest physical specimens of the known world. They are the most popular figures of their day.

These athletes are the subjects of poets, chiseled in marble, and painted on canvas. Cicero complained they were afforded more fame than the conquering generals of Rome. The statues of past champions line the entrance leading to the stadium. It is the dream of every young boy to become one of these athletic gods.

The Race

The main feature is the five-event pentathlon, which consists of the long jump, the javelin and discus throws, wrestling, and the footrace. By far and away, the most popular of these events is the footrace. It is called the *dromos*, a race of one lap around the 600-yard track, a third longer than our present 400-meter tracks. The long-distance marathon race is called the *agon*.

Down on the field, we focus upon a single athlete—a solitary runner. He has trained for ten months under severe discipline and a strict diet. He has spent the last month here in Corinth, working out under the personal supervision of an official. It has been verified that he has trained according to the rules.

This runner jogs to the far end of the track and dips his hands in a bucket of blood. He swears that he has submitted to the rigorous training. Moreover, he agrees to compete according to the rules.

The long-awaited time for the race has now come. This determined runner comes to the starting line, where other competitors are waiting. Every muscle within him is taut. Every nerve is tense. His mind is riveted on one thing—*winning*.

Across the infield is the finish line. There, a ladder-like pedestal is strategically positioned, and on it hangs the most sought-after prize in all the Roman Empire—the victor's crown. This highly lauded laurel— the *stephanos*—will be awarded to the winner of this footrace. It is for this crown that these athletes have diligently trained for months, even for years. It is for this crown that they have pushed and punished their bodies to masochistic limits.

Only one runner will win this crown. Nothing can be held back to secure it.

Inside the stadium, we feel the electricity in the air. The atmosphere is crackling with excitement. The buzz in the crowd is highly charged.

The *Bema*—the Judge's Seat

In the center of the field is a solitary object that leaves an indelible mark on every Christian who enters this stadium. To the side of the track, near the finish line, is a wooden platform. This elevated stand is rectangular, mounted by a series of steps. Upon the platform rests a seat.

Upon this chair sits the umpire, the presiding judge of the games. This seat is called, in the Greek language, the *bema*. It is to this *bema* that every athlete must report after he runs his race.

Back at the starting line, the runners take their mark. With the start of the race, the world's fastest athletes explode out of the starting blocks. They resemble thoroughbreds coming out of the gate. As the race unfolds, it looks to be dead even as the runners head down the backstretch. They come around the final turn and sprint for the finish. A mere hundred yards lay between them and glory. Two runners push to the finish, neck and neck. The finish is too close to call. The crowd is silent in suspense.

Every eye strains and focuses upon the *bema*, awaiting the judge's decision. Which runner will be awarded the winner's wreath? The umpire's call will be final.

As the athletes approach the judge's stand, we feel the sting of regret as the umpire disqualifies an undisciplined runner who violated the rules. We feel remorse as the judge passes over the other runners who lost the race. From these athletes, he withholds the cherished prize.

But we are going to be thrilled by the vivid spectacle as the judge of the games takes the wreath of leaves and calls out the winner's name. When he does, the athlete steps forward and stands before the *bema*. The judge takes the wreath and crowns the head of this new victorious champion.

With this recognition, the stadium explodes into a deafening roar. The crowd spontaneously begins chanting his name. The applause is deafening.

This one moment of glory makes all the countless months and years of training worthwhile. The new champion circles the track in a customary victory lap. He proudly holds aloft the cherished victor's crown for all to see.

The Judgment Seat of Christ

It is against this background that the apostle Paul writes to the Corinthians, "We must all appear before the judgment seat of Christ, that each one may be recompensed for his deeds in the body, according to what he has done, whether good or bad" (2 Corinthians 5:10).

As they heard these words read, every Corinthian knew exactly the context of Paul's statement. The Isthmian Games, held just outside of

Corinth, were intimately familiar to these early believers. Just as an athlete would appear before the judge's seat following his race, they understood that every Christian will one day appear before the judgment seat of Jesus Christ to be judged and rewarded.

This scene was a very vivid picture in the minds of the early Christians. It became a constant focus of their Christian lives. Likewise, it must grip our hearts and compel our lives as we follow Christ. We must run the race that God has set before us—and be in it to win it!

Making this connection, Paul wrote, "Do you not know that those who run in a race all run, but only one receives the prize? Run in such a way that you may win…They then do it to receive a perishable wreath, but we an imperishable" (1 Corinthians 9:24-25).

By those words, the apostle made it clear that every believer must run to win an imperishable crown. We could call it Heaven's Heisman. Paul must have been a keen observer of sports. His frequent use of athletic illustrations in Scripture shows he was intimately familiar with the realm of sports. He frequently pointed to the world of athletics to communicate key truths about the Christian life.

In this chapter, I want us to consider several factors concerning the judgment seat of Christ. *Who* will appear before the judgment seat of Christ? *Why* will we appear? *How* will our performance be assessed?

The People Assembled

First, *who* will appear before the judgment seat of Christ? The Bible teaches that at the end of life's race, every Christian will be summoned to appear before this judgment seat. If you have trusted Jesus Christ to be your Savior and Lord, you will surely stand there. Paul wrote, "We must all appear before the judgment seat of Christ, that each one may be recompensed" (2 Corinthians 5:10). The language—"we," "all," "each one"—is all-inclusive of every Christian.

Can you even imagine what a day that will be? We will stand before the *bema*, face-to-face before heaven's Judge, Jesus Christ. We will behold His nail-scarred hands and His nail-pierced side. We will look upon His majestic face. We will gaze upon His dazzling, unveiled glory.

As believers, we will not see Him as He once appeared, as the suffering servant of the Lord (Philippians 2:6-7). Nor as the humble carpenter from Nazareth. We will see Him as He is—the King of kings and Lord of lords (1 John 3:2), the unrivaled King of heaven and earth, sovereign and awesome, holy and righteous, the Judge of all creation.

It is before this glorified Christ, this enthroned Lord over all, we will appear. The apostle John, in his description of the exalted Christ (Revelation 1:9-20), gives us a fore-gleam of what this experience will be like. The aged apostle was given a vision of the risen Christ, standing preeminently in the midst of the churches. He is clothed as a king in a regal robe flowing to His feet. He is girded as a priest with a golden girdle across His breast.

In this vision, Christ's head and hair were white like the fairest wool and virgin snow, indicating the unstained purity of His holy character. His piercing eyes were like a flame of fire, penetrating deeply into the hearts and lives of men. Nothing escapes His all-seeing eyes.

The strong feet of this Christ were like burnished bronze, glowing in a red-hot furnace, depicting the ironclad strength of His judgments. His sovereign decrees cannot be annulled or appealed. There is no higher court to which any can appeal.

When this Judge speaks, His voice is like the sound of many waters, drowning out every other voice. All excuses and arguments of men are muted. His verdicts alone are heard. In His right hand He holds seven stars, portraying His protective care over His spiritual leaders, who speak God's Word.

Out of His mouth comes a sharp, two-edged sword that represents the sovereign authority and truthfulness with which this Judge speaks. All His judgments are right and true. And His face is shining like the sun, dazzling in its splendor, revealing the supreme majesty of His divine person.

When John saw this glorified Christ, he fell at His feet like a dead man. He was struck in awe, terrified.

It is before this same Christ that you and I will one day stand. We will be equally awestruck as He reviews how we ran the race.

This appearance before heaven's Judge will occur at the end of time. It will not take place during the race. Our prize awaits each of us after the race, at the consummation of this age. Jesus says, "Behold, I am coming quickly, and My reward is with Me, to render to every man according to what he has done" (Revelation 22:12). It is before this glorified Christ that we will one day stand.

The Purpose Assigned

Second, *why* will we appear there? What is the purpose of the judgment seat of Christ?

The intent is not to see if we shall be admitted into heaven. For every believer in Christ, the issue of eternal salvation is already settled. The moment we personally trusted Jesus Christ as our Savior and Lord, we received eternal life. We were just as certain for heaven that moment as if we had already been there 10,000 years.

This eternal prize to be awarded is not our salvation. None of us could ever run fast enough to gain a right standing before God. Salvation is the gift of God, freely given without cost. It can be neither earned nor deserved. Christ won salvation for us through His death on the cross. He offers it as a prepaid gift. Only by faith in Christ may we receive it.

So, what is the judgment seat of Christ all about?

The purpose of this judgment seat is for Christ to review our spiritual lives and determine how faithfully we ran the race He assigned us to run. He will judge the stewardship that He entrusted to us. The issue is not our salvation. Rather, it is the review of our service.

When we stand before Christ, it will be more than a mere appearing. The word *appear* means to be made manifest, to be stripped of every outward façade. To appear means to be laid bare, to be carefully examined and openly revealed.

In that day, we will be fully known by Him. The Bible says, "There is no creature hidden from His sight, but all things are open and laid bare to the eyes of Him with whom we have to do" (Hebrews 4:13). "The Lord...will both bring to light the things hidden in the darkness and disclose the motives of men's hearts; and then each man's praise will come to him from God" (1 Corinthians 4:5). How we ran the race will be played back before us.

Paul stated that the purpose is "that each one may be recompensed for his deeds in the body, according to what he has done, whether good or bad" (2 Corinthians 5:10). Following this review, Christ will reward the good deeds we did in our bodies. The word *recompense* means to receive your due, to receive the just payment coming to you. While standing before His judgment seat, we will receive from Christ His eternal reward for our faithful sacrifice. We will receive an incorruptible crown.

In that final day, Jesus will distinguish between our good and bad works. Our good works are all that we do to glorify Christ, those things that count for eternity. They are the gold, silver, and precious stones (1 Corinthians 3:12), or the good works that will be recognized and rewarded by Christ.

Right now counts forever.

What About Our Sins?

Conversely, our bad works are useless things we do that are of no eternal value. These are not necessarily evil or sinful things, but are worthless things—inconsequential things that we do that have no bearing on the cause of Christ for eternity. These are useless works of wood, hay, and straw. Sad to say, they bring no reward.

Will our personal sins be revealed in that day?

If that were the case, none of us would be able to stand. Be assured, as Christ sorts through our good and bad deeds, no sin will be manifested. Jesus has already covered our sins at the cross. They will never come up again.

Think of it this way. In high school, I played quarterback for our team that ran the triple-option offense. After the season, my football coach was asked to speak at the NCAA coach's convention on how to run the triple option.

To best communicate this, he spliced together a highlight film of our best plays. It showed none of our bad plays—only our good ones. Any team could look fairly good if only their good plays are shown.

But at some point over the years, this highlight film became lost. All our good plays can never be seen again. I have our old game films, and watching those reels is discouraging. Only my fumbles, incompletions, and misdirections remain. My best runs and touchdown passes are gone. I wish it could have been the opposite. Why not my bad plays gone and only my good plays remaining?

At the judgment seat of Christ, it will be exactly this way. All of our sinful deeds have been erased by the blood of Christ, and only our good works remain. God has recorded all our good deeds and the attitudes behind them. At the judgment seat of Christ, our lives will be replayed and reviewed by Christ. God has already permanently edited out our sins and has spliced together only our righteous works.

We Will Give an Account

In that last day, we will give an account of ourselves to Christ. As a servant before his master, so will we stand before Him. He will assess how faithful we have been with what He has entrusted to us. He will examine how faithfully we have invested our lives in His kingdom.

This day of final accountability before Christ is coming. It matters *how* we run life's race. Jesus Christ will be there at the finish line, and He will review our race.

The Performance Assessed

Third, *how* will Christ assess our performance? *How* will He determine if we won the race or not?

To be sure, God does not see as we see. We are limited to look only upon the outward appearance, but God penetrates into the heart (1 Samuel 16:7). As God evaluates the race, He identifies the winners differently than the world does. Jesus said, "Many who are first will be last; and the last, first" (Matthew 19:30; see also 20:16). Many apparent winners here will be losers in that last day. And many who seem to be losers by this world's estimation will be winners then.

Things will seem so different then. Many losers will be winners, and winners will be losers. It will take another world to reveal who the true champions are.

The Criteria for Victory

What will be the divine criteria of His final judgment? What will be the standard of His test? I want to suggest five questions we must ask ourselves so that we can know how to achieve victory on that final day.

Am I Running the Right Race?

First, we must ask ourselves, "Am I running the right race?" There are many tracks open before us. If we are to win, we must run the right race, the one divinely laid out before us. The crown awaits those who get on the right track and run in the right direction.

God has a plan for each of our lives. This plan is called His will. Success in life is doing the will of God, no more and no less. Each of us has a purpose here. That purpose is found in carrying out His purpose. This plan includes what I do, how I serve Christ, where I live, who I marry, where I attend school, and more. God has everything about my life all planned out, both big and small. Winning is finding and doing God's will. Victory belongs to those who run the right race.

Are you running the right race? Are you fulfilling God's purpose for being here? Are you running on the right track in the right direction?

The 1929 Rose Bowl is indelibly etched in gridiron lore as the showcase for one of football's most unforgettable plays. California was playing Georgia Tech, with the Golden Bears leading 7-6 in the first half. Georgia Tech had the ball deep in their own territory with their backs against their own goal line.

Then it happened. A Tech runner fumbled the ball, and a California defender, Roy Riegels, recovered the loose pigskin. That is when the unthinkable occurred.

As Riegels attempted to advance the ball, he became turned around. In the confusion of the moment, he lost his sense of direction. Roy took off for the end zone, and ran what would be the race of his life. Tragically though, Riegels was running the *wrong* way!

The crowd shouted in horror, which only made him run faster. The twenty…the thirty…the forty…the fifty! Only fifty yards separated Riegels from the end zone and infamy. By this time, Riegels's teammates took off in hot pursuit. Benny Lum, a speedy California halfback, was closing in on him, shouting, "Roy, Roy, stop!"

But Roy assumed that his teammate was cheering him on. This made him run even faster.

As Riegels reached the goal line, Lum tackled his own teammate from behind. Roy had run the wrong way, and almost scored a touchdown in the wrong end zone.

Can you imagine his shock when he realized his mistake? Sure, he was running fast. But in the wrong direction!

At the judgment seat, Christ will review which race we ran. He will ask, "Did you run the right race? Did you run in the right direction? Did you score in the right end zone?"

Do not end up being shocked on that final day.

Run the right race.

Am I Running According to the Rules?

Second, we must ask, "Am I running according to the rules?" Every athlete must compete according to the established rules of the game. Paul wrote, "If anyone competes as an athlete, he does not win the prize unless he competes according to the rules" (2 Timothy 2:5). Breaking the rules will bring a penalty or, worse, disqualification.

An athlete must adhere to the rules. There can be no pushing another runner. No leaving the track. No shortcuts through the infield. No drugs or steroids. These are the governing rules. If someone violates these rules, it will always bring painful consequences in the end— mostly likely, disqualification.

Even so, you and I must follow the Word of God as we run the race. We must run God's race God's way if we are to receive God's reward. We must live our lives and serve Him according to His Word.

It is possible for a runner to cross the finish line first, be cheered as the winner, and yet be disqualified at the judge's stand. The crown will be given to someone else if that person did not compete according to the rules.

It is critically important that we run according to the rules in God's Word. We must obey what He desires for us to do in every area of our lives. Our personal lives. Our business lives. Our home lives. Our ministry lives. Our relationships. Our values. All things must be governed by the Word.

If we are to have victory at the *bema,* obedience is necessary.

The potential danger of disqualification is what Paul meant when he wrote, "I discipline my body and make it my slave, so that, after I have preached to others, I myself will not be disqualified" (1 Corinthians 9:27). If we fail to keep the rules, we may suffer disqualification.

Am I Helping Others Win?

Third, we must consider, "Am I helping others win?" There is a reward for those who help other runners in the race. Let me explain.

Jesus Christ said, "He who receives you receives Me, and he who receives Me receives Him who sent Me" (Matthew 10:40). To "receive" means to bring into one's care. When you help another Christian, whether offering financial, material, emotional, or spiritual help, you are actually receiving or serving Jesus Christ Himself. And when you serve Christ, you are, likewise, serving God the Father. An inseparable unity exists between God the Father, God the Son, and believers. When you receive one, you actually receive all three.

Jesus further explained, "He who receives a prophet in the name of a prophet shall receive a prophet's reward; and he who receives a righteous man in the name of a righteous man shall receive a righteous man's reward" (Matthew 10:41). A prophet is one who proclaims God's Word. While a righteous person lives God's Word, a prophet declares it. Both are worthy of receiving a reward, yet they do not receive the same reward. A righteous person will receive a righteous person's reward. A prophet will receive a prophet's reward.

Here is the encouraging part: When I give support to a prophet or a preacher, I actually share in his reward. When I help him win his race, I share in his victory. The one who helps another participates in his reward.

But what about helping those who are less high-profile than a spiritual leader? Do we need to serve everyday, salt-of-the-earth people like you and me? Absolutely!

Jesus continued, "Whoever in the name of a disciple gives to one of these little ones even a cup of cold water to drink, truly I say to you, he shall not lose his reward" (Matthew 10:42). These "little ones" are the least in God's kingdom. Perhaps they are new believers or those who go largely unnoticed in life. Regardless, Jesus said that when we serve one of these little ones, it will not go unnoticed by God.

Any service rendered toward another believer is seen by God as being done to Jesus Christ Himself. Whether it be helping a preacher, a support worker, a new Christian, or even giving a mere cup of cold water to a thirsty disciple, such a deed will be rewarded by God.

Sometimes our ministry goes unnoticed by others. But it never goes unnoticed by God, who keeps heaven's accounts. The Lord will one day reward us for helping others in the race, whether they be teachers, prophets, or widows.

How are you serving other believers? Is there something you can do to help another runner today?

Am I Still Running?

Fourth, we must ask ourselves, "Am I still running?" It matters little if we are running the right race but do not finish the course. If we are to receive the crown, we must finish strong.

The great New York Yankee catcher Yogi Berra once said, "It ain't over 'til it's over." In other words, it matters little if we have an early lead yet fail to finish with perseverance. Victory is won at the finish line, not in the starting blocks. The end of the race is where it counts most.

One of the greatest champions who ever lived, the apostle Paul, wrote about the end of his race: "I am already being poured out as a drink offering, and the time of my departure has come. I have fought the good fight, I have finished the course, I have kept the faith; in the future there is laid up for me the crown of righteousness, which the Lord, the righteous Judge, will award to me on that day; and not only to me, but also to all who have loved His appearing" (2 Timothy 4:6-8).

If we are to have the crown, we must finish strong.

Picture a sprinter who explodes out of the starting blocks. No runner has ever started this fast. He is way ahead of the field, running the race of his life. Then, suddenly, something strange occurs. Toward the finish, he pulls up and stops running altogether. He then walks up into the grandstands and sits down to watch the race with everyone else. Everyone he had passed earlier now passes him.

Guess who wins the crown? Not the one who started well, but the one who finished well. No matter where you are in the race, keep running until you reach the end.

In the 1972 summer Olympic games, America's hope for the gold medal in the 1500-meter run was a runner named Jim Ryun. He had run in the 1968 games, but was beaten by a better man. For the next four years, Ryun rigorously trained to bounce back and bring home the gold. He spent countless hours in grueling practice, which required early mornings and late nights. He sacrificed it all for this one chance at victory.

At the starting line, he stood next to the finest 1500-meter runners from around the world. The gun sounded, and the race began.

But with little more than a lap to go, something tragic happened. Jim inadvertently stepped in the path of another runner. They both fell to the infield track, and the rest of the pack left them far behind. All hopes of victory were banished.

Bruised and in pain, Jim got up with no chance of winning the gold. He nevertheless finished the race alone. He came in dead last. There was no prize, no glory, no medal—only stinging defeat.

But in defeat, Jim Ryun showed himself to be a champion. By finishing the race, he revealed the true character of his heart. Winners, even if they stumble, always finish strong.

I can see the *bema*—the judgment seat of Christ—on the last day. The Lord is passing out His rewards. It may be that a believer who tripped and fell early in life's race but got up and finished the race without quitting will be the gold winner in that final day. Many of the last will be first.

Do you find encouragement in this truth? It may seem that others are way ahead of you. It may appear that they are doing so much more for Christ. Do not become discouraged and quit. The race is not yet over. Be faithful, and press on. Finish the race like Jim Ryun did. Heaven's Heisman may be awaiting you.

Am I Running with the Right Motives?

Fifth, we must ask, "Why am I running? Is it with the right motives?" Are we running for the approval of others? Or for the applause of heaven? What is the driving motivation of our hearts? At the *bema*, the Judge will bring to light our motives for running.

Paul wrote, "Do not go on passing judgment before the time, but wait until the Lord comes who will both bring to light the things hidden in the darkness and disclose the motives of men's hearts; and then each man's praise will come to him from God" (1 Corinthians 4:5). If we run for the glory of God, we will receive a reward from Him. But if we compete for self-glory, we will forfeit any reward.

The Pharisees stand as Exhibit A of people who expended much energy in running, but with wrong motives. They ran to receive the applause of this world. The result? They have already received their reward—namely, to be seen by others.

Jesus strikes a nerve within us all when He says, "Beware of practicing your righteousness before men to be noticed by them; otherwise you have no reward with your Father who is in heaven" (Matthew 6:1). If we run God's race simply to steal the spotlight, God will withhold His reward. But if we sacrifice this world's applause for heaven's glory, God's praise will await us at the end.

The Oscar-winning movie *Chariots of Fire* is based on the quest of Harold Abrahams and Eric Liddell to win gold medals in the 1924 Olympics, something they both accomplished.

There is an obvious difference between Abrahams and Liddell. Abrahams runs for himself, but Liddell runs for the glory of God. Two classic scenes in the movie contrast these two motives for running.

In the first scene, Eric's sister, Jennie, mistakes her brother's love of running for rebellion against God. She pressures him to return to the mission field in China, where they both were born and their parents served Christ. Jennie is upset because Eric missed a mission meeting.

So he decides to have a talk with her. They walk to a grassy spot over-looking the Scottish Highlands.

Clutching her arms, Eric tries to explain his calling to run: "Jennie, Jennie. You've got to understand. I believe God made me for a purpose—for China. But He also made me fast!—and when I run, I feel His pleasure!" Eric lived for God's pleasure.

The other key scene in the movie occurs one hour before the final race of the Olympics. While his professional coach and trainer gives him a rubdown, Harold Abrahams laments, "I am twenty-four and I have never known contentment. I am forever in pursuit, and I do not even know what it is I am chasing."

Both men were awarded a gold medal.

But only one won his medal for God.

At the judgment seat, the Lord will disclose the motives of our hearts. If we ran for the glory of God, then our prize will come from Him.

In the ancient Greek games, only one runner could win the prize. But in God's race, we can all be winners. We are not competing against one another, but against the course. By this, we can all win.

I do not know about you, but that thought lights my fire. Let us run for the Master until we cross the finish line and collapse in His arms.

The Prize Awarded

What will I win at the end of the race? In ancient athletic games, a fragile, leafy crown was awarded to the winner. This garland—called the victor's crown—was a collection of pine leaves, wild olive leaves, parsley, celery leaves, or ivy woven together.

In the Isthmian Games, the prize was a pine wreath. With this crown came instant fame, high acclaim, and hero status. Winners were immortalized, much as sports figures are today. These wreaths were received and lauded with great pride. But in a few days, they would soon wither and discolor.

Making a striking comparison, Paul contrasted this perishable, earthly crown with the imperishable crown of Christ. What can be said about this eternal reward?

First, heaven's crown is called "the unfading crown of glory" (1 Peter 5:4). It is a glorious crown that will never lose its beauty or value. Ancient athletes were awarded floral wreaths that fit atop their heads. But they quickly faded away. I have a box full of rusted old trophies, moth-eaten letter jackets, and yellowish newspaper clippings. They are all tarnished and faded; their glory is past and forgotten.

But our heavenly crown of glory will be unfading and last throughout eternity. It will be incorruptible and timeless, retaining its value forever. This crown, often called the shepherd's crown, will be given in recognition of selfless labor for Christ in His kingdom.

Second, it is called "the crown of righteousness" (2 Timothy 4:8), reserved for those who have lived and competed righteously. That is, they have run the race in conformity to God's Word. This crown belongs to those who competed according to God's rules. As we saw earlier, Paul said, "If any one competes as an athlete, he does not win the prize unless he competes according to the rules" (2 Timothy 2:5). This verse teaches that just as an athlete must play according to the rules, so a believer, if he is to win God's reward, must adhere to the requirements of His Word.

Third, it is called "the crown of life" (James 1:12)—a reward that will bring the highest joy and gladness. A believer's time on earth will not be spared trials and sorrow. Those who follow Christ will surely walk through persecution and difficulty for His name's sake. Some Christians will even be called upon to die a martyr's death. But in heaven, there awaits a crown of life, which represents fullness of joy and happiness. This accolade is promised to those who love the Lord amid much suffering.

Fourth, it is called an imperishable wreath (1 Corinthians 9:25), in stark contrast to the temporal fame that the world offers. Its value will not diminish with time, nor in eternity.

When we stand before Christ, we will long to hear Him say to us, "Well done, good slave" (Luke 19:17). In that last day, to receive the Master's approbation is all that will matter. Then Christ will take an incorruptible crown, shining with resilient glory, and place it upon our heads—the emblem of God's approval for a race well run.

In that grand moment, our hearts will pound with excitement.

Tears of joy will flood our eyes. An overwhelming feeling of awe will grip our hearts. Thrilled by this spectacle of heaven's King, we will prostrate ourselves before His throne.

After our Lord reviews and judges our lives, He will justly determine the measure of our eternal reward. Perhaps He will signal one of the angels to bring the crowns. Then Jesus Christ Himself will place those crowns upon our bowed heads.

A deep sense of humility will immediately grip our hearts. In an act of worship and adoration (Revelation 4:10), we will then cast our crowns back at His feet. This reciprocal act will signify that all that we did to receive it was done "from Him and through Him and to Him" (Romans 11:36). He alone called us into the race. He alone empowered us in the race. He alone was the motivation throughout the race. He alone deserves our crowns.

The Giver of the Crown

Finally, *from whom* will this crown come? The simple fact is, it will come from Jesus Christ Himself. In that final day, it would be meaningful to receive anything from Him. Any recognition from His blessed hand will be worth more than gaining the whole world. The real glory is found in who the giver is, not in the crown itself.

Allow me to illustrate.

One of the happiest days of my family's life was when my younger brother, Mark, graduated from the University of Tennessee Medical School. It was an especially meaningful time because my father was a professor in that same school, serving on its distinguished faculty. My brother had always wanted to be a doctor like my dad.

The entire family gathered for Mark's graduation with great pride and anticipation. The graduation service was very impressive, adorned with all the pomp and circumstance of a high academic ceremony. After the commencement address, the graduating class lined up single-file at the front of the stage on which were seated the president of the medical school and the entire faculty. One by one, each of the graduating seniors walked across the platform to receive his or her diploma from the president.

As the moment came for my brother to walk across the platform, our chests were swelling with pride. Our buttons were popping. My mother had dispatched my sister, camera in hand, to the foot of the platform for a close-up picture.

But as Mark stepped onto the first step of the platform, something strange occurred. My father, outfitted in his finest academic regalia—a black robe with multicolored doctoral stripes, topped with doctoral mortarboard—was seated in the faculty section, located onstage immediately behind the president. Just as Mark prepared to mount the stage, my dad rose to his feet and began sliding down his row to the aisle.

I thought, *Dad, what in the world are you doing? Wherever you are going, now is the wrong time!*

My father walked down the aisle and turned left to approach the very center of the platform—right where the president was standing. How embarrassing! Every eye was now focused on my dad.

He walked right up to the president as my brother proceeded across the stage. Dad took my brother's diploma from the president's hand and, to our total surprise, personally handed my brother his doctoral diploma.

He shook my brother's hand as my sister's camera flashed.

Unknown to us, there is a long-standing tradition at the medical school that a faculty member with a child graduating could personally bestow the diploma.

How meaningful to Mark! Not only did he receive his diploma, but he received it from his role model, our beloved father.

If I could amplify the emotion and significance of this graduation scene a million times a million, it would fail to capture the full impact of that final day when we will walk across the stage of eternity. The presiding Judge of heaven and earth, the Lord Jesus Christ, will be standing there. Our hearts will leap out of our chest with emotion as we come before His throne and kneel as our Savior takes the eternal crown and places it upon our heads.

And we will hear Him say, "Well done, My good slave. You ran the race that I set before you, and you won."

That last day will make all the painful toil of running the race become absolutely meaningless. Memories of all our difficult self-discipline and sacrifice will fade away. It will all be worth it when Jesus Christ Himself places our crowns upon our heads.

What is winning? It is winning God's approbation on that final day. It is winning Heaven's Heisman—and nothing less.

3

The Thrill of Victory
(and the Agony of the Feet)

t is time I come clean with you. We are into this book too far for me to masquerade any longer. I have got to get this off my chest.

I do not run.

That is right. I do not even jog. And here I am writing a book about running a race.

I dislike almost everything about running. I do not like the pain, the gasping for air, the bursting lungs, the throbbing knees, the sore ankles, the numb arms. I do not like any of it.

Why would anyone jog? Have you ever seen a happy jogger? No, and you never will. Runners are always taking their pulse. I suppose to make sure they are still alive.

If God loves me and has a wonderful plan for my life, it cannot include running.

Golf is my favorite sport. It has to be any Christian's favorite sport too. Which sport do you think would be better? One known for Heartbreak Hill, or one identified with the Amen Corner? See my point?

In the early years of my ministry, a young man named Tom Jones joined our church. For the three previous years, Tom had been the starting quarterback for the University of Arkansas Razorbacks. He was a great athlete from a very athletic family. His brother, Bert Jones, was the number one pick of the 1974 NFL draft, an all-pro quarterback for the Baltimore Colts. His father, Dub Jones, starred with the Cleveland Browns.

Tom suggested we start running together several evenings a week. Fresh out of college, he was still in impeccable shape. My wife had encouraged Tom to help get me in better shape for preaching. Trust me, though—no one has ever accused me of being short-winded in the pulpit. In a moment of insanity, I agreed. Two days later, we met at the local junior high track for our first "workout."

I knew I was in trouble when Tom showed up with a stopwatch. "I want to check our times for each lap," he said stoically. Good grief! All I wanted was to get my heart rhythm up, and he was turning this into an Olympic tryout.

"Let us run about twelve laps [three miles] and see how we do," Tom said, as if a Cotton Bowl bid was still at stake. "No problem," I lied. I was too prideful to admit I would never make it.

We started jogging, Tom setting the pace. It was a very fast pace, I might add—a pace I might use to run one lap if I could keep it up. Tom was jogging, I was sprinting.

"One minute, forty-five seconds," he said as we finished the first lap. All I could think was, *Only eleven laps to go. I will never make it.*

By the third lap, I felt like I would die. I could barely hold my head up. My mouth was drier than sun-bleached sand. Perspiration was pouring out of me. Red and yellow sunspots were blurring my vision. My lips were becoming chapped. My mind was playing games with me: *Quit, you fool. He's ten years younger than you.* To which I answered myself, *You're not going to let some kid in your church beat you, are you?*

I looked over at Tom and noticed he had barely broken a sweat. We made eye contact, and he actually smiled at me. Smiled? Sad to say, he was enjoying this!

By the fourth lap, I was planning who would speak at my funeral. I was praying for the second coming, or any kind of divine intervention. Eight more laps. How can I get out of this?

Finally, I had a breakthrough. I blurted out, "Tom, you look a little tired. I think we need to stop and fellowship for a while."

Tom nodded and slowed to a stop. I crashed and burned. Have you ever seen a grown man do a spread eagle on a cinder track? Face down.

I mumbled, "Tom, why do we not have some prayer together while I am down here on my knees."

That was more than three decades ago, and I am proud to tell you I have not jogged since. I will not even jog my memory. My nose will not even run.

Why not? All my friend Tom could tell me was that if I jogged today, I might add five, maybe ten, years to my life. In other words, my reward for jogging was still a long way off. Jogging would not help me until I was much older. The benefit seemed too far away. Too distant. Too removed.

But if Tom had sold me on the *present* payoff from jogging, I might have taken it up again despite the pain. If he had told me it would help me to sleep better *tonight*, I might have bought into it. Or if he had told me I would feel better *today* and have more stamina to preach *this Sunday*, I might have gone for it.

The same principle holds true for the spiritual life. Knowing there is a future reward in heaven is not always enough motivation to keep us running. Not when everything inside us is screaming, "Quit! Drop out of the race!"

You and I must know there is a present-day payoff, right now, today. In other words, there must be something in it for us in the here and now.

In the last chapter, I told you about Heaven's Heisman—the future reward awaiting us at the end of the race. This chapter will focus on the present reward. Sure, we know that the heavenly reward is important. But I also want you to know what running God's race will do for your life today. This year. This month. This week. This very day.

Giving Up One Kingdom to Gain Another

Jesus Himself said there is a present payoff to running His race. Listen to the words of the Master: "Truly I say to you, there is no one who has left house or wife or brothers or parents or children, for the sake of the kingdom of God, who will not receive many times as much *at this time* and in the age to come, eternal life" (Luke 18:29-30, emphasis added).

Did you hear that? "*At this time!*" That means right *now*. Today. In this life. On this earth. Immediately.

We must ask ourselves: "In what way do I 'receive many times as much at this time'?"

As I unpack these words of Jesus, I first want to put out a disclaimer. I am not espousing a name-it-and-claim-it Christianity. I am not advocating a health, wealth, and prosperity gospel. You know, "My God shall supply all your *greeds* according to His riches in glory" (2 Televangelists 4:7).

If name-it-and-claim-it were the game, Jesus failed to practice what He preached. The Son of Man had no place to lay His head. He possessed only the coat on His back. There was no second home in Egypt. No yacht on the Nile.

What was Jesus saying?

You will notice a cause and effect. Our Lord gave a condition followed by the result. We must leave house, wife, brothers, parents, and children, all for the kingdom of God. If we do, we will receive many times as much in this lifetime, and eternal life in the age to come. We must leave behind our kingdom to receive His kingdom.

Mark's record says, "He will receive *a hundred times as much* now in the *present age*, houses and brothers and sisters and mothers and children and farms, along with persecutions" (Mark 10:30, emphasis added). Jesus was saying we will receive hundreds of houses and brothers and sisters and mothers and children and wives.

What does that mean? To find out, we must look at the context. These verses immediately follow the account of the rich young ruler. Here is how the story begins.

"A ruler questioned Him, saying…'What shall I do to inherit eternal life?'" (Luke 18:18). We all wish people were approaching us asking this question. He was inquiring, "What must I do to be saved?"

Who was this man? He was young, rich, and powerful (Matthew 19:20,22). He was a walking success story. He was honest, devout, wealthy, prominent, highly respected, and influential. He had everything going for him.

Everything, that is, except God.

Notice how Jesus responded to this man. He used evangelistic ways that do not quite fit our methodology. There were no points and a prayer. He just used the Word of God to expose this young upstart's self-righteous egotism and to unmask his dire need for the transformation of his heart.

"You know the commandments," Jesus said, listing numbers five through nine. "Do not commit adultery, do not murder, do not steal, do not bear false witness, honor your father and mother" (Luke 18:20).

In other words, Jesus was saying, "Just be perfect."

"All these things I have kept from my youth," was the reply. In other words, "No problem here. Of course I am morally perfect. Why do you ask? Next question, please."

But Jesus saw through the outer façade into the man's heart. Our Lord saw the greed, the materialism, the worldliness, the self-centeredness. What He saw was a spiritually bankrupt heart—empty and void.

With the skill of a deft surgeon, Jesus cut to the real issue of this man's heart: "One thing you still lack; sell all that you possess and distribute it to the poor, and you shall have treasure in heaven; and come, follow Me."

Jesus was not saying the rich young man must buy his way to heaven. This man's problem was that money—and the controlling power that goes with it—had become his master. His god was gold. His pursuit was possessions. Jesus was saying, "You must follow a new Master. I must become your Lord. Transfer your life and all your possessions under My authority."

Or it is no deal.

This wealthy man considered his money. Then Christ. He went back to itemizing his money. Then back to Christ. Which would it be? It was a moment of decision. Who would be his God? Money, or the Master?

The decision was cast, and money and power won.

This young exec turned on his heels and vanished. He left sad and grieved. His face fell, dejected. Why? He could not have it both ways. His money was too much to give up.

Jesus watched him as he faded into the horizon, then turned to His disciples and said, "How hard it is for those who are wealthy to enter the kingdom of God!" (Luke 18:24).

Yes, it is hard for the rich to be saved. Hard because they have more "things" to forsake. Hard because they have to stand in line like everyone else to receive a free gift. Hard because they are more tied to this world. Hard because it is difficult to forfeit the power and control that comes with money.

How hard?

Jesus said, "It is easier for a camel to go through the eye of a needle than for a rich man to enter the kingdom of God" (verse 25).

That is hard, as in impossible. Camels do not fit through the eyes of sewing needles. It is impossible for a person who wants to keep control of his life and money to become saved.

The disciples took a big gulp and swallowed hard. "Then who can be saved?" they asked (verse 26).

Jesus explained, "The things that are impossible with people are possible with God" (verse 27). In other words, only God can save lost human souls. We cannot buy our way. Nor can we earn our way. Nor can we decide our own terms for following Christ. Only a gracious work of God in our hearts can pry loose the ironclad grip of the world so that we might follow Christ.

You can hear the wheels turning inside Peter's head.

Peter then said to Jesus, "Behold, we have left our own homes and followed You" (verse 28). Interpreted, this means: "Lord, we *have* already done what this young man refused to do. We *have* transferred the ownership of all our life and all that we possess to You. We *have* sold out to You. We *have* taken that step of faith to follow You."

Listen to Peter's words once more: "Behold, we have left our own homes and followed You." What else do you hear? Reading between the lines, Peter is asking, "Lord, what is in it for us?" Or, "Read for us the benefit clause of the contract one more time."

Benefits? Jesus responded, "Truly I say to you, there is no one who has left house or wife or brothers or parents or children, for the sake of the kingdom of God, who will not receive many times as much at this time and in the age to come, eternal life" (verses 29-30).

That is the benefit clause for following Christ. Here is a present pay-off for running God's race. There is a benefit at this time, as well as in the age to come. One is present, the other is future. The former is temporal, the latter eternal. Jesus promised houses and family now, and eternal life later.

So what do we gain *now*?

Presently, we "will receive a hundred times as much now in the present age, houses and brothers and sisters and mothers and children and farms" (Mark 10:30). Hundreds of houses. Hundreds of brothers, sisters, parents, and children.

Here is how it works. When I entered God's kingdom, I left behind my old life—a life without Christ. I surrendered the control of my life to Him. I reassigned all my life possessions to Him. I renounced myself and recognized Christ as the rightful Lord over my life. I chose to assign my chief loyalty to Him over any earthly relationship, whether with my wife or children, my brothers or parents.

But in giving up, I gain. In fact, I gain far more than I ever give up. In leaving behind the world, I enter into God's family and gain a new network of spiritual brothers and sisters around the globe. I also gain welcome into hundreds, even millions, of homes. I now have a common bond and kindred spirit in Christ with those believers.

I gain the support, encouragement, and strength of hundreds and millions of these new spiritual siblings. As I have needs—whether they be spiritual, material, emotional, or financial—my new spiritual family rallies to meet them. And as I see needs in the lives of other Christians, I give to help them. All that I possess is available to share. This is because I have transferred the ownership of all I have to God. Then, as He makes me aware of others' needs, I am to share with them. I give because my possessions no longer belong to me, but Christ and to those who are in His kingdom.

Do not write off our Lord's words. He is not talking about a communist approach to living. He is not saying the state owns your possessions. This is Christianity, where you hold your possessions, not the government. You are now a steward over them for God, who owns them all.

If we will leave it all, we will gain it all. If we will give it all up to follow Christ, there is a new network of support into which we enter.

We can receive hundreds of houses. Hundreds of brothers, sisters, parents, and children. Today. All by entering into the network of God's kingdom.

An Eternal Benefit

But, to be sure, there is also an eternal benefit in following Christ, one that endures forever. Jesus added to our benefit clause these words: "And in the ages to come, eternal life." Eternal life begins right now and continues throughout the ages to come.

Eternal life refers primarily not to an eternal length of years, although that is true. The emphasis here is upon the quality of life we receive. Literally, this means the life of the ages to come. It is the supernatural, eternal life abiding in our souls now. It is not adding eternal years to our life, but eternal life to our years.

This eternal life begins the moment we receive Jesus Christ. As Jesus Himself promised us: "He who hears My word, and believes Him who sent Me, has eternal life, and does not come into judgment, but has passed out of death into life" (John 5:24). "Has" is present tense. Jesus said he who believes *has* eternal life—right now.

I used to think eternal life would begin the moment I entered into heaven. If I could just hold out faithful to the end and make it to heaven, I would then be safe at last. Under this scheme, eternal life would begin then, in eternity.

But that is not what the Bible teaches. Eternal life does not begin once we enter heaven. It began the moment we received Christ into our lives. At our conversion, the life of eternity with God in heaven forever came into our earthly life.

This eternal life continues forever, throughout eternity future. This life remains uninterrupted, never to be forfeited. And it has already started in this life.

Jesus said, "My sheep hear My voice, and I know them, and they follow Me; and I give eternal life to them, and they will never perish, and no one will snatch them out of My hand. My Father, who has given them to Me, is greater than all; and no one is able to snatch them out of the Father's hand" (John 10:27-29).

That is eternal life that lasts *forever*! What is settled for eternity can never be lost within time. Once converted to Christ, our salvation is signed, sealed, and delivered. We are always safe in the Father's hand. Every believer is eternally secure in the Shepherd's fold.

Specifically, I want to note several key aspects of this eternal life into which we have entered.

Knowing the Eternal Christ

First, eternal life means knowing Christ, beginning now and forever. Jesus prayed, "This is eternal life, that they may know You, the only true God, and Jesus Christ whom You have sent" (John 17:3). Eternal life is an entirely different dimension of living, unlike anything we have ever known or experienced.

Eternal life is not just getting man out of hell and into heaven. It is also getting God out of heaven and into man. By this, a believer receives a new quality of life, a supernatural life. It is the life of God in the soul of man.

The moment we entered into a personal knowledge of Christ, we entered God's race. With every step of the race, we grow to know Christ more intimately. The apostle Peter wrote, "Grow in the grace and knowledge of our Lord and Savior Jesus Christ" (2 Peter 3:18). While finite man can never completely know an infinite God, we can grow to know Him better.

It has been my privilege to meet some special, famous people. I have met several US senators and governors. I have met multiple Heisman Trophy winners, baseball and football Hall of Famers, and Super Bowl MVPs. I have met golfers who have won The Masters and the US Open. I have met gold medal winners in track.

But as special as it is to meet a famous athlete or politician, that is nothing compared with knowing Jesus Christ. The greatest privilege in the entire world is to know God and His Son, Jesus Christ. We were made in God's image with the capacity to know Him. Our hearts were made to know Christ, who is the fulfillment of our deepest longings. This is eternal life.

Some people try to fill that void with other relationships. But none will satisfy except knowing Christ. A round world will not fit in a triangular heart. Augustine said that our hearts are restless until they find their rest in God.

Let us clarify exactly what it means to know Christ. The New Testament Greek word for "know" (Greek, *ginosko*) refers to experiential knowledge, or what we have come to know not merely by observation, but by firsthand experience. Knowing Christ means to personally experience a relationship with Him. It means to have communion with Him— internally, intimately, and continually. Just like we know another person, we know Jesus Christ, only more deeply.

Some people say, "Jesus Christ lived two thousand years ago across the ocean in a distant land. He's a part of ancient history. How can I possibly know Him *today*?"

Although Christ was crucified, He rose from the grave. He is alive! We cannot know a dead man. We can only know someone who is alive. Because Jesus Christ is alive today, we can know Him personally. When we receive Christ into our lives, He comes to live within us (Colossians 1:27). He establishes His royal residence within our souls. His indwelling Holy Spirit gives us the knowledge of Christ.

Knowing Christ is much the same as knowing another person. What are the marks of a close relationship with another person? Intimacy. Communication. Transparency. Self-disclosure. Mutual support. Commitment. Concern for the other person's feelings. All this and more characterizes a believer's relationship with Jesus Christ.

What a world of difference there is between merely knowing *about* Christ and actually *knowing* Christ. It is the difference between possessing mere intellectual facts about someone and having the experiential knowledge of that one. It is the contrast between knowing with the head and knowing with the heart. It is the difference between empty religion and eternal life. Knowing Christ is so much more than merely knowing facts about Him as an important historical figure. To know Christ means to have personal fellowship with Him.

For example, consider this: I used to know *about* Augusta National and The Masters Tournament. I had read several books about The Masters. I had talked to others who had played golf at Augusta. I had memorized all the holes. I knew all about the course's rich history. I was a walking encyclopedia on The Masters. But I had never attended. I only knew about it from a distance.

But then came that day when I traveled to Augusta, Georgia, and was privileged to attend The Masters myself. I walked the lush fairways. I climbed the steep Georgian hills. I smelled the blooming azaleas. I felt the crowd's excitement. I met some tour players. I experienced the mystique of The Masters firsthand. Previously, I had only known about Augusta National from a distance. But then I acquired a personal, first-hand experience of it.

Multiply that privilege a trillion times a trillion times a trillion, and we only begin to scratch the surface of the privilege of what it means to personally know Jesus Christ in our hearts.

How much better to know the Master than The Masters!

God wants us to know Him, first and foremost. He does not want a performance, but a relationship. Christ is more interested that we know Him than that we be in the race for Him. This is especially true if our running is empty and void of a growing intimacy with Him.

Receiving Eternal Forgiveness

Second, eternal life means receiving God's forgiveness, now and forever. Jesus said, "God so loved the world, that He gave His only begotten Son, that whoever believes in Him shall not perish, but have eternal life. For God did not send the Son into the world to judge the world, but that the world might be saved through Him" (John 3:16-17).

Eternal life is a right standing with God. The guilt and burden of our sin is removed. We are forgiven. Our sins are washed away. All our sins—past, present, and future—are taken away, and we receive the perfect righteousness of Jesus Christ.

The apostle Paul wrote, "Not having a righteousness of my own derived from the Law, but that which is through faith in Christ, the righteousness which comes from God on the basis of faith…" (Philippians 3:9). This righteousness that comes from God means that despite being guilty, we receive a right standing of acceptance before the Holy Judge of the universe. By faith alone, we are given an acquittal in heaven's court. We are declared righteous and given a perfect standing before God.

When we believe in Jesus Christ as our Savior, God sees us through the perfect, imputed righteousness of the Lord Jesus Christ. He sees us dressed in the holiness of His sinless Son. In the great exchange of the cross, our sins are charged to the account of Christ, and His righteousness is charged to us.

Clearly, this perfect righteousness that we have is not from ourselves. It comes from Jesus Christ. We cannot give ourselves a right standing before God.

A right standing before God must come from God. It is a free gift that He gives to undeserving, sinful, wrath-deserving people like you and me. And this gift is received by faith alone: "By grace you have been saved through faith; and that not of yourselves, it is the gift of God; not as a result of works, that no one may boast" (Ephesians 2:8-9).

By His death on the cross, Jesus Christ alone provides this gift. The perfect life He lived is charged to our account as though we had lived without sin. Next to our name, God records "the perfect righteousness of Jesus Christ." Once guilty and condemned, God reckons to us the perfect righteousness of Christ. We are unconditionally accepted before Him. Once forgiven, God will never bring our sins back up again.

If I gave you a deposit slip for my bank account, and you deposited your money with my deposit slip, it would be posted to my account. I have not earned it, nor worked for it. It is simply placed into my account, and it becomes mine. That is the way salvation occurs. When I believe in Christ, His righteousness is transferred into my account in heaven. Though I have not earned it, a right standing before God is legally mine.

A man was telling his close friend about an argument he had recently with his wife. "Oh, I hate it," he said. "Every time we have an argument, she gets historical."

The friend replied, "You mean hysterical."

"No, I mean historical," he insisted. "Every time we argue, she drags up everything from my past and holds it against me."

Aren't you glad God never gets "historical" with us? Once forgiven, He never dredges up our past sins as evidence against us. Our sins are placed beneath the blood of Christ forever.

What does Christ's righteousness have to do with my running God's race? It means that I run this race *not* in order to achieve a right standing before God. I do not strive to gain His acceptance. I do not compete to enter His kingdom. Instead, I run because I am freely forgiven by God. I run out of love for Him, not out of guilt. That is a world of difference.

Think of what powerful motivation it is to run to win. I run without any fear of His condemnation at the finish line. Paul wrote, "Having been justified by faith, we have peace with God through our Lord Jesus Christ" (Romans 5:1)

If I were running a race and knew there was a strong probability that I would be assassinated at the finish line, how fast do you think I would run? Believe me, I would slow down to a snail's pace. I would prolong being shot as long as possible. In fact, I would stop running altogether. I would do anything to avoid being shot. I would absolutely dread the finish line. I would even reverse my field and run the other way—anything to avoid finishing the race.

That is how many view the Christian life. But just the opposite is true in God's race. When we entered His race, we received Christ's perfect righteousness, which, in turn, gave us a right standing before God. Therefore, Jesus awaits us at the finish line with open arms of love and acceptance. He calls us with an encouraging voice. That divine acceptance impels us each day to run for His glory.

We run not with a morbid, unhealthy self-preoccupation, scared about whether or not God will receive us. Instead, we push forward, knowing He has already accepted us in Christ.

Eternal Strength to Persevere

Third, eternal life means I have God's supernatural grace within me that enables me to live the Christian life. His power strengthens me to run the race in a way that glorifies Him.

Paul said, "I can do all things through Him who strengthens me" (Philippians 4:13). God's power indwells us in the person of the Holy Spirit, whom we received at our conversion. Our problem is that we so often fail to tap into His power that is always there. We are like the man who was pushing his car up a hill only to discover he merely needed to turn the key and ignite the powerful engine. How much better it is to turn on the power and enjoy the ride. So it is in the Christian life.

Running is a demanding sport, draining every ounce of energy a person possesses. Running God's race saps all our power. We soon become depleted mentally, emotionally, and physically. That is the nature of running. It is full of uphill climbs, obstacles to overcome, winds to endure, and the scorching sun that leaves us feeling empty.

At times, we grow so weary that we want to pull over and stop running. But the race of life demands that we keep moving forward. We cannot stop. There are no yellow caution flags to stop this race, no pit stops. Just the daily grind.

To run life's race, we must have the power of God. In our weakness, God's power is perfected. The very divine power that raised Jesus Christ from the dead is available to us for living the Christian life. This supernatural strength energizes us to run life's race. By His grace, we are raised to walk a new resurrection life in Christ.

We are like the man who went into a hardware store one Saturday morning to buy a saw. Seeing an easy mark, the salesman showed him a fancy chain saw. He commented that it was their best seller with the latest in technology, and guaranteed it to cut ten cords of firewood a day.

The inexperienced customer was impressed with the sales hype and bought the chain saw on the spot.

Later that day, this same man returned to the store, chain saw in hand, looking somewhat haggard, exhausted, and exasperated. "Something is wrong with this saw," he moaned. "I worked as hard as I could and only managed to cut three cords of wood. I could do four cords with my old-fashioned saw."

Looking confused, the salesman said, "Here, let me try it on some wood we keep out back." They went to the woodpile, the salesman pulled the cord, and the motor roared to life.

The customer leaped back and exclaimed, "What is that noise?"

We can be much like this exasperated customer, attempting to live the Christian life in our own strength. But we have God's power within us, enabling us to do what is otherwise impossible. We have the power to resist temptation and love the unlovely. We have the power to rejoice in trials and overcome the world. We have the power to resist the devil and witness for Christ. We have the power to break old habits and live our new life in Christ. We have the power to run God's race.

I once flew from Charlotte, North Carolina, to Little Rock, Arkansas, via Atlanta, where I was to preach early the next morning. Unfortunately, my flight was very late leaving Charlotte, which caused us to circle Atlanta for the longest time. When we finally landed in Atlanta, it was exactly one minute *after* my flight to Little Rock was scheduled to leave.

I made a mad dash through the terminal, down the escalator, and to the underground tram just in time to miss the departing tram. I had no time to wait for the next one. My only hope was to run to the next terminal a few hundred yards away. So I took off running.

As I sped on foot and dodged my way through crowds of travelers, I noticed a moving sidewalk on my right. I leaped onto it. It began moving me to the next terminal, but still not fast enough. So, I did the only thing a desperate man would do. I began running on the moving sidewalk.

You cannot believe how fast I was able to run. I was flying! I passed everybody, even the tram! I was at the next terminal in no time. I then bounded up the moving escalator to my terminal and sprinted down to my flight's gate—just as they were closing the plane's door.

The smiling flight attendant said, "I guess you were just supposed to make this flight." Interestingly enough, I was flying to Little Rock to preach on God's providence.

The moving sidewalk made the difference. It enabled me to run faster and longer than I ever could have in my own strength. I was running, but the moving sidewalk gave me an advantage, propelling me forward at an unusually fast pace. I ran, but with a far greater power enabling me.

That is precisely how the resurrection power of Christ works in our lives. God has a race for us to run, and we are responsible to run it. We must make maximum effort to put one foot in front of the other. Yet as we do, the dynamic power of God within us energizes us, propelling us forward. By His Spirit, we are divinely enabled to run faster, longer, and straighter than we ever could have on our own. As we run by faith—yielding our life to Christ—He releases His supernatural power in us, which propels us forward.

The prophet Isaiah said, "Those who wait for the LORD will gain new strength; they will mount up with wings like eagles, they will run and not get tired, they will walk and not become weary" (Isaiah 40:31).

Indeed, this is supernatural power!

Do you see the present payoff for running God's race? Do you want this immediate benefit? You can have it! There is a network of relationships—the family of God—all pulling with you to help meet your needs. Hundreds of houses and family members are available for your good. Eternal life is yours, now and forever. Because you know the pardon of Christ, the power of Christ is all yours.

Run for Your Life!

I began this chapter by telling you about Tom Jones, a great quarterback for the Arkansas Razorbacks. I want to conclude by telling you about another great Razorback—Don Horton—who was involved in a play that will forever be etched in Arkansas football history.

The year was 1957, and Arkansas and Texas A&M were clashing in the biggest game of the year. The Aggies came to Arkansas undefeated and on the fast track to a coveted national championship. Coached by the legendary Paul "Bear" Bryant, the Aggies boasted the player who would go on to become the 1957 Heisman Trophy winner, John David Crow, as well as other noted future NFL greats like Gene Stallings, Jack Pardee, and Bobby Joe Conrad.

Late in the game, Texas A&M was clinging to a 7-6 lead. The Aggies were driving the length of the field for a second touchdown, which would seal the victory and pave the way to the national title. They were keeping the ball on the ground, eating up precious time on the clock. Arkansas was out of timeouts, and the game clock was running out. On all counts, the Razorback cause seemed hopeless.

With A&M only a few yards away from the game-clinching touchdown, the players lined up with a receiver split wide to the left hash mark. He was covered by a lonely Razorback defender, Don Horton.

Then the unthinkable occurred.

Roddy Osborne, the Aggie quarterback, threw a pass into the left flat. Don Horton, the Arkansas defensive back, gambled and stepped in front of the Aggie receiver. Guessing right, Horton intercepted the pass on the dead run. He was now running full speed with the ball in his hands, heading for the Razorback end zone!

Before him lay ninety yards of green grass, glory, and fame. A national upset seemed clinched. His name surely would be recorded in Arkansas history for as long as football is played in the Ozarks.

Horton, a high school track star with blazing speed, set off on the run of his life. As he sprinted down the east sideline, the Arkansas student body was on their feet, cheering and hollering, delirious with excitement. The Aggies' national championship crown was about to be denied them.

Suddenly—out of nowhere—came a streaking blur. It was Roddy Osborne, the Aggie quarterback who had thrown the interception. Pursuing Horton all the way down the field, he came running like a madman.

Though blessed with only average speed, Osborne was narrowing the gap. Somehow he ran down the lightning-fast Horton at the Aggie eighteen-yard line. Even though the slower Osborne had farther to run, he, nevertheless, overtook the faster Horton, making the game-saving tackle. No one on the field had possessed the speed to catch Don Horton that day, yet the slow-footed Osborne ran him down.

Arkansas could not score from the eighteen-yard line, and Texas A&M hung on to preserve the victory, 7-6. They finished the season number one, and claimed the national championship.

After the game, reporters huddled around Bear Bryant in the Aggie locker room and asked, "How could Roddy Osborne possibly catch Don Horton?"

The Bear growled, "Horton was only running for the game-winning touchdown. Osborne was running for his life."

So it is for every Christian. We too are running for our lives, motivated not by fear, but out of gratitude for the undeserved benefits of God's grace.

We run with a higher calling—a heavenly calling—yet with earthly benefits we can experience today. Right now. In this life. On this earth. Today.

4

Pump Up
and Air Out!

Do you want to run a marathon?

Great! But first I need to break some news to you. This is deeply profound, so you had better read this sitting down. Are you ready for this? No one just wakes up one morning and, on a whim, impulsively decides, "I think I will run a marathon today." You might as well say, "I think I will swim the Pacific Ocean today."

Can you imagine anything so ridiculous? If you tried to run a marathon without getting into shape, you would never make it. You would run as far as you could—in most cases, not far—and then lay down utterly exhausted.

Do you realize how long a marathon is? It is twenty-six-plus miles. Most summer vacations are not that long. You get frequent-flyer miles at that distance. Twenty-six miles? You pass through three time zones. See America, run a marathon!

Any race that long requires months of rigorous training, perhaps even years. No one would dare to run a marathon without first getting in shape. It is too demanding and too long.

Yet this is precisely how many people are living their Christian lives. They attempt to run God's race without ever training, without getting into shape, and they are utterly exhausting themselves in the process.

As Christians, we should learn from the marathon runner. A runner must be committed to rigorous training in order to succeed. If he is to win, he must train countless hours. Let us turn back the calendar again to the first century.

An Ancient Training Ritual

In the ancient Olympic and Isthmian games, a long-distance runner would begin training a minimum of ten months in advance. He would submit to rigorous discipline in order to win. His goal was clear, his purpose sure. In addition to maintaining his running routine, he would undergo a strict and highly disciplined regimen of eating, sleeping, and exercising right. He was intent on honing his body into the best possible shape in order to run for one specific purpose—namely, to win.

One month before the games, this athlete would move to Corinth, ten miles from where the Isthmian Games were held. There he would submit to training on site under the watchful eye of a personal coach. This final training stage meant early rising and spending long days of lifting weights, running exercises, and pushing himself to the limit. He would do all this to prepare to run the famous marathon. Any success he might experience would be due, in largest measure, to the intensity of his preparation. Nowhere is such rigorous training more necessary than in the marathon.

So it is in the Christian life.

If we are to run God's race—a lifelong marathon—we must submit to serious training. We must get in shape if we are to win the longest race of our lives.

Bobby Knight, at one time the winningest college basketball coach, said, "The will to win is not nearly as important as the will to prepare to win." This principle is true in the spiritual realm as well. As believers, we must prepare to win the race set before us through rigorous training, discipline, and hard work.

We entered God's race the day we were converted to Christ. And we will run this race until the day we die. If we are to run victoriously, we must constantly submit ourselves to rigorous spiritual training

The Basics to Winning Heaven's Crown

This chapter focuses upon training to win heaven's crown. It explores the spiritual discipline necessary to win in God's race.

The key passage that epitomizes this spiritual program is 1 Timothy

4:7-11. The apostle Paul wrote, "Discipline yourself for the purpose of godliness; for bodily discipline is only of little profit, but godliness is profitable for all things, since it holds promise for the present life and also for the life to come" (verses 7-8).

Paul was saying, "Get yourself in shape. Strengthen your commitment to Christ. Develop your spiritual muscles. Get your mind disciplined. Build up your faith." This involves four key basics: (1) a strong commitment, (2) a special diet, (3) a strenuous workout, and (4) a sure hope. I want us to consider each.

A Strong Commitment

First, if I am to be a strong runner, I must be firmly committed to a training program. Working out is not easy. Discipline is hard work. If I do not make a solid commitment to getting in shape, I will start the training process only to soon falter, fail, and fall by the wayside.

Have you ever decided, "I am going to start running to get in shape?" You probably have at some time. So how do you get started?

First, you buy the newest model of running shoes. They have more gadgets and features than a computer. Then you buy a running suit to look great! You are now ready to begin a lifetime of running.

You see others running. They make it look so effortless. *No problem*, you think. *I can do it too. Why did I not start earlier?*

You map out a course through the neighborhood. It will probably become famous once you make it big as a runner. People will sell maps outlining your first running route. The price of real estate along this route is sure to go up. Once *Runner's World* finds out where you run, there will be no privacy. Such is the price of stardom.

You are ready to launch your new running career. Everyone at the office knows all about it. You have told them you are now an official runner—two miles, at a slow pace.

Your first workout is scheduled for early tomorrow morning, before sunrise. This is your maiden voyage. You go to bed rehearsing your acceptance speech for "Newcomer of the Year." But in the still quiet of the early morning hours—buzzzzzzz!—the alarm goes off, sending you through the ceiling. You subconsciously slap the alarm off. It is a lightning-quick chop that would make a black belt envious. You think, *It is so cold, I am going to stay under the warm covers for just a few more minutes.* Before you know it, you have dozed back to sleep. No running this morning.

You reschedule your jaunt for tomorrow morning. No problem. Space shuttles are often rescheduled for a later launch. But as you are watching the evening news, you hear there is a ten percent chance of morning showers. *Hmmm, I better not chance it tomorrow. I cannot afford to get my new running shoes wet.*

Day after day, your creativity approaches genius level as you design new excuses not to run. After a few runs to the mailbox and back, your aspirations to run are dead. Your running career is now history— *ancient* history.

What was the problem? Pure and simple, your grand illusions had no real commitment behind them.

It is one thing to feel warm fuzzies about getting in shape. But it is something else to discipline yourself, morning after morning, to run. Training happens only with the help of a strong commitment. It never just happens by itself.

Do Not Be a Spiritual Couch Potato

Commitment is a lost word today. For too many of us, commitment is a task we absolutely, positively, unequivocally are going to do—until something easier or better comes along. But real commitment is making a solid agreement to do something in the future—no matter what happens. Regardless, sink or swim, it is being firmly obligated to a person or task.

So it is that believers should be committed to spiritual disciplines. But, sad to say, too many people are spiritual couch potatoes. For them, commitment to spiritual discipline means nothing. They have passing moments of great intentions, but zero commitment to get in shape.

They are content to be season ticket holders at church, but never seem to get out of the starting blocks. They are professional spectators, not serious runners.

Serious training begins with counting the cost. Jesus said, "Which one of you, when he wants to build a tower, does not first sit down and calculate the cost to see if he has enough to complete it? Otherwise, when he has laid a foundation and is not able to finish, all who observe it begin to ridicule him, saying, 'This man began to build and was not able to finish'" (Luke 14:28-30).

The fact is, it will cost us a high price to be God's champion. That price is never marked down. Godliness is never on sale. Genuine spirituality offers no cash-and-carry deals. It always requires paying the full price of hard work and strenuous exercise. Plus tax.

The Cost of Commitment

What will it cost us? Spiritually, it will cost us time, hard work, and self-denial.

First, *it requires our time.* If we are to be in shape, it will require invested time in prayer and Bible study. These disciplines must be fixed priorities in our everyday lives. These faith-builders are nonnegotiable. It will require bringing our schedule into submission to our spiritual goals. It will necessitate that we say no to many other things.

Time has been called a seamstress, specializing in alterations. Let me warn you: No matter how busy you become, do not cut out Bible study and prayer. Not if you want to win.

Are you willing to pay this price?

Second, *it requires hard work.* Spiritual fitness requires concerted effort in digging into God's Word. Bible study always demands our intense concentration. It takes an expenditure of mental energy to remain focused to master, memorize, and meditate upon Scripture.

Are you willing to pay this price?

Third, *it requires self-denial.* It will require saying no to the world and yes to God. It will require resisting the devil and obeying God. It means you must decrease, and He must increase.

Are you willing to pay this price?

If the answer is yes, then purpose in your heart to take these first steps out of the starting block. Drive the stake down. By God's grace, say, "I will pay the price to get into the Word, no matter what the cost."

Just do it!

Remember, paying the price has eternal dividends. Working out in God's Word and pushing yourself in prayer is like making a deposit in a bank. You are investing in your future. One day there will be a spiritual payoff with compound interest. In the end, you will be crowned as a spiritual champion for Christ.

What most characterizes a true champion is his heart. He is known for his will to win. He is marked by his resolve to train, by his determination to pay the price. The difference lies deep in the heart.

The Heart of a Champion

A man went to his high school reunion accompanied by his twenty-year-old son. He could hardly wait to find his former football coach and show off his muscular son, who was now playing college ball.

After introducing his son, the beaming father asked the coach, "Who is the bigger man?"

The coach looked at the aging man, now bald and bulging. He then checked out his growing, bulky son. Clearly the son was now bigger, taller, and stronger.

But the coach suddenly grabbed at the father's chest, clutching his shirt right over his heart. He said, "This is how I still measure a man. By his heart."

That is how God measures a man as well. The Lord weighs his heart. A long-distance race goes not to the swiftest of foot, but to the strongest of heart.

In 1 Samuel 16:7, the Lord tells us plainly, "Do not look at his appearance or at the height of his stature...man looks at the outward appearance, but the LORD looks at the heart." Proverbs 4:23 adds, "Watch over your heart with all diligence, for from it flow the springs of life."

The first step toward winning the crown of life is making a heart commitment to pay the price in rigorous training. Everything else flows out of this. The heart must be firmly committed.

A Special Diet

Second, Paul pointed out the importance of consuming in the Word. He said we are to be "constantly nourished on the words of the faith and of the sound doctrine" (1 Timothy 4:6). Just as a proper, balanced diet is critical to a marathon runner, so it is to the Christian.

I am the last person in the world to talk about this. It has been suggested that I eat from the three basic food groups—McDonald's, Wendy's, and Burger King. But a champion runner must rise above what's popular and maintain a special diet for energy and health. Better food leads to higher energy.

Strenuous workouts can burn an extra 1500 calories a day. Without a high-energy diet, fatigue will take over and prevent an athlete from reaching his goal. But the fatigue factor can be avoided through a strict diet.

Devouring the Word of God

Just as carbohydrates provide fuel for the body, so the Word of God provides high-energy food for the Christian life. Spiritual exhaustion can be avoided through ongoing nourishment from the living and abiding Word.

Nourishment is the key word here. We are to feed on the right food—God's Word—and digest it and absorb it into our spiritual system. This means drawing the necessary nutrients and energy supply from God's Word for fuel that will enable us to run God's race with endurance.

We must constantly nourish ourselves on God's Word. We cannot settle for a mere sporadic meal here and there. Instead, we must feed regularly, even daily, on the Scriptures.

Irregular eating habits will kill a runner's energy level. Skipping meals can leave him drained and fatigued. This same thing will happen with our spiritual stamina if we do not maintain consistent, regular feeding on God's Word.

We should set aside time every day to read and devour God's Word. At a minimum, fifteen minutes each day is needed, probably more. We must constantly feast on God's Word so we have the spiritual energy we need to run God's race successfully.

Longing for the Word

The apostle Peter wrote, "Like newborn babes, long for the pure milk of the word, so that by it you may grow in respect to salvation" (1 Peter 2:2). God's Word, like nutritious milk, contains what is needed to produce our spiritual growth and maintain our health. Believers must crave the Scriptures. If we long for it, we will devour it.

Jesus says, "Man shall not live on bread alone, but on every word that proceeds out of the mouth of God" (Matthew 4:4). God's Word is like bread—it is a basic staple in any Christian's diet. It is our true daily bread. So we must devour it if we are to have the spiritual energy that will enable us to run the race and win.

Paul referred to God's truth as "milk" and "solid food" (1 Corinthians 3:2). Like nutritious milk and substantial food, Scripture is absolutely necessary for our spiritual development and strength.

David testified, "How sweet are Your words to my taste! Yes, sweeter than honey to my mouth!" (Psalm 119:103). God's Word, like honey, is sweet, satisfying, and provides lasting energy. This is why we must savor it.

Jeremiah wrote, "Your words were found and I ate them, and Your words became for me a joy and the delight of my heart" (Jeremiah 15:16). We must feed our minds and nourish our hearts on Scripture. It is undeniable that we must eat and enjoy the Word.

The Bible remains the "breakfast of champions." We must eat at God's training table every day and be nourished by His Word.

Five Daily Nutrients

Below are five strategic steps for receiving consistent spiritual nourishment from the Scriptures. Remember, these require commitment and discipline. This is necessary if we are to run and win the race.

Master the Word

The first step is to *master God's Word*. We must read and study God's Word to strategically grasp its truths. Paul said, "Be diligent to present yourself approved to God as a workman who does not need to be ashamed, handling accurately the word of truth" (2 Timothy 2:15).

This presentation to God requires mastering the essential truths of His Word.

This means you must have a workout schedule—a game plan—for reading the Bible. You should read through the entire Bible systematically, rather than scan bits and pieces at random. Or, you can set up a daily schedule of reading a few chapters from an Old Testament book and then a few chapters from a New Testament book. You could follow this pattern until you have finished both Testaments. Or, you can read the same book in the Bible through several times consecutively. Each reading will reveal new and hidden truths.

As you read God's Word, give attention to the context, the historical setting, and key words, especially those that are repeated, emphatic, and highly theological. These will help shed increased light on the verses you are reading.

You will want to pay special attention to the following: Who is speaking? To whom is he speaking? What is the historical background? What was the intended application for that day? What does it mean for believers today?

Ask God, as the psalmist did, to open your spiritual eyes to His truth: "Open my eyes, that I may behold wonderful things from Your law" (Psalm 119:18). Ask Him to plant His message in your heart, like precious seed in the soil, so that it will germinate, sprout, and bear fruit. Ask the Holy Spirit to enlighten your mind and direct your life accordingly.

Magnify the Word

The second step is to *magnify God's Word*. That is, elevate its place in your life. Give it a place of preeminence. Recognize its authority. Obey its commands. Follow its examples. Apply its principles. Claim its promises. Heed its warnings. When the Bible speaks, God speaks.

Follow Paul's advice to the believers at Colosse: "Let the word of Christ richly dwell within you" (Colossians 3:16). Allow Scripture to settle down and be at home in your heart. Make it the absolute authority of your life. Permit it to set deep roots in you, and it will bear precious fruit in your life.

Obey it. Live it. Follow it.

Memorize the Word

The third step is to *memorize God's Word*. We retain God's Word in our heart by memorizing it. The psalmist testified, "Your word I have treasured in my heart, that I may not sin against You" (Psalm 119:11). To treasure His Word means to hide it, like a valuable treasure, in your heart. This is the opposite of letting it go in one ear and out the other.

Memorizing God's Word allows the Holy Spirit to better reprove, correct, and train you to win the race. Hide it in your heart, and you will be empowered.

Our Lord Jesus Christ memorized much of God's Word—probably all of it. He was able to quote it because it was hidden in His heart. He carried it with Him wherever He went. In the wilderness, our Lord was tempted three times by Satan, and each time He resisted by citing God's Word. He said, "It is written…It is written…It is written" (Matthew 4:4,7,10).

If Jesus Christ, the perfect Son of God, memorized God's Word, we certainly need to do likewise. If we are to run victoriously, we need to have it memorized in our minds.

Meditate on the Word

The fourth step is to *meditate on God's Word*. Meditation suggests digesting the meal you have eaten. The word *meditate* is well illustrated by the way a cow chews her cud throughout the day. The cow is extracting every tasty tidbit and healthy nutrient from her food. We too must chew on God's Word, over and over, until we understand it correctly, appreciate it fully, and grasp its meaning personally.

As the psalmist declared, "Your servant meditates on Your statutes… Make me understand the way of Your precepts, so I will meditate on Your wonders" (Psalm 119:23,27). If we are to endure in the race, our minds must be stayed upon the truth of Scripture.

Minister the Word

The fifth step is to *minister God's Word*. God has committed to all believers the message of reconciliation (2 Corinthians 5:19). As His servants, we must speak and teach God's Word to others. When we counsel others, we must use the wisdom of His Word. When we encourage others, we can share the comfort of the Word. And when we confront others, we can use the authority of the Word to challenge them.

The more we minister God's Word, the more it will become a part of us. All believers are ministers for Christ and as such, we are to be spreading His Word to others (Ephesians 4:12). Whether from a church pulpit, a business office, a school classroom, or wherever we live, every Christian is to be about the business of spreading God's Word.

These five steps are all necessary for a healthy spiritual life. First there must be a constant intake of the Word, and then there must be an outflow of it from us into the world.

Dry River, Stagnant Swamp, Mighty River

Our lives will be either like a dry creek bed, a stagnant swamp, or a mighty river.

A dry creek bed has no water flowing into it. It is lifeless, with nothing growing in it. This pictures a person's life with no intake of God's Word. Such a person is spiritually dead.

One who is like a stagnant swamp has an inflow, but no outflow. The water flows in, but just sits there, going nowhere. Soon the stagnant water begins to stink. This swamp pictures a Christian life with an inflow of God's Word, but with no outflow into the lives of others. The Word just sits there, self-contained. Lifeless. Stinking.

Conversely, a mighty river is characterized by constant movement and flow. The water is not stagnant, but always moving. As soon as it flows into a given area, it continues to move onward. This pictures a believer's life in which the Scriptures are constantly flowing in and through a willing heart, touching and impacting others. This healthy dynamic is the final stage of a good spiritual diet.

Strenuous Workout

The third step in training is undergoing a rigorous exercise program. Strenuous workouts, Paul said, are necessary: "Discipline yourself for the purpose of godliness; for bodily discipline is only of little profit, but godliness is profitable for all things, since it holds promise for the present life and also for the life to come" (1 Timothy 4:7-8).

The Discipline of Discipleship

The word *discipline* refers to the effort of exercising, training, and working out. It pictures someone working out in a gym. It comes from the same word from which we have derived the English word *gymnasium*, which literally means a place where one becomes naked in order to work out. Discipline originally involved stripping down for the purpose of working out. In the ancient world, young athletes worked out in the nude for freedom of movement, and the gymnasium was where they trained. So, *discipline* came to mean the strenuous training an athlete does in a gymnasium to get in shape.

Every successful athlete must train and work out. There are no exceptions. He must exercise, lift weights, do stretching exercises like sit-ups, push-ups, and pull-ups. He does all this for the purpose of getting into shape and keeping his muscles toned so he can win.

"Discipline yourself," Paul said. This is something I myself must do. It is my personal responsibility. No one else can be disciplined for me. As an act of my will, I must choose to engage in the training process.

This discipline is "for the purpose of godliness." Spiritual discipline produces godliness, or devotion to God. Godliness is the virtue of heartfelt reverence and inward piety toward God. It is loving God and becoming like Him.

Sure, bodily discipline is profitable. It strengthens the body and builds character. But it is "only of little profit" because it merely develops the body, not the spirit. And it does so only for now, not for eternity. But spiritual discipline is profitable for the entire person, for time and eternity. Paul said, "It holds promise for the present life and also for the life to come" (verse 8). Spiritual training is far more important because it impacts all of our life forever.

The Power Hour

When I think of discipline, I think of the off-season conditioning drills that I underwent on the football team at Texas Tech. Our winter workouts were from January to March and prepared us for the fall football season in September to November. The victories of the fall season were actually won months earlier in the winter training program. Any advantage we could achieve through our conditioning would often mean the difference between victory and defeat.

Our daily workout program was divided into four fifteen-minute periods. We called it the "Power Hour." It was a demanding training regimen designed to develop and train every aspect of the athlete—the most strenuous sixty minutes you can imagine.

Building Spiritual Strength

First, there was the *weight-lifting room*. The equipment here helped to build up our muscles. Every exercise had specific muscles designed to bulk up and strengthen. No muscle was overlooked or left underdeveloped. Specially designed weight machines could accommodate three or four athletes at a time, each working on a separate exercise.

The athletes advanced through the weight room, pumping the weights as many times as they could. We moved from one machine to the next, like a long train winding through a valley.

Even so, we must do heavy lifting in the Scriptures. Like a weight machine, the Word of God functions to build up our faith and strengthen our commitment to Christ. Paul affirmed this when he said that "the word of His grace…is able to build you up" (Acts 20:32). He claimed that the Word preached and taught is profitable for "the building up of the body of Christ" into a growing knowledge of Christ and Christlikeness (Ephesians 4:12-13).

Only the Word of God can do this. To be weak in the Word is to be weak in faith.

Building Spiritual Agility

Second, we spent time in the *agility room*. Here we did drills that were designed to develop body control, increase coordination, and quicken agility. In a fast and furious fifteen minutes, my teammates and I would run in place, roll sideways, and somersault backward and forward, all in response to our coach's signal.

We were able to do things with our body that we never dreamed possible.

Similarly, we must discipline ourselves to be immediately responsive to the direction of God's Word. We must quickly respond with our entire being—heart, eyes, body, mind, feet—to God's direction for our lives.

We must respond with our *hearts*: "You shall love the Lord your God with all your heart, and with all your soul, and with all your mind" (Matthew 22:37).

We must respond with our *eyes*, "fixing our eyes on Jesus, the author and perfecter of faith" (Hebrews 12:2).

We must respond with our *body*: "Present your bodies a living and holy sacrifice" (Romans 12:1).

We must respond with our *minds*: "Set your mind on the things above, not on the things that are on earth" (Colossians 3:2).

We must respond with our *feet*: "How beautiful are the feet of those who bring good news of good things!" (Romans 10:15).

Building Spiritual Quickness

The third workout station was the *wind sprints*. These were run on the football field itself and were designed to develop our speed and quickness.

We would line up and run fifty-yard wind sprints at a coach's signal. We would have about thirty seconds to catch our breath. Then another coach would signal us to sprint back to the first coach. This would be repeated quickly for the entire fifteen-minute period. Quite frankly, I still break out in a sweat just thinking about this.

As speed is vitally important to any athlete, so it is for the Christian. We must be quick to *hear* God's Word. James instructs us to be "quick to hear, slow to speak and slow to anger" (James 1:19).

We must be quick to *obey* His call. Concerning Christ's first disciples, Mark wrote, "Immediately they left their nets and followed Him" (Mark 1:18). So it must be with us. "Immediately" is the key word in the Gospel of Mark. The early disciples responded immediately to our Lord's call. Delayed obedience is no obedience.

Further, we must be as quick to *share* God's Word as Jesus Himself was: "They went into Capernaum; and immediately on the Sabbath He entered the synagogue and began to teach" (Mark 1:21). Jesus began teaching the Word immediately.

Building Spiritual Endurance

The fourth workout station was *running the stadium bleachers*. Running the long climb to the top of the stadium and then back down to the base was the chosen method of self-inflicted torture. The purpose was to build up our stamina, endurance, and perseverance, not to mention our character. We were ready to die, but we kept pressing on, nonetheless. No matter how much pain we were suffering, we could never quit.

The Christian life is, likewise, a long, uphill climb requiring much endurance. It demands our protracted obedience over the long haul. Paul urges his Philippian readers to "press on toward the goal for the prize of the upward call of God in Christ Jesus" (Philippians 3:14). Always pressing upward must we be running.

All such spiritual training requires our strenuous effort. We cannot be halfhearted about it. Getting in shape is all or nothing. For a marathoner, it requires all-out effort and exercise. So it does for the believer.

Paul said, "It is for this we labor and strive" (1 Timothy 4:10). For what do we labor and strive? For spiritual mastery over our minds, hearts, and wills. For this, we must work hard in all our disciplines.

No athlete can effectively train who has an aversion to pain. There is an old, tested and true football adage: "No pain, no gain." An athlete must labor and strive in his training and workouts if he is to know gain on the field.

"Labor" means to work to the point of exhaustion. It pictures pushing oneself to the limit. "Strive" is an athletic word meaning to agonize in an athletic contest. It represents the pain involved in working out and competing. This was so true that the first-century marathon was simply called the *agon* because it was so agonizing.

All four areas of training are needed. Not merely two or three. We must build up our strength through God's Word, prayer, and perseverance under trials. We must increase our speed by being quick to obey the Word. We must develop our personal control through our sensitivity to the Holy Spirit's guidance. And we must increase our endurance through our faithful service to Christ. All this is necessary if we want to be spiritual champions where it really counts.

A Sure Hope

Training is hard work—but not without hope. A runner must believe that his training will pay positive dividends. No athlete would work out with consistency and intensity if he did not strongly believe, deep down inside himself, that his training would increase his chances of winning the race.

A Confidence in Future Glory

An athlete must have hope—a steadfast confidence about the future. He must possess, and be possessed by, a hope that his long hours of training will bring him a reward. It is the hope of winning a crown that keeps his fires of motivation burning brightly through the rigors of training.

This is precisely what Paul talked about when, after calling us to "labor and strive," he said, "We have fixed our hope on the living God, who is the Savior of all men, especially of believers" (1 Timothy 4:10). Paul knew his discipline was invaluable because it would yield a great spiritual reward. His hope expectant was set, not on himself, but on the living God.

As we discipline ourselves for godliness, laboring and striving to be godly, we must have hope in God. We must have a confident assurance about the future that is burning brightly within us, motivating our maximum effort in training.

In a word, hope is a God-confidence that the race will go well. If I train well, I will win the race. If I discipline myself, I will one day taste His victory.

Three-a-Days in Mississippi

I had that kind of hope years ago during what we called "two-a-days." For those of you who have played football, I'm sure the memory of two-a-days still sends a chill up your spine. Those hot August pre-season practices—actually, we had three-a-days—were so tough, so demanding, and so grueling that by comparison, the season was a cool breeze.

While other students were on summer vacation, those of us who were on the team went through the ordeal of these blazing infernos of preseason workouts.

I experienced them at two levels—first in high school, and then in college. Both were something I will never forget. In high school, we went south to Greenwood, Mississippi, for an entire week of two-a-days. We rented a deserted Air Force base—sleeping in barracks, eating in the mess hall, and practicing on the massive marching field.

Have you ever been in the Mississippi Delta in the scorching heat of August? It is hot, humid, and steamy—and that is before sunrise. You break out into a sweat just lying on your bunk.

For a solid week, we practiced and scrimmaged against each other. Goal-line offense. Goal-line defense. Punt coverage. Kickoff coverage. Passing game. Running game. Tackling practice. Blocking practice.

One thing about three-a-day practices—nothing compares with putting on a sweat-filled jersey, then putting on pads that you can squeeze the sweat out of, like slime out of a dirty sponge. Sweat that is a few hours old is the only thing cold on a hot August day in Mississippi.

Why would anyone in his right mind subject himself to a week of insanity like this? Only one thing drove us to do so—a commitment to prepare for victory.

Training today means victory tomorrow.

Two-a-Days in West Texas

In college, I played for Texas Tech University. That is the good news. The bad news is that Texas Tech is located in west Texas. That meant two-a-days under the blistering, scorching hot Texas sun in August.

While all my classmates were sitting in air-conditioned homes or offices, we were working out in an empty stadium in order to prepare for the coming season.

The first day back meant running what we called the "Red Raider

Mile." We had to run it under an individually assigned time. If we didn't beat that time, we would not have the "privilege" of participating in two-a-days.

Jones Stadium had a newly installed Astroturf playing field. Practicing on it was like playing on a hot skillet. As you looked across the field, you could barely see the other goal line because of the intense August heat rising from the synthetic turf.

No one would dare walk on the field barefoot. Two pairs of socks and taped ankles were the only way to avoid heat blisters. One day we put a thermometer on the field and the mercury shot up to 110 degrees and burst the glass.

So there we were, practicing twice a day in this inferno. Killing ourselves. Pushing ourselves beyond danger limits. Suffering sunstrokes. Ignoring dehydration. Ignoring exhaustion. Ignoring leg cramps. Going on despite seeing red, yellow, and orange sunspots. Some teammates losing five pounds a day in body liquids. Finding new personal limits every day.

Why would any sane person do this?

I will tell you why. Because victory always comes at a high price. You must pay the cost of discipline, training, and getting in shape.

Training today means victory tomorrow.

The High Price of Godliness

What is true in the world of athletics is equally true in the kingdom of God. Spiritual victory always comes at a high price. Like football or any other sport, it requires our discipline, training, and getting in shape. It requires working out and preparing one's self to compete.

Maybe you are saying to yourself, "I do not think I can discipline myself to undergo such rigorous training. I have never gone through anything like that before. The task seems to be too big for me to get in shape."

I want to encourage you with some wonderful news. We have a Coach who is in the business of taking raw rookies like you and me and molding us into world champions. He has an unparalleled record at producing winners out of losers.

His name is Jesus Christ.

Two thousand years ago, our Lord took some burly fishermen and whipped them into spiritual shape. He disciplined them so much that He called them disciples. And they became world-beaters.

Jesus can do the same in your life. The only prerequisite is for you to submit to His leadership. You must allow Him to train you for the task. He is able to discipline you and prepare you to run the race of faith—and win.

Right now, I urge you to yield yourself completely to Jesus Christ. Allow Him to make you and mold you into the champion He called you to be.

5

Home Court
Advantage

DEE-fense! DEE-fense!"

The Boston Garden crowd is on its feet. Vocal. Rowdy. In a frenzy. The place is rocking. This is the home court advantage.

The Celtics have battled back from a fourteen-point deficit against the Los Angeles Lakers. Twelve unanswered points by the Celtics leave Boston only two points back. Momentum is now wearing a Shamrock green jersey.

"DEE-fense! DEE-fense!"

The Lakers are on the attack, desperately clinging to their lead. Suddenly, Larry Bird strips the ball from Magic Johnson and hits Dennis Johnson with a quick outlet pass. Instantly, the Celtic fast break is in fifth gear. Kevin McHale and Bird fill the lanes. Robert Parish is trailing. Only two Lakers are back.

DJ pulls up at the top of the key. He shuffles his feet. Looks left. Then, lightning-fast, he dishes the ball right to Larry Bird. Instinctively, Bird pulls up at the three-point line. He pulls the trigger. The ball arcs a perfect rainbow toward the goal. Bottom! The ref signals a three-pointer. The Celtics are now up by one!

The Garden crowd explodes. The roar is deafening. Fifteen consecutive unanswered points, and the Lakers are visibly shaken. The Celtic fans have died and gone to heaven.

"DEE-fense ! DEE-fense!"

The Lakers' Magic Johnson works the ball back up court. Dribbling with his right hand, Magic motions the offense with the left. He shouts instructions to James Worthy. But who can hear? Not with this crowd. It is the home court advantage.

"DEE-fense! DEE-fense!"

The Celtics overplay their men and cut off all the passing lanes. The Laker offense is shut down. Stalled. Nothing is working for them.

"DEE-fense! DEE-fense!"

The twenty-four second clock has ticked down to three seconds. In desperation, Magic signals for a timeout in surrender. The Celtics come off the court, and the Garden crowd is at a fever pitch. You can just feel the electricity in the air. Cheering, whistling, foot-stomping. A standing ovation. It is the home court advantage.

No Place Like Home

That was the Boston Garden. When you were talking home court advantage, you were talking the Boston Garden.

There was no place in all of basketball like it. Before it was demolished, other cities had already built new, lavishly furnished arenas with comfortable theater seats. Their teams played in places that, from the outside, look like upside-down spaceships.

Not Boston. They had the Garden. Built in 1928, this hallowed shrine was the most revered home court in the game, as much a part of Boston's storied history as the Old North Church and Bunker Hill.

So much tradition was there. So much nostalgia. The Celtics' world championship banners hung from the rafters above. Sixteen of them. The retired numbers of Celtics past graced the rafters as well—Cousey's 14, Russell's 6, Havlicek's 17.

The parquet wooden floor was laid in checkerboard fashion. It had been chipped, scarred, and bloodied. The Celtic logo was painted on the center-jump circle, with a green leprechaun smiling and balancing a basketball on his finger.

But most of all, Boston Garden was the crowd. The roar. The noise. The intimidation factor. A multitude—14,890 people—rising to their feet cheering.

Home court advantage? You better believe it.

Do Not Leave Home Without It

What is this phenomenon? It is playing before home fans who are fanatically cheering like crazy. It is the high-impact emotion that lifts the home team to a higher level of play. It is the confidence-building energy transmitted from the crowd to the players.

It is the home court advantage. When playing at home, you feel like you can never be beaten. No deficit is too big, no opponent is too imposing, no odds are too insurmountable to overcome. It gets your heart pounding, your adrenaline flowing, your expectations soaring.

Who would not love to play before a hair-raising crowd like this? Be honest. Just once, to hear the roar of the crowd, cheering for you. Just once, to feel the surge of emotion pulsate through your body.

Well, you *can*.

Not at the Boston Garden, which is no more. But someplace far greater, before fans far more fanatical. You can play before a home crowd far more enthusiastic than the ones in the Boston Garden.

I am talking about running before heaven's grandstands and receiving the applause of heaven. The home court advantage of heaven causes all earthly applause to pale into insignificance.

The Bible says, "Therefore, since we have so great a cloud of witnesses surrounding us, let us also lay aside every encumbrance and the sin which so easily entangles us, and let us run with endurance the race that is set before us" (Hebrews 12:1).

Did you get that? God's Word is saying that as we run, we are surrounded by "so great a cloud of witnesses." The imagery is clear. When we become Christians, we enter into a heavenly arena. We run before a packed stadium. The crowd is cheering in a frenzy. The roar is deafening.

Maybe you are saying, "I do not ever recall hearing heaven cheer for me. The last time I obeyed God or resisted a temptation, there was no roar in my ears."

We must hear with spiritual ears if we are to be tuned into heaven's roar. In this chapter, I want to amplify the applause of heaven. I want to turn the volume up so that it is impossible for you not to hear it.

The Heavenly Crowd

First, we must identify heaven's home court advantage. Who is cheering in this "cloud of witnesses"? Where are they?

They are *not* the angels, sitting on clouds, plucking their harps, playing heaven's fight song to the tune of Notre Dame's "Victory March." They are *not* seraphim with golden pom-poms and emerald-jeweled megaphones, shouting, "Give me a F...add an A...try an I...T...H. What have you got? FAITH! Say it again. FAITH!"

They are *not* B-team believers who did not make the varsity but are cheering us from the sidelines. They are *not* holding up "John 3:16" signs to us from the grandstands like that omnipresent person on television who holds those signs up at pro football games and golf tournaments.

So, who is this "cloud of witnesses"?

These witnesses are members of God's "Hall of Faith" named in Hebrews 11. These are the past champions who have run God's race victoriously. They are spiritual victors—the winners of Heaven's Heisman. They are the stalwarts of the faith who have won heaven's prize. They are God's heroes who have taken their place in heaven's grandstands.

The imagery in this verse is of an earthly saint running life's race. As weariness sets in, he is tempted to slow down—maybe even stop running. But he hears the cheers of these great men and women who are now in heaven, shouting words of hope and screaming encouragement. Their applause provides inspiration and gives a second wind to this discouraged runner. Suddenly, he is propelled forward with renewed strength and a burst of hope.

This is heaven's home court advantage.

I want us to focus now on Hebrews 11. The chapter is known as God's Hall of Fame, or God's Hall of Faith. It is the inspired record of Old Testament believers who lived victoriously by faith.

Call the roll of Hebrews 11, and it is like a who's who of Old

Testament champions. Past winners like Abel, Enoch, and Noah are seated in its stands. Legendary heroes like Abraham, Isaac, Jacob, and Joseph are there.

On the other side of the stadium, yesterday's victors include Moses' parents, Moses himself, Joshua, and Rahab. World-beaters like Gideon, Barak, Samson, and Jephthah are in their places. So also are conquerors like David, Samuel, and the prophets. These are the "cloud of witnesses."

Heaven's Home Court

Can you hear them yet? These champions of old are cheering for *us*! Heaven is in an uproar. They are on their feet. Clapping. Stomping. Whistling. Encouraging us onward. This is heaven's home court advantage.

They have already faced every formidable foe we face. And they won a decisive victory by faith. Because they triumphed, they *know* we can win by faith. They are yelling, "Go for it! Trust God! You can do it."

In the present hour, we may be living at the end of this age. We could be running the last lap of history. All the saints down through the ages are now in heaven. Heaven's grandstands have never been so packed. The apostle Paul is there. So are Martin Luther and John Calvin. George Whitefield and Jonathan Edwards. Your grandfather who knew Christ is seated. Perhaps your mother. Your brother. All these spiritual champions are there, cheering us on. We may be running the final race of history.

What encouragement this is to run and not falter, to run and to win!

In school, I ran anchor on our relay team. Every school in Fort Worth, Texas, entered several relay teams in a big, year-end, citywide track meet.

After each event, athletes who were done competing would sit in the grandstands. Gradually, the stands became fuller and fuller. When it came time for the final race, *everyone* who had already run was in the stands. Momentum built as the fastest runners toed their marks for this once-around-the-track finale, before the biggest crowd, to win the most cherished prize.

As anchor, I was running against the fastest athletes in town. I was nervous, but I loved the thrill of the competition.

The starter announced, "Runners to their mark…get set." And then the gun fired. Our lead runner exploded out of the starting blocks. As our team entered the backstretch, the race was too tight to determine the lead. Four schools were tied, and one of them was us!

Into the last curve we came. Stride for stride. Nip and tuck. It was up to me.

I turned my eyes down the track and began to accelerate as the baton was placed into my hand. With eyes riveted on the finish line, I could feel the energy of the people in the crowd as they rose to their feet and cheered us on. The roar from the grandstands electrified me! My heart leaped out of my chest as I ran like the wind.

Never looking back, never faltering, with only one thought in mind—victory—I pushed through the finish tape. Only then did I glance over my shoulder to see that we had won.

I remember looking up into the stadium. My teammates were cheering and yelling. By winning this final race, we also won the track meet and the bragging rights around town. It was sweet!

In like measure, you and I are running a race—God's race—and heaven's grandstands are packed. Its past champions are cheering us on. Our hearts ought to leap out of our chests!

Do you hear the crowd?

Are you inspired by their urging?

Moses is yelling, "Go for it!" David is pumping his fist and saying, "You can do it!" Joshua cups his hands and shouts, "Go forward by faith! Run with all your might!"

This is the home court advantage.

The Silent Cheers

"Time out!" I hear you saying. "Are you telling me I am supposed to hear voices? I have never heard any audible voices. Not once. All I hear are grunts and groans as my feet relentlessly pound the ground."

Or, you may be thinking, *Hey, I have never won a race! I never hear anyone cheering!*

You are right. There are no audible voices to hear. Heaven's applause is actually much louder. It is a silent applause. Let me explain.

Hebrews 12:1 does *not* say that these people actually watch us from heaven. It does *not* say they are witnessing the race. And I'm afraid watching me run would be more hell than heaven.

This passage is saying they are *bearing* witness to us. Their lives—the way they ran their race by faith—silently scream encouragement to us. They are not actually watching us. Instead, they are inspiring us by the testimony of their lives. They are demonstrating to us that in our race, faith is sure to win the victory. They have run God's race by faith—often through impossible circumstances—and have endured victoriously. Their stories should inspire us to follow in their footsteps.

These witnesses—Abraham, Moses, Joshua, and all the rest—put their faith in God and won the prize. On the basis of their examples, we can do the same. Their past victories cheer us on. But it is a silent cheer. It is not their voices we hear. It is their lives we observe, which motivate and inspire us.

Since we cannot actually hear the cheers, we need to look carefully at the example of their lives.

A Walk Through Heaven's Grandstands

I want us to walk through heaven's grandstands now and "hear" what these heroes are saying to us.

Hebrews 11 is all about faith. The chapter begins, "Now faith is the assurance of things hoped for, the conviction of things not seen" (verse 1). Faith is the total commitment of one's life to God. It is an inner confidence and a settled conviction that God can be trusted in the midst of life's challenges to fulfill His promises. The word *faith* means belief, trust, confidence. It is taking God at His Word, relying upon His grace, and living daily on that basis.

Faith is the firm conviction that God is always at work on our behalf and will come through for us. Faith is not a blind leap into the dark. It is not wishful positive thinking, nor is it presumption.

True faith remains confident in and obedient to God's Word no matter what our circumstances.

As we look at these past champions, let us be reminded that they were ordinary people like you and me, people who knew failure as well as success.

Noah got drunk. David committed adultery. Abraham told lies. Sarah laughed at God. Moses was a murderer. Jacob was a deceiver. Rahab was a harlot. Despite their momentary failures, they overcame by faith and won their race.

We can overcome by faith too. Remember, we have the home court advantage.

I want us to meet these heroes. Let us hear from them now.

Abel: "Worship by faith!"

Abel is seated first in heaven's grandstands. He has had his season tickets for ages. The life of Abel inspires us to worship God by faith. In Hebrews 11 we read, "By faith Abel offered to God a better sacrifice than Cain, through which he obtained the testimony that he was righteous, God testifying about his gifts, and through faith, though he is dead, he still speaks" (verse 4).

God desired that Abel and his brother Cain worship Him through a blood sacrifice. Only through the blood of an innocent sacrifice could they approach holy God. But Cain chose to bring the fruit of the fields. He tried to access God through his own good works. Abel, however, obeyed God and brought a blood sacrifice. By faith, Abel acknowledged his sinfulness and God's unapproachable holiness.

A blood sacrifice? Abel could have reasoned that it is not intellectually acceptable. He could have calculated that it is socially uncultured, uncouth, and uncivilized. Bringing such a sacrifice may not have made any sense.

But because of Adam's fall into sin, a transgression that affects us all, God requires a blood sacrifice to enter His presence. Ultimately, Abel's blood sacrifice prefigured the cross of Jesus Christ. Today, our faith, likewise, must be in the blood sacrifice of Christ to take away our sins.

Those of us who have trusted Christ have, at one time or another, been ridiculed for our commitment to Him. We have taken flack for our faith.

We can identify with the persecution Abel received. What was especially bad is that resistance came from within his own household. The same often occurs in our tight circle of relationships. Those whom we are closest to may end up hurting us the deepest.

This cold, hardened world will persecute us too. We expect that. But when the cold shoulder of a sarcastic putdown comes from one of our own family members, it cuts deep. Those wounds hurt the most.

Abel shouts encouragement to each one of us personally to trust in the blood of Jesus Christ. No matter how foolish this world may consider the cross to be, we must come to God through the blood of Christ. This requires victorious faith.

Do you hear his encouragement?

Enoch: "Walk by faith!"

Next, the life of Enoch inspires us to walk with God by faith. Hebrews 11 continues, "By faith Enoch was taken up so that he would not see death; and he was not found because God took him up; for he obtained the witness that before his being taken up he was pleasing to God" (verse 5).

Enoch walked with God in an ungodly society (Genesis 5:22,24). He sought a close, personal fellowship with God. He was devoted to knowing God. He kept his heart fixed on God. Despite living in a corrupt society, Enoch would not compromise his walk of faith.

In this pagan culture, Enoch was a dynamic witness. He proclaimed a message of judgment that his sinful generation resented and resisted (Jude 14-15). He confronted his world and refused to become a part of its godless system.

Enoch inspires each of us to seek God with all our hearts in the midst of a decadent society. Hebrews 11:6 tells us, "Without faith it is impossible to please Him, for he who comes to God must believe that He is and that He is a rewarder of those who seek Him."

We must stand out as pure lights in a dark world. We must be different to make a difference. I said different, not weird. Some Christians act just plain odd. I am not calling for that. Instead, we must be morally and ethically different from this world.

As believers, we must remain insulated from the squeeze of the world's godless value system. Insulated, not isolated. We are to be in the world, but not of it. Only then can we reach the world for God.

How do we remain pure? Like Enoch, we must remain focused on God and live by faith.

Noah: "Work by faith!"

Now let us hear about Noah. The writer of Hebrews said, "By faith Noah, being warned by God about things not yet seen, in reverence prepared an ark for the salvation of his household, by which he condemned the world, and became an heir of the righteousness which is according to faith" (verse 7).

God told Noah that He was going to destroy the world through a flood. But before He carried out His plan, Noah was to build an ark—a giant ship the length of one-and-a-half football fields—and get his family safely on board.

What a work of faith this was! Keep in mind Noah was 500 miles from the nearest sea. And it had probably never rained on the earth before this time. Yet he worked for 120 years—alone—to build this ark on dry land.

Can you not hear the laughing, jeers, and ridicule of his neighbors? They were all sneering, "His elevator must be stuck in the basement." "He has got rooms to rent upstairs. Unfurnished." "His lights are on, but nobody is home."

Yet Noah worked by faith. Despite standing all alone in the world, he obeyed God and did God's work.

We too must work by faith, and at that, often alone. Are you trying to build a godly family? Or a godly business? Noah inspires faith within us to stand alone for our convictions. Even if others around us ridicule us, we must do God's work by faith.

Can you hear him encouraging you?

Abraham: "Follow by faith!"

Here comes Abraham. He is seated on the fifty-yard line of heaven's grandstands. His credentials follow:

> By faith Abraham, when he was called, obeyed by going out to a place which he was to receive for an inheritance; and he went out, not knowing where he was going. By faith he lived as an alien in the land of promise, as in a foreign land, dwelling in tents with Isaac and Jacob, fellow-heirs of the same promise; for he was looking for the city which has foundations, whose architect and builder is God (verses 8-10).

Abraham lived in Ur, an idolatrous, vile, and pagan city. He was a successful businessman there. God called Abraham to pack his bags and go to an unknown land. There, God would establish a nation through his loins.

Abraham obeyed the call of God. Not knowing where he was going or how it would work out, he left behind his home and estate. He severed his family ties. He abandoned the security of comfortable surroundings for an unknown world. Abraham went forward by faith, not knowing where God would lead him.

God may be launching you into a new career. He may be leading you into an entirely new venture. A life of faith may mean leaving your comfort zone and security to step out in a new direction. It will require making a break with the world's system in order to follow God's direction for your life.

Remember, wherever God guides, He provides. Our responsibility is to follow His leading. His responsibility is to meet our needs. You are safer out on a limb with the Lord than standing on solid ground without Him.

Draw encouragement from Abraham. Just as God led this patriarch, so He will lead you.

Sarah: "Wait by faith!"

Here comes the head cheerleader now—Sarah. We continue in Hebrews 11: "By faith even Sarah herself received ability to conceive, even beyond the proper time of life, since she considered Him faithful who had promised" (verse 11).

God had promised Abraham that a chosen nation would come through his children. That meant Sarah must bear a child. But she was past the age of being able to conceive. One day, Sarah could wait no longer on God, and she sent her maid, Hagar, to lie with her husband to help God's plan. Her impatience on God's perfect timing created Ishmael. The result has been problems for generations and centuries to come.

Years later, when Sarah was ninety years old, God again promised a child in her old age. This time, Sarah trusted God to do what was humanly impossible. She had faith that God would give her a baby despite the fact that she was long past the age of being able to conceive.

God kept His word, and the result was Isaac, a son of promise.

Maybe you are growing tired of waiting on God. Impatience haunts most of us. We want instant everything. Perhaps you are in danger of taking matters into your own hands.

Sarah shouts to us, "Wait patiently by faith. God's timing is perfect."

Patience, it has been said, is letting your motor idle when you feel like stripping the gears.

A man was driving home and came to a red light. As he sat there idling his motor, the car behind him began honking emphatically. Honk! Honk!

The man waved in the rearview mirror, pointing upward to the red light.

Honk! Honk!

The man signaled again, pointing upward to the red light. Honk! Honk!

That was all the man could stomach. He jumped out of his car and walked back to the car behind him. He was furious. Livid.

"Are you blind? Anyone can see the light is red. Will you stop that honking before you drive me crazy? You are giving me a pain I cannot locate!"

To which the man replied, "Your bumper sticker says, 'Honk if you love Jesus.' I was just telling you I love Him too."

It is hard to let your motor idle. It is difficult to just sit still.

But Sarah says, "Wait patiently by faith—God's timing is perfect!" Just remember, you will never be too old to serve God. You are never past your prime in God's economy. It is always prime time with God.

Moses: "Overcome by faith!"

Who is next in the grandstands? Is that Charlton Heston? No, I am sorry. That is Moses! Hebrews 11 recaps Moses' life: "By faith Moses, when he had grown up, refused to be called the son of Pharaoh's daughter; choosing rather to endure ill-treatment with the people of God than to enjoy the passing pleasures of sin; considering the reproach of Christ greater riches than the treasures of Egypt; for he was looking to the reward" (verses 24-26).

Moses grew up in Egypt, the wealthiest, most advanced civilization in the world at the time. He was a prince, the son of Pharaoh's daughter. He lived in the palace in the lap of luxury. He had all this world could offer—prestige, pleasures, possessions.

At age forty, Moses had to make a choice whether to become a full-fledged Egyptian or to join his own people, Israel. Moses said no to the honor of the palace and said yes to life among the slaves.

Moses did not seek the world's prestige. He sought God's will. There would be no rat race for Moses. He chose the right race.

We live in constant danger of the world squeezing us into its mold (Romans 12:2). Satan is ever luring us to conform to his system. We must repeatedly sacrifice present riches for an eternal reward. The world's system looks alluring, but we must say no and choose to pursue spiritual reward.

How will we stay on track in God's race?

By faith.

Faith does not buckle and fold under the world's pressures. It keeps looking for the eternal reward, not earthly treasures. It focuses upon the invisible, not what is seen.

Moses' life inspires us to live for eternal reward in the midst of material prosperity. He motivates us to seek heaven's applause rather than earthly approval.

There was a man in our church named Ken who is a champion golfer. A few years ago, Ken was on the verge of turning pro, only to discover that golf was requiring too much time and keeping him away from his family. It had become all-consuming.

From deep conviction, Ken made the painful decision to walk away from a certain career on the tour. He refused to be squeezed into the mold of the world. He chose to follow Moses' example and live for future reward rather than earthly acclaim.

So must we learn to say no to the world.

Israel: "Forward by Faith!"

Here is a big section in heaven's coliseum—the nation of Israel. The writer of Hebrews 11 notes a few highlights of its history: "By faith they passed through the Red Sea as though they were passing through dry land; and the Egyptians, when they attempted it, were drowned. By faith the walls of Jericho fell down after they had been encircled for seven days" (verses 29-30).

Moses led the children of God out of Egypt to go to the Promised Land. But the journey and conquest were not without challenges. The nation soon found itself in an impossible situation.

With the Red Sea in front of them and Pharaoh's army closing in behind them, the nation of Israel had nowhere to go. They knew they could not defeat Pharaoh's legions. This crisis necessitated that they trust God to defeat their enemy. They put their faith in God, and He parted the Red Sea and led them to their deliverance.

Once in the Promised Land, the nation still had to move forward by faith. The impregnable walls of Jericho stood between them and their entrance into the land. God called for complete faith, and said He would defeat Israel's enemies. At Jericho, they looked to God by faith, and He again defeated their foe.

The Christian life is a steady advancement forward. We are to be always moving onward by faith. We must move forward into the fullness of God's blessing, forward into Christlikeness, forward in the conquest of our foes.

What is your Red Sea? What walls are obstructing your spiritual advancement? When impossible obstacles stand in our way, God enables us to advance forward by faith.

Listen to this encouragement!

Judges, Kings, Prophets: "Fight by faith!"

Here is another large section in heaven's arena. These are the spiritual leaders of Israel—probably sitting in the press box high above—encouraging us to fight our foes by faith. Hebrews 11 says, "Gideon, Barak, Samson, Jephthah…David and Samuel and the prophets, who by faith conquered kingdoms, performed acts of righteousness, obtained promises, shut the mouths of lions, quenched the power of fire, escaped the edge of the sword, from weakness were made strong, became mighty in war, put foreign armies to flight" (verses 32-34).

Gideon was outnumbered by the Midianites 135,000 to 300—yet conquered by faith. Barak triumphed over the Canaanites. Samson single-handedly slew the Philistines. Jephthah faced impossible odds and won. David fought Goliath and won. Samuel fought against idolatry and immorality and won. The prophets, from Samuel to John the Baptist, stood for God's truth and won.

In every case, they were victorious by faith.

Daniel obeyed God even though it meant being thrown into the lion's den (Daniel 6). Because he lived by faith, God protected him. Daniel's friends Shadrach, Meshach, and Abednego were thrown into the fiery furnace because they refused to worship the statue of the Babylonian king (Daniel 3). But God protected them.

David escaped the sword of Goliath and Saul. King Hezekiah was about to die, and prayed. God gave him health, and he lived fifteen more years. Elijah and Elisha both raised the dead sons of women. The faith of these prophets brought those children back from the dead.

As Christians, we face impossible odds every day. Our battles are just as real as in the ancient days. The Canaanites still outnumber us. The Goliaths are always looming over us. Our race is still against the grain of society.

No matter how impossible the odds, we too can triumph by faith. It is, after all, our home court advantage.

Others: "Suffer by faith!"

Finally, we arrive at those who were martyred for their faith. Unknown on earth, these are the undisputed champions, well-known in heaven. These are those who

> were tortured, not accepting their release, in order that they might obtain a better resurrection; and others experienced mockings and scourgings, yes, also chains and imprisonment. They were stoned, they were sawn in two, they were tempted, they were put to death with the sword; they went about in sheepskins, in goatskins, being destitute, afflicted, ill-treated (men of whom the world was not worthy), wandering in deserts and mountains and caves and holes in the ground (Hebrews 11:35-38).

Sometimes God does not design the battle to be immediately victorious. In such cases, courageous faith must continue in the face of suffering. Faith that conquers quickly is great faith, but faith that perseveres despite suffering is even greater.

Jeremiah suffered mockings, brutal whipping, and imprisonment (Jeremiah 20:2,7). Zechariah was stoned (2 Chronicles 24:20-22). Isaiah was sawed in half, tradition tells us. Others were tortured to deny God. Still others wandered in poverty, having to forsake everything the world had to offer.

These spiritual champions were "men of whom the world was not worthy" (Hebrews 11:38). The world thought these victors to be unworthy. But God received them into heaven, where they were welcomed home and recognized as having a faith worthy of applause.

They are screaming encouragement to us!

Faith in Adversity

The baseball career of former San Francisco Giants pitcher Dave Dravecky was ended when his arm had to be removed. His future in the game was amputated. Why would he still have any faith? Why would he continue to walk with God?

It was Dravecky's unshakable confidence in God, who can do only what is right, that continued to sustain him and his family through a time of unspeakable agony.

What keeps Dave going is that he can "hear" with his heart the urging, the encouraging, the compelling applause from this great cloud of witnesses.

This is heaven's home court advantage.

And it is your advantage.

Here are examples of real men and women, just like you and me, who ran God's race by faith and won. These champions are screaming encouragement to us to worship, walk, and work by faith. Follow and wait by faith. Overcome and go forward by faith. Fight and, if need be, suffer by faith. That is what these champions are yelling to us.

Can you hear it?

The Applause of Heaven

Some years ago, a great football coach by the name of Lou Little coached at Columbia University. A young man who was not a particularly good player tried out for the varsity team. While not nearly good enough to make the team, he had such an irrepressible spirit and contagious enthusiasm that Lou thought, *This boy would be a great inspiration on the bench. He will never be able to play, but I will leave him on the team to encourage others.*

A Strong Faith in Christ

As the season went on, Coach Little grew in his admiration and love for this boy. He was especially impressed by the manner with which the boy cared for his father. Whenever his father came to the campus, the boy and his father would always be seen walking together arm in arm. This was an obvious indication of the close bond between them. They could be seen on Sunday mornings walking to and from the university chapel. It was obvious they possessed a deep faith in Christ.

One day, Coach Little received a telephone call. He was informed that this boy's father had just tragically died. He would have the difficult task of telling the boy. With a heavy heart, the coach informed his player of his father's death. The boy immediately left to go home for the funeral.

A few days later, the boy returned to the campus, only two days before the biggest game of the season. Coach Little walked up to him and said, "Is there anything I can do for you? Anything at all? I will be glad to do it for you."

To the coach's astonishment, the boy said, "Let me start the game on Saturday!"

Lou was taken aback. He thought, *I cannot let him start. He is not good enough.* But he remembered his promise to the boy and said, "All right, you can start the game." Coach Little rationalized, *I will leave him in for a few plays, and then take him out.*

In God's Starting Lineup

The day of the big game arrived. To everyone's surprise, the coach started this boy who had not played in a single game all season. On the very first play from scrimmage, the boy singlehandedly made a tackle that threw the opposing team for a loss. Coach Little was shocked.

The boy played inspired football, play after play. In fact, he played so exceptionally that the coach left him in for the entire game. The boy led his team to victory, and he was voted the outstanding player of the game.

When the game was over, Coach Little approached the boy and said, "Son, what got into you today?"

The boy replied, "Do you remember when my father would visit me here, we would walk arm in arm around the campus? My father and I shared a secret that nobody here knew. You see, my father was blind—and today was the first time he ever saw me play!"

As the boy's father's presence in heaven powerfully influenced his earthly effort, so this cloud of witnesses in Hebrews 12:1 should inspire us to run victoriously. No, heaven's heroes do not actually watch us as we run. But the examples of their lives can influence us profoundly as we run the race.

As we run God's race, let us listen for the applause of heaven and draw strength. Let me tell you one more time—it is the home court advantage.

Shhh! What is that I hear from above?

"DEE-fense! DEE-fense!"

6

Removing
All Encumbrances

Come with me to the ancient Greek games. As the fastest runners in the Roman Empire gather at the starting line, the tension and pressure are mounting. They are about to run the race of their lives. The crowd rises to its feet in anticipation.

The runners begin to remove their outer warm-up robes. Nothing must slow them down. They then remove their loose-fitting tunics. No garment must cause any wind drag.

Then, in a startling move, the runners remove the rest of their clothing. They strip down. Completely.

These athletes have stripped down so nothing—absolutely nothing—will slow them down. They will do anything to gain an advantage over the competition. They are willing to risk the embarrassment of public exposure. They must run without any encumbrance. They do all this to win the crown.

Removing All Hindrances

The runners' muscles and finely tuned bodies ripple in the open arena. With sculpted torsos that look like they have been chiseled out of marble, they resemble exquisite masterpieces. These are the finest athletes in the ancient world.

These men are possessed with a burning passion to win at any cost. So they removed all encumbrances that would hinder a swift performance. All to capture a crown.

Just as the first-century athletes stripped down to run with maximum speed, we must strip away every spiritual encumbrance that would impede our progress in God's race. Pursuing the ultimate prize requires laying aside anything that would slow us down.

Hebrews 12:1 says, "Therefore, since we have so great a cloud of witnesses surrounding us, *let us also lay aside every encumbrance*" (emphasis added).

Too many of us run as if outfitted with layers of restrictive clothing and with heavy weights. We must strip down and run unencumbered. We must take it all off!

In this chapter, we will look at what it means to "lay aside every encumbrance." What are encumbrances? Where are they to be found? How can we detect them?

What Are Encumbrances?

First, let us consider what encumbrances are.

Picture with me, if you will, an athlete approaching the starting blocks attired in a three-piece suit, a heavy overcoat, and wingtip shoes. How ludicrous! Yet many of us are running God's race as if we had such excess baggage. We are hindered by layers of restrictive clothing and heavy weights.

Shedding Our Encumbrances

The word "encumbrance" in Hebrews 12:1 means a weight, a bulk, a mass of something heavy. It refers to either body bulk or excess weight. It refers to any unnecessary weight that would slow down a runner. In ancient times, an athlete would train by wearing leg weights. But when he approached the starting line, he would shed those weights, along with any warm-up clothes.

This is *not* talking about sin. Hebrews 12:1 contrasts an "encumbrance" with "the sin which so easily entangles us." There is a difference.

An encumbrance is simply something amoral or neutral in our life that works in a counterproductive way. It weighs us down, diverts our attention, saps our energy, and dampens our quest for the ultimate prize.

It is excess, superfluous baggage.

Legitimate things can become weights that hold us back—love of home and family, love of country, love of comfort, contentment with a job, security at work. Even such good things can become weights to hold us back in running—and winning—the race of faith.

Whatever Impedes Our Speed

In discerning God's best for our life, not all our choices are between good and bad. Many of our decisions are choices among what is good, better, and best. An encumbrance may simply be something good that keeps us from the best. Winning God's race requires choosing the best over the good and the better.

In short, an encumbrance is not a sin per se. It is just anything that prevents God's best.

A runner in training might choose to give up drinking colas. Not because drinking colas is sinful. But because too much syrupy sugar and carbonated water might hinder his best performance and affect his mind. In a spiritual sense, watching a football game on television could work the same way. There is nothing morally wrong with watching sports on television. In fact, it can be a form of recreation that provides beneficial rest and stimulation. But if watching a football game keeps you from Bible study or prayer, then a good thing has become a hindrance to the best thing. The good becomes the enemy of the best.

The problem is not in what the encumbrance *is*, but in what it *does* and what it keeps us from. *Good* things become *bad* things when they keep us from the *best* things.

The question we must ask is, How fast do I want to run God's race? Fast, faster, or fastest? If fast, then I can carry some excess baggage. If faster, I can carry a little baggage. But if I want to run my fastest, then I must lay aside *every* encumbrance.

The Bare Essentials

The story is told of a group of people who were preparing to climb Mount Blanc in the Swiss Alps. On the evening before the climb, the guide outlined the prerequisite for reaching the top. Due to the difficulty of the climb to the top, it was necessary to take only the bare essentials of equipment. All unnecessary accessories must be left behind.

A young Englishman refused to listen. He proceeded to bring along an extra blanket, a cap, and a fancy notebook in his backpack.

On the way to the summit, the guide began to notice certain items left behind in the snow. First the blanket. Then the notebook. Later the cap.

Finally, when they reached the top, they discovered this Englishman had jettisoned everything unnecessary along the way.

This epitomizes what must happen in our lives spiritually if we are to win the race. Every unnecessary weight must be cast aside if we are to make it to the top. We must let go of the good if we are to achieve the best.

Running with maximum speed requires stripping down. Even small encumbrances can keep us from victory. The difference between victory and defeat is often very small.

Even Small Weights Hinder

The famous runner Gil Dodds was once preparing to run a race. After a series of stretching exercises, Dodds ran several warm-up laps around the track. Just before the race began, he stopped and quickly changed into a different pair of track shoes.

One of the onlookers asked Dodds why he was changing his shoes. Dodds tossed one of his warm-up shoes to the inquirer. Then one of his racing shoes.

The man was still puzzled. There was no detectable difference between the two shoes. Both looked the same. Both seemed to weigh the same.

Then Dodds explained. There was indeed a difference. The warm-up shoes were slightly heavier than his racing shoes. Though the difference in weight was small, shedding even that seemingly insignificant amount of weight for the race could spell the difference between victory and defeat.

The same is true about our spiritual lives. No encumbrance, large or small, can be tolerated in our lives. Not if we are to win. The Word of God says to "lay aside *every* encumbrance" (Hebrews 12:1, emphasis added). Not some, but *every*. So every encumbrance must go. Anything that would hold us back must be relinquished.

What Must Be Laid Aside?

If stripping down is really a factor in winning, then let us identify some areas of potential excess baggage in our lives.

I think we have to admit that most of us suffer from too much baggage. Too many irons in the fire. Too many balls in the air. Too many competing demands. Too many good things crowding out the best things.

Let us examine three key areas where encumbrances may need to be laid aside.

Hindrance 1: Career Crunch

First, we need to talk about our work life and the demands we face there. We must guard against becoming so caught up in our career that our spiritual and family life end up suffering. The squeeze of the marketplace can be a death grip.

Work, in and of itself, is not bad. In fact, work is good. The Bible teaches that hard work is honorable. God lovingly assigned man the responsibility to work and manage the earth (Genesis 1:28). This divine assignment was made before the entrance of sin into the world. That means work was a part of paradise. Today, long after the fall into sin, man still works for the glory of God (Colossians 3:22-24). And he can find great enjoyment and fulfillment from his professional pursuits.

However, the growing demands of time on the job and the drain of emotional energy at the office can become heavy weights. Encumbrances. Hindrances. Excess baggage.

When that happens, the good crowds out the best. We soon find ourselves winning at work but losing in God's race.

Our work can become a big, heavy weight that holds us back in running God's race victoriously. When we become so wrapped up with our careers that we have little time and energy left for God, His kingdom, and our families, we are hindered severely in the race.

No one is immune from this trap. Not even ministers. Even something as noble as doing God's work can become a hindrance to doing the more important things in life. For me, I can become so busy with my ministry that I neglect time alone with my family.

Crunch Time at Home

Let me show you how I can blow it.

A few years back, my wife asked that I be home by 5:00 pm. She and our boys needed to leave home by 5:30 to get to the church for a children's program rehearsal. She knew she had to ask me because I had been coming home later and later each evening.

Sure enough, I was met with another church emergency at 4:30, and I came dragging home at 5:45. As I drove home, God's Spirit convicted me that I should have postponed solving this crisis until the next day. Most "emergencies," after all, can wait until the next day.

As I walked into our kitchen, my sweet wife burst into tears. "You promised you would be home by five. John almost killed himself by falling out the back door. Andrew and James are being rowdy. Grace Anne needs your attention. And I am burning dinner!"

"But, sweetheart," I replied, "I was taking care of an emergency at church that came up and would not go away without my help. I had to help a person."

Still hurt because my lateness was becoming a pattern, my wife said (tongue in cheek), "Well, maybe I need to set up an appointment to see you. That is the only way I am going to be able to talk to you."

Ouch! She was right.

The Tyranny of the Urgent

Our work can easily crowd out the more important matters in our lives. Like family. Like God. Maybe God Himself needs to say, "Well, maybe I need to set up an appointment to see you. That is probably the only way I am going to be able to talk to you."

Maybe you can relate to how I blew it. We can let the tyranny of the urgent crowd out the best. When that happens, repeatedly buck-ling to the demands of work becomes a hindrance.

We must not allow the crunch of career demands to crowd out what is truly best in life. If we make that trade-off, we will surely lose the race.

Our passion for the marketplace too often crowds out what is most important in our lives. When that happens, these imbalances become an encumbrance. A ball and chain.

Have you ever wrestled with this tension? Have you ever felt the growing demands at work subtly crowding out your devotional time with God? Squeezing out your family time? Pushing out time to serve the Lord? Are you too busy to notice?

Well, this is too convicting. We need to move on.

Hindrance 2: Pastime Passions

We need to talk about how we spend our free time. Recreation is not sin. Hobbies and entertainment are not sin. But they can become encumbrances if not checked, which will slow us down in the pursuit of heaven's prize.

It could be fishing or hunting. It could be golf or tennis. Or it could be working around the house. Whatever you like to spend your spare time doing can become a hindrance if it begins to crowd out the best.

Sure, recreation is good and needed. I believe it is a part of the Sabbath principle taught in the Bible. Just as God worked six days on creation and then rested, so we must have regularly scheduled rest from the stress of our occupations. We need physical rest. Emotional rest. Spiritual rest. Without rest, we will snap and break, like a tightly wound rubber band.

But recreation, something good, can keep us from the best things. In other words, recreation is a means to an end, but not an end in itself. Our passion for recreation can displace our passion for winning God's crown.

A Double Bogey at Home

For me, it is golf. That little white ball is my mental break. I confess, I love golf with a passion. Some years ago my children gave me a tooth-brush that was inscribed, "I love golf." That says it all.

Can you imagine a greater way to be outdoors than to be on a beautiful golf course? Riding in a cart? If I die on a golf course, I will go from glory to glory.

I recently went with a friend to play golf. We decided to drive to a golf course about two hours away. The night before, I went into my ritual to get ready, like a bride preparing herself the night before her wedding day.

I got my golf clubs out and cleaned them. Again. They were already clean enough to eat off. But you cannot take chances with such things.

I took the car up to the corner and filled it with gas. I had the oil checked. I cashed a check at the grocery store to be ready for any emergency. I laid out my golf clothes for the next day. I even packed an extra shirt in case I spilled something. I polished my golf shoes. Replaced the shoelaces.

I called the golf course to ask exactly how long it took to drive there. I reviewed the directions with the receptionist. I then watched the weather forecast and earnestly prayed and fasted for good weather the next day.

As my wife and I retired to bed that night, I think she felt a bit neglected. She said gently, "Why can you not get this organized for our family trips? You never plan ahead like this for our vacations."

Ouch! She was right again.

I can let golf get out of hand. When it does, it becomes an encumbrance in my life. It holds me back from running God's race. It can paralyze my real priorities. Like time with my family. Like time with God.

Is there any hobby or entertainment in your life like that? Could it be in danger of crowding out the best in your life?

The Encumbrance of Entertainment

Another recreational hindrance can be television. Years ago, I made the choice not to subscribe to cable television. My kids thought we were the Beverly Hillbillies. Before they discovered oil.

I made this "radical" decision for two reasons. First, because I did not want many of those cable programs available to my children. And second, because I knew I would become addicted to ESPN. If I had access to this all-sports network, it would ruin my life. I might be tempted to watch it every night. No, I *would* watch it every night. To the neglect of my family. To the disregard of time in God's Word. For me, it would become an encumbrance, slowing me down in the best things.

You ought to see us on family vacations. The moment we check into a hotel, we immediately turn on ESPN. I tell my wife that I am spending personal time with my boys.

What is your pastime passion? Working on your car? Grooming your yard? Building something in your workshop? Being mesmerized by your computer?

Now, these are not sins. They are innocent things. Legitimate. Good things. But they can become encumbrances and hold us back from running the race well.

Hindrance 3: Ministry Overload

Here is a third hindrance that must be stripped off. We carry excess baggage when our ministry for Christ becomes too all-consuming. If it pushes out our time alone with God, our ministry becomes a hindrance to what is the best. Our work for God must never take away from our worship of God. That, my friend, is a bad trade-off.

Do not get me wrong. Ministry is important. As a pastor, I am committed to ministry. My job is to equip the body of Christ to do ministry (Ephesians 4:11-12). Every believer must serve in God's kingdom. Christlikeness requires girding oneself with a towel and serving others (John 13:1-17).

But this must never crowd out our personal worship of God. The most important thing about us is our knowledge of Christ (John 17:3). We must constantly grow to know and love Him in a deeper, fuller, richer way (2 Peter 3:18). Our service for Christ must flow out of our personal walk with Christ. Worship first; work second.

Sometimes we get so busy serving Christ that we neglect our heart devotion with Him. Our quiet times get put on the back shelf so we can keep up with the busy hustle and bustle of ministry. That is the good competing with the best. It is also the ultimate buy high, sell low.

Sitting at Jerusalem

There are two ladies who can teach us a lot about this lesson. They are Mary and Martha (Luke 10:38-42). One day Jesus came to their house, and Martha began serving Jesus in the kitchen. She rolled up her sleeves and got after it!

Guess what Mary did? She just sat there at Jesus' feet. She spent time alone there, drinking in the words of Jesus, adoring His majesty.

Martha was not pleased to be serving solo. She got hot and bothered. "Lord," she complained, "do You not care that my sister has left me to do all the serving alone? Then tell her to help me" (verse 40).

Jesus gently rebuked her by saying, "Martha, Martha, you are worried and bothered about so many things...Mary has chosen the good part" (verse 41).

In other words, "Do not just do something. Sit there!"

Jesus made it very clear. He put the cookies on the bottom shelf. Do not sacrifice your personal worship on the altar of ministry. Serving Christ is good. In fact, it's very good. But worshiping Christ is the best. The very best.

A Relationship, Not a Performance

I must confess to you that I struggle with maintaining this priority. As a task-oriented, impatient, take-charge kind of person, my tendency is to *do* for Christ. This often comes at the expense of worshiping Him. Sitting is not my natural tendency, even when it is at His feet. But sitting is what He wants. I must not let ministry mania crowd out my time alone with God in Bible devotions, prayer, or personal worship.

God does not want a performance. He wants a relationship. We must be careful not to discard the best for something as noble as serving God.

What about you?

Does ministry madness ever crowd out your heart relationship with Christ? If so, it is a hindrance in running the race. It has become a heavy weight, slowing you down.

Watch over your heart. Do not allow it to grow cold and distracted from God. Choose the best. Choose to worship Him, first and foremost. *Then* serve Him.

What Is *Your* Baggage?

It is not enough for us to talk about encumbrances in broad categories. We must get specific about identifying the hindrances that are in our lives. I want to give you some principles for identifying them.

In an airport, each traveler must identify his own baggage after his flight and match his claim check against the baggage tag. Over the loudspeaker, a voice repeatedly warns people not to pick up someone else's baggage. Be sure to identify your own baggage.

The same is true spiritually. We need to identify our own baggage. We must spot our *excess* baggage so we can lay it aside. Now, it would be presumptuous for me to identify your baggage. It would be legalism for me to attempt to identify for you the excess baggage in your life. What is a hindrance for me may not be a hindrance for you, and vice versa.

Each Christian must decide for himself which encumbrances must be laid aside. Only the Spirit of God can point out these weights to each believer.

Below are some questions that, when properly applied, can help you determine the personal hindrances you need to lay aside. While the Bible is explicit about identifying sin, encumbrances fall in a gray area because they are usually a matter of good versus best rather than right versus wrong. The apostle Paul assists us with identifying these gray areas in 1 Corinthians 6–10.

As you consider these questions, you must decide for yourself what to remove. Ask the Spirit of God to point out these weights. Then resolve to take decisive action. Only then can you run to win. Apply each of the following questions to every area of your life.

Is It Profitable for Winning?

Paul writes, "All things are lawful for me, but not all things are profitable" (1 Corinthians 6:12; see also 10:23). "Profitable" means advantageous, beneficial, helpful. Is this thing to my advantage? The price of carrying excess baggage is terribly high and thus unprofitable.

An athlete must do only those things that will bring victory. If he is serious about winning, then anything that is not expedient to winning must be closely monitored and restricted.

"All things are lawful" does not mean that "anything goes." It means that all things that are not unlawful are lawful. The Bible explicitly teaches that some things are unlawful. For example, "You shall not commit adultery" (Exodus 20:14). Period. This means you have no right to experience intimate relations with anyone other than your own spouse. You will recall that there are a few more of these commandments.

All other things in your life are lawful. God has made all things for you to freely enjoy. But not all things that you have a right to do are profitable for winning the race.

A runner who wants to win must say no to some things to which he has a right to say yes. He will deny himself certain foods and activities simply because they will not contribute to winning. He will avoid anything that might hinder his winning.

You must ask yourself: Will doing this enhance my spiritual life? If not, strip it. Will it cultivate godliness? If not, strip it. Will it be to my advantage? If not, strip it. Do not ask, "Can I do this and get away with it?" Rather, you should ask, "Will this profit me spiritually?"

If the answer is no, strip it.

Will It Bring Me into Bondage?

Paul next wrote, "All things are lawful for me, but I will not be mastered by anything" (1 Corinthians 6:12). This means nothing must be allowed to control or dominate your life except God and His will for your life. Your body, your passions, and your drives must be controlled by God alone. You must not be dominated by work, recreation, ministry, or anything else except God.

If a championship runner is to compete victoriously, he must not allow anything to master him. Nothing must control his body or dull his senses. His body must be free of all substances. He cannot let drugs, alcohol, or controlled substances bring his body into bondage. Addictions destroy.

A believer could become enslaved by something in which he has freedom to indulge. If he is to win the race, he must not allow anything to hold such a grip on his life.

Do not allow anything to master your life. Not sports. Not work. Not alcohol. Not anything. Rather, yield your life entirely to Christ. By the power of the Holy Spirit, lay aside any encumbrances. By divine grace, strip them off.

Will It Cause Others to Stumble?

Paul wrote, "But take care that this liberty of yours does not somehow become a stumbling block to the weak" (1 Corinthians 8:9). A stumbling block is something that causes another person to trip and fall in the course of the race.

A runner who interferes with the progress of another runner will be disqualified. It matters not how well or how fast he is running. If he causes another to trip and fall, he will be put out of the race.

What in your life may cause a weaker runner to stumble?

Will It Weaken My Faith?

In 1 Corinthians 10:23, Paul added, "All things are lawful, but not all things edify." Again, this does not mean that sinful things are lawful. Rather, it means that things not forbidden by Scripture are lawful. But this does not mean that all things edify. Those things that edify us must be our dominant pursuit.

The word "edify" here refers to building up other people to increase or strengthen their faith. Whatever contributes to spiritual growth is profitable. But whatever weakens one's faith must be discarded.

If a Christian is to run God's race to win, he *must* be strong. Weak legs will never cross the finish line first. So anything that weakens him must be laid aside. It is not worth it.

What is it that weakens your faith? What deludes your commitment to Christ? What waters down your resolve for Him? Whatever it is, let it go.

Will It Keep Others from Entering the Race?

Paul further wrote, "Give no offense either to Jews or to Greeks... just as I also please all men in all things, not seeking my own profit but the profit of the many, so that they may be saved" (1 Corinthians 10:32-33). This is to say, we should not abuse a freedom that would lead to offending an unbeliever or repel him from entering the race.

It is important that you run your race in a way that encourages others to enter the race. You must never keep them from entering the race. How important it is to God that others be saved and enter the race. So it must be important to you as well.

Think about it. Most people are led to faith in Christ through the witness of another. Rare is the conversion that occurs in a human vacuum. Usually, God uses one life touching and impacting another life to bring that unbeliever to faith in the Savior.

How you conduct your life, therefore, is of monumental importance. By your life, you can influence a seeking unbeliever closer to Christ. Or, tragically, you can influence another away from Christ.

What kind of an impact are you having? Do not give someone else an excuse to continue rejecting Christ.

Will It Glorify God?

Finally, Paul wrote, "Whether, then, you eat or drink or whatever you do, do all to the glory of God" (1 Corinthians 10:31). Here is the all-inclusive principle that governs and guides all our actions. It is that God should be glorified in everything we do. We must test all things in our life by whether or not they bring glory to God.

Runners in the Olympics have a higher motive for running than mere personal fame. Uniquely, they run for the glory of their home city or country. In the Roman Empire, they ran for the glory of the emperor. Likewise, we run with a higher motive than personal glory and reward. Our highest passion must be to run for the glory of our great God.

Does this glorify God? Will it exalt Him? Will it honor Him? If it does not, then let it go.

These are all significant questions to ask. They can help tell us the difference between good and better and best. But they will be utterly useless if not personally applied and practiced. Right now matters forever. No encumbrance is too precious to discard. Nothing must slow us down!

It Is Time to Strip Down

You can get out of the rat race and be in the right race. You can set your heart on Heaven's Heisman. You can train and discipline yourselves for godliness. You can hear the roar of heaven's grandstands and be inspired to push to the finish line. But if you are encumbered and hindered by excess baggage, everything else is to little avail. You are merely plodding. You are not running to win!

The one who will win is the one who has stripped away all unnecessary encumbrances. He has laid aside all excess baggage. He has rid himself of all expendable weights.

Until there is a fire burning in your heart to count the cost, to pay the price, to lay aside the hindrances, none of this matters. The passion to win for the glory of God must be an all-consuming fire that energizes you to sacrifice, discard, and divest yourself of petty hindrances that are keeping you from God's best.

Have you stripped down?

Are you running to win?

Starting Blocks
and Stumbling Blocks

A determined marathon runner is crouched and coiled at the starting line, ready to explode. He nervously shakes the stiffness from his legs. In the pit of his stomach, he feels this is his race to win. He hears, "Runners to your mark...set...go!"

As the runners leap from the starting line, he jostles for the lead. His legs are strong. His stride fluid. His breathing effortless. His arms relaxed. His eyes focused. His head still. He is running like a well-oiled machine. All systems are go.

His feet are barely touching the ground. He passes one runner after another and pushes to the front of the pack. Every time he passes a runner, he feels another burst of energy.

He can hear the crowd cheering. A rush of adrenaline shifts him into a higher gear. This is *his* race to win!

The runners leave the stadium and wind through the streets of the town. This runner pushes himself to new limits. He discovers hidden reservoirs of previously untapped energy.

Many miles later he returns to the stadium the lone leader. His dreams are about to become reality. His many months of training are about to pay off. Victory is sure! The crowd is on its feet cheering him fanatically.

He glances over his shoulder to confirm that the lead is his alone. He is the only runner back in the stadium. He savors the moment. This is *his* race to win!

One Small Stone, One Major Fall

Suddenly, the unthinkable happens. A loose object lies on the track. A small stone. Unseen. Undetected.

As the runner approaches, his foot comes down directly on the stone. His ankle twists. He stumbles.

Frantically, he tries to gain his balance. But it is too late. His stride is broken.

He extends his hands to brace his fall. But to no avail. He crashes headfirst into the track. He hits the ground hard. He rolls over several times. He has wiped out.

As a result of the fall, his entire body is jarred. His knees are ripped open. His flesh is torn apart.

His competitive drive screams for him to get back up. Instinctively, he scrambles to his feet. But he immediately collapses back to the ground. His ankle is twisted too severely.

Other runners now begin to reenter the stadium. He can hear the crunching of the cinders as their feet sprint past him. He can taste the blood flowing from his cut lip. The sweat streams down his face. He drags himself off the track. Dejected. Shattered. Defeated.

The Agony of Defeat

The sound of the crowd cheering for another winner is a dagger thrust into his heart. Tears of regret flood his eyes. The agony of defeat fills his heart. Victory was *his* until this fatal fall.

A look of anguish covers his face. Bitterness sours his spirit. Months of training are now wasted. His boyhood dreams have become a nightmare. Lifelong hopes are dashed.

From the edge of the track, his eyes search for that dreaded object, for what caused his fall. He sees it.

A small stone. A mere pebble.

He limps over to the stone. He glares at it. A simple rock. He picks it up in disgust and hurls it off the track. The margin between victory and defeat is this hellish stone.

How could anything so small have caused such devastating consequences? It is just a small stone.

Or is it?

Pointing Out the Stumbling Blocks

Let me ask you: If you were sitting in the stands that day and knew the stone was there, would you not have warned the runner? Especially if you wanted to see him win? Would you not have pointed out the pebble?

Surely you would have.

To spare him the pain. The humiliation. The loss.

If you cared anything at all for the runner, you would have warned him and pointed out the stone.

As we run the race of life, there are stumbling blocks in our path. Small. Imperceptible. Yet destructive. Dangerous. Fatal. From where God sits, He sees them all. And in His Word He has revealed them to us. To warn us. To prevent our stumbling. Why? Because He wants us to win!

So Close, So Far Away

It is possible to be running God's race—with victory certain—and then to suddenly, without warning, stumble and fall. What tragedy! One moment running full speed. Wide-open. Unhindered. Then in the next split second—BOOM !—to stumble and fall. And land flat on our face.

This is the bone-jarring reality of the Christian life. It happens.

Hebrews 12:1 warns, "Therefore, since we have so great a cloud of witnesses surrounding us, let us also lay aside every encumbrance and *the sin which so easily entangles us*" (emphasis added).

It is bad enough to be slowed down by a heavy weight. We discussed that in the last chapter. But it is even *worse* to stumble and fall because of an entanglement. Far worse! The tragic stumbling because of sin will be the focus of this chapter.

I must warn you—this chapter is a hard-hitting look at sin. But no less hard-hitting than what sin hits us with. So strap it on. Here comes a hardball look at sin.

That Three-Letter Word

First, let us look at this little three-letter word *sin*. S-I-N. It appears to be a small stone. What does God say about sin? I fear we have become so desensitized toward sin that we no longer take the small stones seriously.

The word *sin* (Greek, *hamartia*) means to miss the mark. To miss the way. To deviate from the path. To go wrong. Sin is missing God's standard of right and wrong. It is falling short of God's glory (Romans 3:23). This is no small stone.

Sin is pictured as a fall. The original sin of Adam is called "the fall." Sin trips us up and causes us to stumble. It knocks us off our feet, puts us on the ground, and brings defeat. Sin is a crippling hindrance to running life's race.

As we run, there are stumbling blocks that can "so easily entangle us." These stumbling blocks can lead us into sin and bring its devastating consequences upon us.

What is a stumbling block? The word (Greek, *skandalon*) originally meant the trigger stick of an animal trap on which the bait was placed. It means to lure or ensnare into destruction. It is a snare, a trap. A cause of disaster. A temptation to sin. An occasion to fall.

Stumbling Blocks to Watch For

We Christians encounter various stumbling blocks. James 3:2 says, "We all stumble in *many* ways" (emphasis added). What are the different ways we stumble? To answer that question, we need to consider the different stumbling blocks we will encounter: Satan, the world, our flesh, other believers, and God Himself. Wise is the person who is aware of each.

Stumbling Block 1: The Devil

First, Satan lines our path with stumbling blocks. The Bible teaches that there is a real devil who opposes the work and people of God. The word *devil* means "one who slanders," or "one who trips up." The devil is a stumbling block who trips us up in the race.

As we run God's race, we are sure to encounter the devil's snares and traps, shrewdly camouflaged and strategically placed.

What are these devilish snares?

Temptations. Temptation to abandon God's will. Temptation to put our self-interests before God's. Temptation to seek our own will rather than God's. Temptation to work our own agenda, not God's.

The temptation itself is not sin. But it is the stumbling block that leads to sin.

Peter's Plan

En route to the cross, Jesus predicted His own death. He told the disciples that He must go to Jerusalem to suffer, be killed, and be raised on the third day (Matthew 16:21). This was all a part of God's plan.

When Peter heard this, he took Jesus aside and rebuked Him: "God forbid it, Lord! This shall never happen to You" (verse 22). In other words, "Lord, I love You and I have a wonderful plan for Your life." Peter was attempting to divert Jesus from God's plan. He was saying, "Surely God does not want You to face this."

Jesus saw through these words to the deadly source—*Satan*! He responded immediately, "Get behind Me, Satan! You are a stumbling block to Me; for you are not setting your mind on God's interests, but man's" (verse 23).

Peter's well-intended words, prompted by Satan, were a stumbling block. A temptation to abandon God's plan. An enticement to pursue his own will, not God's.

To Go Our Own Way

Satan will do the same in our lives. He will attempt to wreck our race. To disrupt our running. To divert our direction. And he will do it by enticing us to follow our own desires, to go our own way, to make our own path.

Satan's chief temptation is that we leave God out of the picture. He wants us to forsake God's eternal perspective and see life from a mere human, temporal perspective. He lures us to focus upon man's interests, not God's.

For Christ, the temptation was to abandon the cross and pursue earthly success. It will be the same for us. Our seduction is to abandon heaven's reward for men's applause.

We must always maintain an eternal perspective. Every decision must be made in light of God's eternal plan for our life. We must always ask, "Which decision will leave the greatest mark on eternity and bring the greatest glory to God?" Satan would have us think solely about what is personally expedient. This is a stumbling block we face day after day.

False Teaching

Here is another stumbling block of Satan: false teaching—anything that does not square with God's Word.

Mark it down: Satan is a liar. Worse, he is the father of all lies (John 8:44). He is the architect of doctrines of demons (1 Timothy 4:1). Satan will tempt us to abandon God's Word and follow his lies. This has been his modus operandi since the garden.

Even within the safe confines of Christian fellowship, Satan's stumbling blocks of false teaching can be found. Jesus said to the church at Pergamum, "I know where you dwell, where Satan's throne is…But I have a few things against you, because you have there some who hold the teaching of Balaam, who kept teaching Balak to put a *stumbling block* before the sons of Israel, to eat things sacrificed to idols and to commit acts of immorality" (Revelation 2:13-14, emphasis added).

This devilish doctrine of Balaam, Jesus asserted, was hatched in hell. Specifically, it taught that God's people should marry unbelievers and join their spouses' idolatrous worship. Christ warned strongly against this worldly compromise because, since He indwells believers, such practices brought Him into union with Satan.

This same stumbling block is still laid by Satan today. It is the temptation to fellowship with the world. To become like it. To adopt its standards. To follow its lifestyle. To laugh at its jokes.

Where are you being lured away from the authority of God's Word? How are you in danger of compromising Scripture? Are you a stride away from losing the race?

Stumbling Block 2: The World

We need to stop here for a moment to catch our breath. Before I point out the second stumbling block, I already know some of you are not going to want to hear this. You are going to want to turn the page. Maybe even close the book.

But before you do, let me just remind you of the title of this book: *In It to Win It*. We cannot be winners in God's race unless we deal successfully with this second stumbling block. Head-on.

The second stumbling block is the world. Like Satan, the world lays its obstacles before us as we run God's race.

Jesus emphatically said, "Woe to the world because of its stumbling blocks! For it is inevitable that stumbling blocks come" (Matthew 18:7).

The world is the invisible system of evil in society that is opposed to God. Headed by Satan, it is the organized system that is hostile to God and founded on self, greed, and pride. It opposes and contradicts all that is godly and Christian. God is ignored, forgotten, and ultimately rejected by all participants of this world system.

As we Christians run the race, the world is contending for our minds. The evil system around us is vying for our hearts and our souls with evangelistic fervor. It is relentlessly seeking to squeeze us into its mold. To prompt us to adopt its godless values and lifestyles. To trap and ensnare us as we run God's race.

But we cannot love the world and God at the same time. The two are mutually exclusive. The apostle John told us, "If any one loves the world, the love of the Father is not in him" (1 John 2:15).

In the next verse, John described the seductive lure of the world: "For all that is in the world, the lust of the flesh and lust of the eyes and the boastful pride of life, is not from the Father, but is from the world." With this threefold enticement, the world stirs up within our hearts a strong desire for satisfaction through wrong desires.

"The lust of the flesh" is the world's appeal to our physical desires. Sensuality. Immorality. Pornography. Drugs. Alcoholism.

"The lust of the eyes" is the seduction of our eyes with the world's goods. It breeds a materialism that must have more and more of the world. Lust causes us to become obsessed with the glitter of things.

"The boastful pride of life" tempts us to self-elevation, arrogance, egotism, and obsession with our own importance. It is the drive for popularity and prestige.

We all encounter these stumbling blocks. There seems to be no end to their seductive attempts to mislead and corrupt us. We must resist the attraction of the world (Romans 12:2). We must not become entangled with the world's values, lifestyle, and godless philosophy. These are dangerous stumbling blocks.

Let me tell you quite candidly—I struggle with the attractions of the world. There have been allurements in my life and still are. The same is true for all believers.

Having once had a taste of the world's "good life," we know how hard it can be to resist the fleshly attractions. Materialism can spin its web around our hearts. It is hard to cut the cords and remain unstained.

As you push to get ahead in the world, do not become entangled with the world. As Christians we are *in* the world, but not *of* the world. We are to have our boat in the water, but no water in the boat.

Stumbling Block 3: The Flesh

Here is a third stumbling block: our flesh. This one is not so obviously seen because it arises from within. It is hidden within our hearts. It is our sinful flesh that trips us up.

When the Bible speaks of the flesh, it is not referring to the skin that covers our body. The flesh is our sinful human nature. It is called the old man, the old self, the body of sin. It contains our self-centeredness that leads us away from God. It is the evil inclination that lurks within us, an internal propensity for evil that still pulls us toward sin.

I want to disclose four sometimes subtle but always deadly ways the flesh rears its ugly head.

Pride

First, *pride* can cause us to stumble. This is the chief destructive obstacle within our flesh. Solomon recorded, "Pride goes before destruction, and a haughty spirit before stumbling" (Proverbs 16:18). Pride causes us to run God's race with our nose in the air. No wonder we fall.

Arrogance comes in many disguises. It is often in the form of male ego, the drive to be number one at all costs, glorying in the world's approval, the quest to be the best regardless of whom it hurts. The attention is on the unholy trinity of me, my, and mine.

Muhammad Ali once spoke of himself before his 1971 title fight with Joe Frazier thus:

> There seems to be some confusion. We're gonna clear this confusion up on March 8. We're gonna decide once and for all who is king! There's not a man alive who can whup me. [He jabs the air with half a dozen blinding lefts.]
>
> I'm too smart. [He taps his head.]
>
> I'm too pretty. [He lifts his head high in profile, turning as a bust on a pedestal.]
>
> I AM the greatest! I AM the king! I should be a postage stamp—that's the only way I could get licked. [1]

By the way, Ali lost to Frazier. Need we say more?

Greed

Second, *greed* is another stumbling block within. It is the drive for more and more and more. Greed is an insatiable appetite that is never content with what you have. It is the restless passion to always want more.

The Bible says, "They will fling their silver into the streets and their gold will become an abhorrent thing…They cannot satisfy their appetite nor can they fill their stomachs, for their iniquity has become an occasion of *stumbling*" (Ezekiel 7:19, emphasis added). Despite having silver and gold in abundance, the heart's appetite is not satisfied. It must have more. Always more. The sin of greed is a sure occasion of stumbling.

The story is told of a great ship that, years ago, struck a reef and began to sink. The people on the ship had only a few minutes to escape. So they abandoned all their belongings and fled to the lifeboats.

One man, however, ran back to his stateroom and filled his pockets with his money and jewelry. This took just long enough to ensure that no room was left in the lifeboats for him. The man put on a life jacket and jumped overboard with his pockets full of his personal belongings.

But, as his friends looked on from their lifeboats, they saw him hit the water and plummet to the bottom like an anchor.

The weight of the money and jewelry was too great to allow him to float. He sank to his death because his greed would not let him release his death grip on his material possessions. A death grip it literally was.

Greed often fills us with what becomes our own destruction.

It is reported that when John D. Rockefeller, one of the world's richest men, was asked how much money was enough, he replied, "Just a little bit more."

Greed bears this mentality: Get all you can, can all you get, sit on the lid, and let the rest of the world go to hell.

Are you driven by the desire for more? Always more? Always bigger? Always better? This is the stumbling block of greed.

A Loose Tongue

Third, a *loose tongue* can cause us to stumble. James wrote, "If any one does not *stumble* in what he says, he is a perfect man, able to bridle the whole body as well" (James 3:2, emphasis added).

Few stumbling blocks can trip a believer more easily than a dangling tongue. Our tongues can get so long that we trip over them as we run.

A woman once came to John Wesley, convicted of her gossiping. She confessed that she wanted to put her sinful tongue on the altar. Wesley replied curtly that he did not think the altar was large enough.

Another time, a young lady said to Wesley, "I think I know what my talent is."

Wesley said, "Tell me."

"I think it is to speak my mind," she replied.

"I do not think God would mind if you buried that talent," Wesley said. [2]

Men, this is not just a problem for women. Our tongues too can cause us to stumble.

We hurt ourselves when we hurt others with our tongue. Like the man who knocked himself out trying to throw his boomerang away, our hurtful words come back to haunt us. What goes around comes around. That is especially true about our words.

Always speak as if you were in the presence of Christ. Say nothing that would be inappropriate if He were present. Because He *is* present.

Sexual Lust

Fourth, *sexual lust* is another fleshly stumbling block that we must avoid. Jesus said, "Everyone who looks at a woman with lust for her has already committed adultery with her in his heart. If your right eye makes you *stumble*, tear it out and throw it from you...If your right hand makes you *stumble*, cut if off and throw it from you" (Matthew 5:28-30, emphasis added).

Do not misunderstand, please. Jesus was not calling for self-mutilation. Even a blind man can lust. He was saying we must deal radically with lust in our heart. We must take drastic steps to resist and remove it.

I will deal with this subject of lust more fully in chapter 11. In fact, I will devote the entire chapter to it. For now, let me say that sexual lust must be mastered.

Personally, I have found the best defense is a good offense. Both in football and with lust. Defeating lust requires an all-out, aggressive saturation of my mind with the Word of God.

I am an intently single-minded person. Very monothematic. When my mind is dwelling on God's Word and His holy character, then it is not free to wander onto what is wrong and forbidden. Meditating on God helps avoid this major stumbling block.

Paul wrote, "Whatever is true, whatever is honorable, whatever is right, whatever is pure, whatever is lovely, whatever is of good repute, if there is any excellence and if anything worthy of praise, dwell on these things" (Philippians 4:8).

These are the primary entrapments of the flesh: pride, greed, a loose tongue, lust. They are hideous, ugly, and deadly. They head the résumé of everyone who loses God's race.

It is not enough to just recognize them. We must resist and replace them with what is holy and righteous. If we are to say no to these enticements, we must say yes to Christ. Yes to His lordship. Yes to His power. Yes to His holiness.

Stumbling Block 4: Other Believers

The fourth stumbling block is very subtle. Would you expect your own teammates in the race to cause you to fall? Probably not. But by their actions and attitudes, they can do just that.

Let me remind you again that we are not racing against one another. My victory does not depend on me "beating" you. Nor vice versa. We are racing against ourselves and the track, not against other believers. Therefore, we can encourage one another to excel without fear of personal loss.

Nevertheless, the influence of other believers is a very real and powerful force, either for good or for bad.

The Bible clearly warns us against causing another believer to sin: "Let us…determine this—not to put an obstacle or a stumbling block in a brother's way" (Romans 14:13). This is a serious offense against Christ, as well as against that Christian.

Conversely, this verse implies that we must be careful not to allow the influence of another believer to cause us to stumble. This can arise from their exercise of Christian liberty (1 Corinthians 8:9). Or it may be something that is clearly sinful (1 Corinthians 15:33). But fellow runners can trip us. And cause us to fall.

The 1984 Olympics will always be remembered for a tragic event. It had to do with Mary Decker of the United States and Zola Budd of South Africa (but she was running for Great Britain) in the women's 3000-meter run.

Midway through the race, Decker and Budd were running even. Stride for stride. Budd, who was running barefoot, slightly clipped the back of Decker's heel. Unintentionally.

Decker went down hard as if she were shot. She was too injured to complete the race. Her stumble caused her to lose in her attempt to win the gold medal.

Not only did it cost her this race, but she also did not run competitively for an extended period of time. It cost her many victories.

The same can happen to you and me. Unintentionally perhaps, other runners can cause us to stumble. Just as we must not be a distraction to others in the race, neither should we allow another to cause us to fall.

That is why we must keep our eyes riveted upon Christ as we run. If we become too focused upon others—their shortcomings, their failures, their opinions, their successes—then we will surely trip and fall over their life.

Throughout the day, Jesus Christ must remain preeminent in our hearts and minds, the object of our adoration and thoughts. Others will fail us often, causing us to fall. But Christ will never fail us. Keep your eyes on Him.

Stumbling Block 5: God Himself

Here is the final stumbling block: God Himself. Would you believe God can be a stumbling block? Yes, I said God. I have purposefully reserved this one for last. It is the most serious stumbling block of all.

Let me first make a disclaimer. I am not saying that God is the author of sin. Nor am I saying that He tempts us to sin. What I am saying is that God allows us to suffer the consequences of our own sin. He places stumbling blocks in our path to knock us down. But He does so in order that we would humbly look up to Him.

In other words, we are knocked down to look up. There can be a time in a believer's life when God must discipline him. God, in love, disciplines us for our good. Yes, God loves us and accepts us just the way we are. But He loves us too much to let us remain in our sin.

His loving discipline seeks to remove us from our sin. Consequently, when we go too far into sin, He will place before us a stumbling block to discipline us. The purpose is to cause us to fall. Often it takes being knocked flat on our backs before we look up to God. He allows us to stumble not to harm us needlessly, but to bring us back to Himself.

Israel's Discipline

Such was the case with God's people, the nation Israel, in the Old

Testament. Their worldliness and immorality became a cause for His divine discipline in the form of stumbling blocks.

In Jeremiah 6:21, God Himself said He would place stumbling blocks before His willfully disobedient and unrepentant people: "Thus says the LORD, 'Behold, I *am* laying stumbling blocks before this people. And they will stumble against them'" (emphasis added).

In Ezekiel 3:20, God states that He will lay a stumbling stone before a once-righteous man who has fallen into apostasy: "When a righteous man turns away from his righteousness and commits iniquity, and *I place an obstacle before him*, he will die" (emphasis added).

Isaiah wrote, "It is the LORD of hosts whom you should regard as holy. And *He shall* be your fear, and *He shall* be your dread. Then *He shall* become a sanctuary; but to both the houses of Israel, a stone to strike and *a rock to stumble over*, and a snare and a trap for the inhabitants of Jerusalem. *Many* will *stumble* over them. Then they will *fall* and be broken; they will be snared and caught" (8:13-15, emphasis added).

Cornerstone or Stumbling Block

Either the Lord is the cornerstone of our lives, or He is a rock over which we stumble and fall. When we fail to build our lives upon His wisdom and truth, we are, sooner or later, subject to His stumbling blocks. Maybe too often, we give Satan credit when it is actually God who is at work in our lives.

Similarly, Jesus Christ will be either a cornerstone or a stumbling block. The apostle Peter wrote,

> Coming to Him as to a living stone which has been rejected by men, but is choice and precious in the sight of God...
> "Behold I lay in Zion a *choice stone*, a precious *corner stone*, and he who believes in Him will not be disappointed."...
> but for those who disbelieve, "The stone which the builders rejected, this became the very *corner stone*," and "A *stone of stumbling* and a rock of offense"; for they *stumble* because they are disobedient to the word (1 Peter 2:4,6-8, emphasis added).

These verses say that when we receive Christ by faith, we build our lives upon Him (Matthew 7:24-25). He becomes our cornerstone, who holds us up and gives strength to our entire life. If we refuse to trust in Christ, then we stumble over Him and are eternally destroyed.

As we run God's race, we must run in close fellowship with Christ. We must continually trust in Him, much as a building constantly rests upon its cornerstone. When we fail to do so, we stumble through our disobedience and fall into serious consequences.

These are the five stumbling blocks we will face: Satan, the world, our flesh, other believers, and God Himself. We must be ever on the alert as we run God's race and not allow ourselves to falter and suffer loss.

Never Say Never!

Perhaps you are saying, "This would *never* happen to me. Why are you talking to *me* about this? I am not going to fall." Such naive thinking only assures the probability that you will fall. Stumbling is an ever-present danger for all of us. No believer is immune. No one is safe.

Take Heed Lest You Fall

The Bible warns, "Let him who thinks he stands take heed that he does not fall" (1 Corinthians 10:12). When we have just come off a spiritual high or victory, we are prime candidates for catastrophe. Many times, our most tragic defeats come on the heels of our greatest spiritual victories.

Peter learned that lesson. Painfully.

The scene is the Upper Room, the night before Jesus was crucified. Our Lord tried to prepare His disciples for what was about to occur by saying, "You will all *fall away* because of Me this night" (Matthew 26:31, emphasis added). To "fall away" means to stumble. Jesus was saying, "You will all stumble tonight. You are headed for a devastating fall in your faith. Your world is about to be turned upside-down."

But Peter—who repeatedly suffered from foot-in-mouth disease—shot back, "Even though all may *fall away* because of You, I will never *fall away*" (verse 33, emphasis added). Peter thought he would never fall. He certainly never meant to, especially not that night. He was saying, "Other runners may stumble and fall flat on their face, but not me, Lord. I will never stumble in the race."

The Fall of Peter

Knowing the human heart, Jesus sadly replied, "This very night, before a rooster crows, you will deny Me three times" (verse 34). In other words, "Peter, you say you will not stumble? You may be running fine now, but tonight you will fall flat on your face. Three times!"

You know what happened to Peter. The Bible records that he did just as Jesus had said. He fell flat on his face. Three times.

Never presume that you are incapable of stumbling into sin. Satan is too cunning. The world is too seductive. Our flesh is too weak. Other believers are too influential. Distractions are too numerous. God is too concerned.

Never say never!

Get Back into the Race

If you are like me, you are saying, "I stumble and fall all the time. Is there any hope for me?" We all stumble. None of us makes it through the race unscarred by sin.

And you ask, "After I fall, can I get back in the race?" Absolutely, you can. Here is how.

Confess Your Sin

First, you must *confess your sin*. First John 1:9 says, "If we confess our sins, He is faithful and righteous to forgive us our sins and to cleanse us from all unrighteousness."

To confess one's sin means to agree with God about one's sin. It is to acknowledge that it is wrong. It is to tell Him that you have fallen short of His glory.

When we confess our sin, God cleanses it by the blood of Jesus Christ. He delights to forgive our sin. He does so fully, freely, and completely. It is His nature to forgive. Once confessed, our sin will never be brought up again.

Forsake Your Sin

Second, you must *forsake your sin*. You must not commit a sin and confess it with the intention of continuing in it—only to fall again. Proverbs 28:13 says, "He who conceals his transgressions will not prosper, but he who confesses and forsakes them will find compassion." This is a call for repentance, which necessitates that we forsake the sin and run from it.

Get Back on Your Feet

Third, you must *get back into the race*. Once you confess your sin, you must get back on your feet and continue running the race. God is a God of second chances. And third chances. And fourth chances.

Peter fell, but he got back into the race. After he denied the Lord, he confessed his sin (John 21:15-17) and resumed his place of spiritual leadership (Acts 1:15). He was the powerful preacher on the day of Pentecost who preached and 3000 souls were saved (Acts 2:3-41).

Jonah fell, but he got back into the race. God told him to go to Nineveh to preach, and he went the opposite direction. He stumbled and fell, and spent time in the belly of a whale. But he confessed his sin and got back into the race. He went to Nineveh, and many thousands of people were saved (Jonah 3).

If you have stumbled and fallen, can you get back into the race? Yes, you can. Confess your sin. Forsake it. And get back into the race and run.

Fallen Runners Can Be Restored

The movie *Chariots of Fire* depicts the life of Eric Liddell and his quest for the Olympic gold medal. Early in the movie, Liddell is running a race in the Scottish Highlands. Many local Scots have turned out to see this "Flying Scot" run.

As the runners make the first turn, Liddell trips and falls flat on his face. The crowd gasps and groans as the race appears to be lost for Liddell. It is a moment of personal decision for the Flying Scot. Will he stay down? Will he concede the race? What will he do?

To everyone's astonishment, he gets back up and reenters the race. Far behind the pack, Liddell runs as fast as he can. Gradually, he overtakes one runner. Then another.

Finally, he captures the lead. Eric Liddell speeds down the final straightaway and breaks the tape at the finish line. He is exhausted, bent over, gasping for air. And then he collapsed. But victorious. He fell, but got back up. He came back to win the race.

A God of Second Chances

That is the message of grace in the gospel of Jesus Christ. Though we fall, we may get back into the race. There are many stumbling blocks—Satan, the world, our flesh, other believers, and God Himself—lurking in our path as we run God's race. There is not a one of us who will not fall at various points in the race. We are all prone to sin.

But when we do fall, it need not mean that we will automatically lose the race. If that were so, we would all lose. When we become entangled with sin, we must confess it, forsake it, and get back in the race. God is the God of second chances—and more.

Please do not misunderstand. There are serious consequences to our sin. But falling does not mean there no longer remains any chance for victory. We may overcome our stumbling blocks through the unmerited grace of God. We may overcome isolated defeats and bounce back to experience His ultimate victory.

Maybe you have been knocked down in life's race. Perhaps you are lying on the track hurt, disappointed, discouraged. Maybe you think you can never win. It could be that you have lost your will to even finish the race.

I have good news for you. Failure is never final as long as there is the grace of God. If you have fallen, you can overcome defeat. If you have stumbled, you can still win the victory.

Do not lie there!

Get back up!

Get back in the race!

You Don't Have to Go to Boston to Run a Marathon

The third Monday in April. If this date means anything to you, you are definitely a serious marathoner.

On this date the Boston Marathon—the world's oldest, longest-standing, and most prestigious race—is run every year. On this date, the finest runners from around the globe gather to run this marquee event. There is nothing like Boston. No other race generates such electricity, nor exudes such mystique.

This third Monday in April is also a state holiday in Massachusetts—Patriots' Day. Over a million spectators are able to line the course to witness this sports spectacle.

With media-filled helicopters hovering overhead, approximately 6000 of the world's elite runners bunch together nervously at the starting line in Hopkington, Massachusetts. Their destination: downtown Boston, twenty-six-plus miles away.

Landmarks of Tradition

Along the route, two memorable landmarks have become ingrained in the rich tradition of the Boston Marathon.

The first is the all-girls school, Wellesley College, located at the halfway point. The student body of this college lines both sides of the course to cheer the runners along. The sight and sound of the enthusiastic coeds provides a much-needed emotional lift and encouragement to the energy-drained runners.

The second landmark is Heartbreak Hill. After passing Wellesley

College, the runners face a series of five ascending hills spread out over the next eight miles. Climb, plateau. Then climb, plateau again, and so forth. This second half of the race is a major gut-check time. The fifth and climactic hill is the shortest—but it is also the steepest. And it comes at the twenty-one mile mark. Heartbreak Hill is exactly that—a heartbreaker. A lungbreaker. A backbreaker.

The difficulty is not only in the steepness of Heartbreak Hill, but in its location. It comes at a point in the race when legs are already exhausted and lungs are ready to burst.

Once past this "cardiac climb," the race leads downhill into the heart of downtown Boston, amid the skyscrapers and many historic buildings.

Approaching the Finish Line

Over the last five miles, anxiously awaiting spectators line both sides of the course, peering into the distance to catch the first glimpse of the oncoming runners. They shout encouraging words of inspiration to the weary racers: "You can do it!" "You are looking good!" "You are almost there!"

As the runners continue their odyssey, they anxiously search the horizon for the red Citgo sign perched high above the city skyline. When they reach it, they know only one mile remains to the end of the race. A sharp right. A turn left. Before them lies the most strenuous straightaway in all of sports. Six hundred agonizing strides down a steel and glass corridor, framed by towering buildings and packed bleachers, toward the finish line of the Boston Marathon.

Amid the shadows of the tall office towers looms the finish line at Copley Square, just in front of the Boston Public Library. Here, in the grandstands nestled between the tall buildings of downtown Boston, over 100,000 supporters await their heroes.

The flashing lights on the motorcycle escort signal the advancing runners as they stride for the finish line. The crowd rises to its feet and responds with a deafening roar of approval. The runners can feel the exuberant energy of the cheering people surge through their numb bodies. Every runner is a hero. If you run and finish this race, you are an undisputed champion.

With the close of each Boston Marathon, another page of history is recorded. These gallant runners have run the race. They have met the challenge. They have finished the course.

Can you not sense the exhilaration as these runners come to the finish line? Can you not feel the vibration of the crowd's roar? Can you not hear the motorcade at the finish? Can you not smell the sweat of the athletes? Can you not taste the victory?

Must We Run in the "Big Races"?

In the world of competitive marathoning, world-class runners must run in the big races in order to establish themselves. They must compete in elite marathons like those held in Boston, New York City, London, Rotterdam, and the Olympics.

You cannot be a champion marathoner by just competing against the local talent. You must go where the big-time runners are.

You cannot be a recognized champion and stay home. To be the best, you must run against the best. Further, you must beat the best. You must travel great distances to face the stiffest competition.

If you are not willing to travel, you will always be a second-class runner. No matter how fast you think you are.

Some people view the Christian life the same way.

They think the "big race" is out there somewhere. They assume that to be a big-time Christian, you need to go across the ocean. To the mission field. To Africa. To Europe. Or at least across the country—to seminary.

But the truth is, you do not need to go looking for God's race far away. It is right in front of you. The Bible says, "Let us run with endurance the race that is *set before us*" (Hebrews 12:1, emphasis added). It is set by God right before us. It is right under our noses. For most of us, it is not "out there" somewhere. Rather, it is right where we live.

In the Christian life, you do not have to go to Boston to run a marathon. God has a championship race for you to run at home. Right where you are. In your office. In your family. In your neighborhood. In your school.

Some people think that unless they go across the country, or halfway around the world, they will remain a second-class Christian. You know, "*Just* a businessman." Or "*Just* a layman."

God's Race for You

But nothing could be further from the truth. In the Christian life, the "big races"—heaven's Olympics—are held every day right where you live.

You do not have to go to the mission field. Nor to seminary. Nor into the ministry. Certainly, God will call a few of us to do that. But most Christians will run God's race right where they are.

It is not the place that counts. It is the race.

Is this not liberating? This truth gives eternal significance to the day-to-day grind of life. Nothing in your life is meaningless. It is all important. This is because it is a part of God's race for you.

This divinely appointed race before you is very simply God's will for your life. No more, no less. God's will is the track on which you run this race of faith. It is important that we understand what this track is and how we can discover it.

God has placed a race—a track—right before each of us. Christians run on a specially prepared track called God's will. God has a plan for each of our lives—a spiritual blueprint called His will. There are several features of God's will that we must grasp if we are to recognize God's track before us.

It was just such a race, much like the Boston Marathon, that the writer of Hebrews had in mind when he wrote, "Therefore, since we have so great a cloud of witnesses surrounding us…let us run with endurance the race that is set before us" (Hebrews 12:1). In this chapter, we want to focus on the last part of this verse: "Let us run with endurance the race that is set before us."

While you may never make it to the Boston Marathon, God has a race for you to run right where you are.

Running the Race Effectively

What must you do to run this race well? I want to give you four key strategies for running God's race. By His grace, you can run like a winner.

Run Your Own Race

Here is the first strategy: *Run your own race.* God has an individual race for each of us to run. No two races are run exactly alike. No two runners are exactly alike. I do not run your race. You do not run mine. You do not have to copy another believer's pace. We each run at our own speed.

No Two Runners the Same

In competitive marathoning, some runners like to jump out with a quick start. Others like to lag behind and make their push at the end. Some like to run in a pack. Others like to run alone. Some like to set the pace. Others like to follow the pace. The point is, no two runners run exactly the same way.

Many factors determine how one's individual race is run. Speed. Body strength. Personality. Emotions. Health. Familiarity with the course. Other runners. Past successes. The most recent race. Weather.

No two runners are exactly alike.

No two races are run exactly alike.

The same is true in the Christian life. As believers in Christ, we each have different spiritual gifts. Different callings. Different temperaments. Different natural talents and abilities. Add to that different backgrounds. Different passions. We are all wired so differently.

God has an individual race for your life. No one else is meant to run your race. If I were to run your race, I would miss God's individual race for my life and vice versa. God has a tailor-made race for each of us.

Please do not misunderstand me. I am not saying there are different roads that lead to heaven. Jesus Christ claims that He alone possesses exclusive passage to the Father: "I am the way, and the truth, and the life; no one comes to the Father but through Me" (John 14:6). Only one road—the bloody cross of Jesus Christ—leads us to the Father. That is the gospel truth.

What I am saying is that there are different individual races for each of us to run. Different lives. Different places. Different circumstances. Different challenges. Different obstacles. Different speeds. Different conditions. God has not cut us out with a cookie cutter. We do not all look alike or sound alike. Neither do we run alike.

I must allow God to be as unique with me as He is with you. You must be who God uniquely made you to be.

Do Not Run Someone Else's Race

Let me illustrate. When I was in college, I had a professor who had a tremendous impact upon my life. He was a successful lawyer who taught business law. He was smart, sharp, and explosively funny, the kind of person to easily connect with a student like myself.

I soon found myself wanting to be just like him. I figured the way to be successful, smart, and sharp was to be a lawyer. So, guess what? I headed off to law school to be like my prof.

But once classes started, I was miserable. Absolutely depressed. I hated it.

I took a leave of absence from school to work for this professor in his bid for the Texas state senate, which he won. He eventually beat George W. Bush in another political race and went to Washington as a US congressman.

It was there, working in his political campaign, that I made a sobering discovery. I was not running God's race for my life. I was running someone else's race. I was trying to be my professor, not the person God had called me to be. I had gotten off track.

This was a painful lesson to learn. But a much-needed one. I must run my own race. Not somebody else's.

This is a key strategy we must follow. Run your own race. Do not run somebody else's race. Be the person God uniquely created you to be.

Follow God's Track

Here is the second strategy: *Follow God's track*. Picture God's race being run on a divinely prepared track. Call it God's will for your life. You do not make up your own route to run. You do not find your own way to the finish line. God has already prepared the track that He has chosen for you to run.

God does not say, "You are here, at point A. I want you to get over there to point B. Now, go find a way. Get there on your own, somehow, some way." I am glad that God has already designed a route to get me where He wants me to be. I simply run God's track, which He has already prepared.

It Was Designed in Eternity Past

The Bible teaches that in eternity past—before you were even born—God planned the path you should take. With infinite wisdom, He laid it all out. With inscrutable genius, He weighed and considered all the possible options and chose the best race for you to run.

Before you even entered the race, God laid out your track to run. He determined when in history you would run your race. Where on the globe you should run it. Who your parents would be. Who your spouse would be. What your vocational calling would be. Your personality makeup. Your spiritual gifts. Where you would serve Him. All this—and much more—was a part of His predetermined plan for you.

This predetermined plan was certainly true for Jeremiah. God chose him to run a race that was mapped out ahead of time. It was planned long before Jeremiah was born. God explained to the prophet, "Before I formed you in the womb I knew you, and before you were born I consecrated you; I have appointed you a prophet to the nations" (Jeremiah 1:5).

It was also true for the apostle Paul. The apostle came to realize he was running a sovereignly prepared race, one planned long before his birth. Every step he ran was a step of destiny. Paul testified, "[He] who had set me apart even from my mother's womb and called me through His grace, was pleased to reveal His Son in me so that I might preach Him among the Gentiles" (Galatians 1:15-16).

This is no less true for you and me.

Our race was specially designed by God from before the foundation of the world. We run with a sense of destiny. Everywhere we run, we arrive by divine appointment. God has a sovereign reason—a divine purpose—for everything that happens in our lives. God has prepared good works for each one of us in which to walk (Ephesians 2:10).

Every day when you get out of bed, you are running into a day specially designed by God to fulfill His purposes. Every stride is a part of His master plan. Every step is divinely appointed.

This track was forged in the heart and mind of God from before time began. This individual race has your name on it.

It Is Constructed on God's Character

A second aspect of this track is its divine character. This track—God's will for your life—is constructed on God's character. The character of the Designer is revealed in the track itself. Because God is good, His will for you is good. Because He is *perfect*, so His track is perfect.

The Bible teaches that the will of God is "good and acceptable and perfect" (Romans 12:2). That means it is the very best track on which to run. "Good" means devoid of any evil. God will not lead us to sin. His will is also "acceptable," meaning that when we discover it, we will like it. It will be acceptable to us.

Back in my college days, I used to fear that if I followed God's will for my life I would have to go to some remote outpost in Africa as a missionary. But then I learned that whatever it is God wills for me to do, He will put the desire in my heart for doing it. He will make it acceptable for me. I would be miserable doing anything else.

His will is "perfect." It cannot be improved upon. If I had a thousand lifetimes to redesign God's track, I could never improve upon it. Because He is perfect, His will is perfect.

I hear people talk about surrendering to the will of God. They talk like it is surrendering to defeat. "Well, I guess I am *stuck* with doing God's will." Get that notion out of your head. God's will is something good that you get in on.

The Lord says, "I know the plans that I have for you...plans for welfare and not for calamity to give you a future and a hope" (Jeremiah 29:11).

Who would not "surrender" to this?

It Encompasses All Your Life

Third, everything that God designs for your life ought to happen on this track. Everything!

No part of your life is excluded from His plan. Paul tells us that God "works all things after the counsel of His will" (Ephesians 1:11). This truth is an all-inclusive statement.

Some people make a false dichotomy in life between the spiritual and the secular. They assume that only the spiritual is a part of God's race—that is, Bible study, prayer, witnessing, church work. The secular, they reason, must not be a part of God's race. Things like work, parenting, recreation.

As a result, a gross misconception arises about the race—the assumption that only certain parts of a person's life are run on the track. But nothing could be further from the truth. God has designed all of it. Every area of your life is included in the race.

This race is not run only on Sundays with a few spiritual pit stops during the week. No way. *Everything* you do is a part of God's race. Everything.

God's race includes your spiritual life and your church life. Sure. It also includes your family life, your professional life, your social life, your recreational life, your community life, and your financial life. Everything about your life is a part of God's race.

It Leads You into the World

Fourth, this track leads into the world. For the most part, it is not run behind the cloistered walls of the church. It is run out in the world.

In the Olympics, only the first and last laps of the marathon are run in the stadium. Almost the entire race weaves through the streets of the city—by the banks, through the marketplace, next to the schools, past the hospital, by the factory. The course snakes through the entire community. Finally, the race reenters the stadium for one final lap in front of the crowd for what many call the most dramatic moment in sports.

God's race is like this. It takes us into the world. Through neighborhoods. Into the business districts. Into the classroom. Into the marketplace. We do not run all our laps within the four walls of the church.

God's track leads us into the real world, where real people need Him. We do not stay within the secluded confines of Christian fellowship. Mostly, we run into the world to impact our community with the gospel of Jesus Christ. We must "take it to the streets."

Jesus commanded His first runners, "Go into all the world" (Mark 16:15). He said, "Go therefore and make disciples of all the nations" (Matthew 28:19). He prayed to His Father for us: "I do not ask You to take them out of the world, but to keep them from the evil one" (John 17:15).

We are to be in the world, but not of the world.

Read the Signs

You may be saying, "Great! I want to follow God's track. But I am not certain where it is. How do I recognize His track for my life?"

That brings us to the next strategy: Read the signs.

Before runners run a marathon, they study the markings and signs along the way. They know that to lose sight of the course for even a short period of time will probably mean losing the race. It means a loss of energy, a loss of time, a loss of opportunities. Perhaps a loss of victory.

Even so, God has clearly marked His race for our lives. The key to knowing God's race is knowing how to read the signs along the way. What are the signs that reveal the way?

Here are seven key signs that let you know how to follow God's track.

Follow God's Word

First, the Bible leads us along God's track. As we run in this world of darkness, we need light to see the track. God's Word is this light—"a lamp to my feet, and a light to my path" (Psalm 119:105). Scripture shines a spotlight before us and reveals the direction in which we should run. His individual will for you is always found within the wisdom and morality revealed in His Word.

How exactly does the Bible—an ancient book written thousands of years ago—reveal God's way to people today? There are several key questions we must ask, the answers to which reveal to us the way. Here they are:

1. Is there a command to obey?

The Bible is filled with divine commands for you and me to obey. There is no question what God's will is in these areas. Our obedience to His commandments leads us precisely into the center of His will.

For example, "Do not get drunk with wine, for that is dissipation, but be filled with the Spirit" (Ephesians 5:18). This is clear-cut. Non-negotiable. Black and white. There is no doubt what God's will is in this matter. His track will always—I repeat, always—be found within the boundaries of obedience to His commandments.

2. Is there an example to follow?

A major portion of the Bible is written in story form—narrative and biographical literature. The first seventeen books of the Old Testament are narrative; the first five of the New Testament are biographical and narrative. These historical books contain the lives of real people who followed God. Their godly lives are recorded as an example for us to follow (Romans 15:4). As we imitate their lives, their walks of faith reveal God's track to us.

Take Daniel, for example. As I read that this exiled prophet placed a higher allegiance on obeying God than obeying government, his life reveals God's way to me for today. When I am confronted with a similar tension between the earthly and the heavenly, I must choose to obey God, not men. Always.

3. Is there a promise to claim?

As a father's will governs the management of his vast estate, so too is the Bible filled with promises from God to His children—to bless, to enrich, to satisfy. God's estate is a vast reservoir of spiritual riches able to meet all the needs of our life. Charles Spurgeon once compared these divine promises to blank checks issued by God to His children. Already signed by God, they are to be cosigned by His children, brought to heaven's treasury, and drawn against the limitless wealth of heaven's account.

For example, Jesus says, "Whatever you ask in My name, that will I do, that the Father may be glorified in the Son" (John 14:13). Just think about the large inheritance that Christ desires to share with us. Of course, the key is praying in Jesus' name—praying for those things which honor and glorify His name.

4. Is there a sin to avoid?

The Bible holds up before us certain sins that must be avoided at all costs. They are clearly out of bounds. For example, "This is the will of God, your sanctification; that is, that you abstain from sexual immorality" (1 Thessalonians 4:3). God's will is always found where sexual purity is maintained. This is a no-brainer. Any step toward immorality is definitely out of bounds and off track.

5. Is there a principle to follow?

A principle in the Bible is a timeless truth tightly stated. It is a short, pithy, practical statement of truth drawn from a passage and used to guide our lives. Principles are broad statements of truth that universally apply to every situation we face. For example, Joshua led the children of God in a march around the city of Jericho, giving a shout of victory as they trusted God to fight for them. The principle is that we should worship before we do anything else. We should praise God in the face of the impossible and watch Him act on our behalf.

Obviously, the better we know God's Word, the better we will know His will for us.

Follow the Spirit's Witness

Second, God's Holy Spirit sets the pace for us along God's track. The Bible says, "All who are being led by the Spirit of God, these are the sons of God" (Romans 8:14). Just as there is the outward, objective witness of God's Word, so there is the inward, subjective witness of the Spirit.

While this verse primarily addresses the Spirit leading us to put to death the sins of the flesh, it does speak, in a general way, to the Spirit leading us in our daily life. The witness of the Spirit is the inner "tugging" we may feel in our heart. It is the divine pressure of the Holy Spirit that urges us to pursue a particular action.

A little boy was out flying his kite on a windy day. The blowing breeze pushed the kite higher and higher until it disappeared above the clouds.

Soon, one of his buddies came up. He looked up and saw only

string ascending into the clouds. But he saw no kite. "Why are you holding onto that string?"

The little fellow replied, "I have got a kite up there."

His friend looked up again. But he still could not see the kite. "I do not see it. How do you know there is a kite up there?"

"Well, I know it is there," he said, "because I can feel the tug."

That is precisely how the inner witness of the Holy Spirit works within us. While we do not see God visibly, we feel the inner tug of the Spirit leading us into God's will. We are constantly in touch with God, sensing His leadership in our lives.

Often, this witness of the Spirit of God is received and recognized through prayer and meditation. The Bible says, "If any of you lacks wisdom, let him ask of God, who gives to all generously and without reproach, and it will be given to him" (James 1:5). Prayer helps us sense the Spirit's inner witness in our heart.

Wisdom, according to J.I. Packer, is the best means to achieve the highest goal. It is the earthly living of heavenly truth that the Spirit applies to our hearts.

When we are confused and do not know which course to pursue, God invites us to pray in order to ask for His wisdom and seek His counsel. Jesus said, "You do not have because you do not ask" (James 4:2). The Holy Spirit gives us the wisdom to discern the course to pursue.

God does not answer begrudgingly. Just as any earthly coach gives counsel to his athletes, so God desires to give wisdom to His runners. When we ask for it, God delights in bestowing such insight in life.

Listen to James again: "He must ask in faith without any doubting, for the one who doubts is like the surf of the sea, driven and tossed by the wind" (James 1:6).

We must ask by faith for wisdom without a wavering doubt. This means without being divided within oneself, without being pulled in two directions. We should not think, *God can!...No, He cannot.* We must believe that God is infinitely wise, unconditionally loving, and ultimately sovereign. Thus, He knows best, wants our best, and is able to bring it to pass, no matter how impossible it seems.

Lloyd John Ogilvie wrote, "Prayer does not overcome God's reluctance to guide us; but it puts our wills in condition to receive what He wills for us."[1] Prayer does not so much change God's will as it finds God's will.

Follow "Sanctified" Common Sense

Third, God's track is followed through "sanctified" common sense. Now, all too often, common sense is just that—common. But what I am talking about is *sanctified* common sense—a Spirit-enlightened common sense through a renewed mind.

God has given us a mind with which we are to make decisions. We are to think rationally, logically, and intelligently in discerning His will. Because we are created in the image of God, He has given you and me the capacity to think, reason, and choose. We are able to sort things out, analyze situations, think things through, make evaluations, have insights, and draw conclusions.

Too often, we think God's will is found in bizarre, unconventional ways. But that is not usually the case. It is through a renewed mind that His will is discovered (Romans 12:2).

I read about a lady who received a brochure advertising a tour of the Holy Land. Because going to Israel was one of her lifelong dreams, she really wanted to go. She had the money, the time, the interest, and the strength. But was it God's will?

Before going to bed, she read the pamphlet once more and noticed that the airplane they would travel on was a 747 jumbo jet. After spending a sleepless night wrestling with the pros and cons, she awoke the next morning. She opened her eyes and *there* was the answer. She just knew it was God's will for her to go to Israel.

How did she know for sure?

She said that when she awoke, she glanced at her digital clock and it read 7:47. That was her "sign" from God. In reality, her mind was already made up and she was grasping for any "sign" she could cling to.

I wonder what would have happened if she had awakened in the middle of the night only to read 1:47? Maybe that would have been a sign to take a smaller plane, like a crop duster.

God has given us brains we can use for figuring things out, although that could be debated based on a lot of what we see on religious television programs. He expects us to use our brains with sanctified common sense.

How did the early church know God's will? Most often, the Holy Spirit worked through a renewed mind. In Jerusalem, the church leaders discovered God's will through what *seemed* good and right: "Then it seemed good to the apostles and the elders, with the whole church, to choose" (Acts 15:22). The apostles, when it came to making a decision, arrived at a conclusion that "seemed good to us" (verse 25). This rational thinking was in conjunction with the inward witness of the Spirit. The Holy Spirit worked through their thinking capacity, which was yielded to God. And that is how the early church made its decisions: "It seemed good to the Holy Spirit and to us" (verse 28). His will just "seemed" right, logical, and prudent.

God also led Paul in much the same way. By his sanctified common sense, he sent Epaphroditus to the Philippians: "I thought it necessary to send to you Epaphroditus" (Philippians 2:25). He simply *thought* it best. No bells and whistles.

A.W. Tozer remarked, "The mind is good—God put it there. He gave us our heads and it was not His intention that our heads would function just as a place to hang a hat." [2]

Follow Your Heart

Fourth, God leads through our hearts just as He works through our minds. When it comes to living the Christian life, the Bible links our minds with our hearts.

A strong compulsion within to pursue a course of action is often God revealing His way to us. J.I. Packer advises us to "note nudges from God that come your way—special concerns of restlessness of heart." [3]

God worked through Nehemiah's heart in order to lead him into His will. Nehemiah recorded, "I arose in the night, I and a few men with me. I did not tell anyone what my God was putting into my mind to do" (Nehemiah 2:12). Literally, "mind" here is the word *heart*. God led Nehemiah by putting into his heart what He wanted him to do. This godly man felt a strong passion and desire to do this for God.

When I consider my own call into the ministry, the leading indicator of God's will for me was this strong desire. It was not something I merely wanted to do. It was something I *had* to do. A holy passion and heavenly compulsion gripped my heart.

When Paul wrote Timothy, he told him this strong compulsion would accompany God's leading men into the ministry: "If any man aspires to the office of overseer, it is a fine work he desires to do" (1 Timothy 3:1).

The verbs employed here are very strong. "Aspires" (Greek, *oregomai*) means a strong aspiration to covet after, as one would for heaven (Hebrews 11:16). "Desires" (Greek, *epithumea*) is even stronger. It is a great desire to long for, to covet after (Luke 16:21; 17:22; 22:15).

So God puts His desires into our hearts. They then become our desires, which lead us into His will and along His track.

Follow Open Doors

Fifth, God's track is also followed by open doors of opportunity. We believe that nothing occurs by random chance. God is the sovereign Lord of heaven and earth who ultimately controls every circumstance of human history. He governs all the events of our lives. As R.C. Sproul says, "There are no maverick molecules on this planet. All are under His control." [4]

Consequently, our sovereign Lord opens doors before us through which we are to run. He prepares a way to travel where there is no way. He lays the track for us upon which we are to run. Further, He removes the obstacles that would impede our progress. These opportunities we call "open doors."

In the New Testament, the phrase "open door" is used five times. In each instance, it refers to an opportunity to move forward in doing God's will. Jesus told the church at Philadelphia, "Behold, I have put before you an open door which no one can shut" (Revelation 3:8). For Paul, God created these opportunities for his service and ministry by placing open doors before him (see 1 Corinthians 16:8-9).

God does the same for you and me. He opens doors, which permits us to follow His track.

Follow Your Strengths

Sixth, God leads through our strengths. Before we can make proper decisions, we must properly know ourselves. We must know our strengths and weaknesses because God generally leads us to exercise our strengths.

Paul told young Timothy, "Pay close attention to yourself" (1 Timothy 4:16). In other words, watch over yourself. Know yourself. Know your gifts, your strengths, your abilities.

The apostle wrote, "I say to everyone among you not to think more highly of himself than he ought to think; but to think so as to have sound judgment" (Romans 12:3). We should know and think about our strengths. We must not overestimate them. But neither should we underestimate them. The verse immediately before this one talks about how to know God's will. We can only conclude that knowing our strengths and gifts is a part of knowing God's will and following His track.

Each of us has an array of God-given strengths and spiritual gifts that we bring to any situation. When presented with a choice concerning where to work or how to serve Christ, go with your strengths. Know what they are and put them into practice.

Knowing God's will involves developing and using our spiritual gifts and natural abilities. This is a matter of stewardship. We must be faithful to utilize and maximize what God has entrusted to us.

Jesus told a parable about a king who went on a journey (Luke 19:11-27). Before he left, he gave ten of his slaves ten minas each. "Do business with this until I come back," he told them.

When the king returned, each slave was called to give an account of what business he had done with the king's money.

One invested well and made ten minas. To which the king replied, "Well done, good slave."

Another made five minas. "Well done, good slave."

But the last failed to invest the king's money. He sat on it, and it brought no return. The king was greatly displeased. He ordered his initial investment taken from this overly cautious slave and given to the others.

The slave was not judged for what he did not have, but for what he *did* have. Not for his weaknesses, but for his strengths.

The lesson of the parable is this: God has entrusted to every believer certain talents. Every believer must be faithful to invest God's entrustment, or face His displeasure.

What gifts, talents, and resources has God entrusted to you? Your wise and aggressive investment of what He has given to your care will lead you into God's will.

No two of us are exactly alike. Each of our individual races will focus upon the wise investment of what strengths God has entrusted to us.

Follow Godly Counsel

Seventh, God leads His way through godly counsel, through the corporate wisdom of others—a spouse, a pastor, a friend, a mentor, a parent, a prayer partner.

The wisdom of Solomon says, "Where there is no guidance the people fall, but in abundance of counselors there is victory" (Proverbs 11:14). "Guidance" here is a nautical term that pictures the steering of a ship into a port. God steers our lives into His will through the wise counsel of others.

Without such guidance, we will stray off course during the race. But with the collective wisdom of other believers, there is victory. Their counsel will help steer us correctly along God's track and toward God's victory.

Do Not Get Off Track

Let me give you one last strategy: *Do not get off track!* This may sound too negative, but it needs to be said.

Unfortunately, the potential exists to get off track during the race. We can misread the signs. We can veer off the course. We can overstep the boundaries and leave the track.

I do not mean to imply that we can lose our salvation in Jesus Christ. Such is impossible. The Bible clearly teaches the eternal security of the believer. Once we become children of God through the new birth, we can never be unborn and put out of the family. Once saved, always saved.

By leaving the track, I mean that it is possible to wander from God's will. We can stray from the clearly marked track that God has laid before us. We do not lose our salvation, but we do lose our way. We lose our sense of direction and precious time.

So we must be careful to stay on track.

When we leave the track to pursue our own path, we must reenter God's track as soon as possible. Precious time is being wasted. If we stay off track too long, we might even become disqualified by God and lose a reward.

Clearly, obedience in the Christian life is important. Every step of the way is critical.

Some Christians, after starting on the right course, become diverted from the track on which God originally set them. They just veer over to the side. They sit down and rest in the grandstands. They become passive spectators rather than prize-winning champions. Some believers even get busy serving in the stands. Selling hot dogs. Taking up tickets. But they are not in the race. They are off track and out of God's will.

The Christian's race begins the moment a believer is born into God's kingdom and ends when he enters God's presence. The interval between is the time he has to complete his spiritual course.

If he strays from his course, he loses valuable time. The only way to complete the course within the allotted time is to stay on course.

We have a limited time to finish our spiritual race. In a sense, we are running against the clock. So, make "the most of your time, because the days are evil" (Ephesians 5:16).

Putting It All Together

This chapter has focused upon the four key strategies for running the race set before us. They will surely lead to victory at the finish line. Do you remember what they were?

First, run your own race. We each run the specific race that God has designed for us. Do not run somebody else's race. Be who God uniquely created you to be.

Second, follow God's track. God has divinely prepared a path for you to run. This track is His will. We must discover and follow God's will for our lives.

Third, read the signs. God's will is not hidden. You will find it by following God's Word, the Spirit's witness, sanctified common sense, your heart, open doors, your strengths, and godly counsel.

Fourth, do not get off track. Be careful not to veer off the path. Do not wander off course. Precious time and energy will be lost.

These strategies are crucial for victory in the race that God has for you.

Are you in it to win it?

9

It's Always
Too Soon to Quit

WINNERS NEVER QUIT. QUITTERS NEVER WIN."
I can still see that sign hanging in our locker room. Plain as day. It had been mounted there by my high school football coach to build character and instill courage within us. The letters were hand-painted onto a stained wooden plaque. But more importantly, that sign would become inscribed upon my heart. And indelibly etched upon my soul.

I can still see it. "WINNERS NEVER QUIT. QUITTERS NEVER WIN."

The message came through loud and clear. This was not rocket science. It would become the bedrock foundation of our every drill, our every practice, our every game.

A quitter? To this day, no word is so revolting or distasteful. The words "I quit" were not allowed in our vocabulary. *Quit* is a four-letter word. I would rather die than quit. Call me anything—just do not call me a quitter.

My coach spent three years building into us the virtue of endurance. Some call it perseverance. Others tough-mindedness. Whatever, it was drilled into us. You just never quit. No matter how impossible the odds. No matter how tough the opponent. No matter how dark the hour. You just never quit.

Never!

A champion *never* throws in the towel. He would rather eat the towel than throw it in.

Endurance means never quitting, regardless of the score. You suck it up and go. If you are playing poorly, you hang tough until you can turn it around. When the chips are down, you buckle your chin strap. You just *never* quit.

What Makes a Winner?

The mark of a winner is his heart. He is distinguished by the will to win. He is possessed by the resolve to never give up. He is known by the drive to always press on to the goal. When the going gets tough, the tough get going.

Call it heart. Call it perseverance. Call it character. Call it whatever you want. God calls it endurance.

Take, for example, a gifted athlete who is blessed with every advantage. He has the size, height, speed, muscles, and strength to be a champion. He is the total package. A physical specimen. Inevitably, he is competing against a less-gifted athlete who is smaller, slower, shorter, less muscular.

So often, the less-gifted athlete beats the swifter and more muscular one. Strange as that is, even Solomon recognized that "the race is not to the swift" (Ecclesiastes 9:11).

What makes the difference?

The edge lies deep within. The difference is the heart. The distinguishing factor is the will to win. A winner has the willpower and staying power to endure in the heat of battle. He overcomes whatever adversity is necessary to win. Whatever the opposition, whatever the difficulty, whatever the mental fatigue or physical pain, he endures all to win.

I can still see that sign: "WINNERS NEVER QUIT. QUITTERS NEVER WIN."

This truth is equally applicable in the Christian life. God's champions never quit. To win the incorruptible crown, we must run with endurance and press on to the finish. Quitters never win. Not in God's race.

The Heart of a Winner

The Bible says, "Let us *run with endurance* the race that is set before us" (Hebrews 12:1, emphasis added). The key word here is *endurance*. That is another way of saying perseverance, or staying power.

This chapter is an anatomy of the heart of God's champion. It is a look at the believer who is pursuing the ultimate prize. If we were to peel back the heart of this champion one layer at a time, what would we discover? At the core, we would feel the vibrant, throbbing heartbeat of a deep commitment to run the race with endurance. Such a runner is resolved to finish the race, no matter what.

Show me what it takes to stop you, and I will show you whether or not you are a champion. I am amazed at what little things eventually stop us in God's race. All too often, they are such petty things, such minimal things that hinder us—hurt feelings, misunderstandings, even trivial pursuits.

I must tell you that this chapter will be both comforting and convicting. It is a two-edged sword that cuts both ways. It will be comforting to those of you who are undergoing a personal trial and testing. This chapter will encourage you to endure and press on because a crown awaits you. You must hang in there.

James put it this way: "Blessed is a man who perseveres under trial; for once he has been approved, he will receive the crown of life" (James 1:12). The one who endures and perseveres through trials will win the crown.

Did you get that?

A crown awaits you if you will persevere in the race.

But at the same time, if you are complaining about your problems and wanting to bail out, this chapter will be most convicting. If you are grumbling your way through the Christian race, this chapter will be a swift kick to the backside. Maybe you have stopped running. Perhaps you have given in to the pain, the weariness, the exhaustion. Then get back in the race! Stop whining—and start winning.

The Virtue of Endurance

Now, let us look at this virtue of endurance and answer three simple questions: What is it? What does it look like? How can I live it?

What Is Endurance?

The Christian life is a long-distance marathon—not a 100-yard sprint. Endurance is more important than sprinter's speed. Most often, the final yards of the race are more important than the opening yards.

The Bible says, "Let us *run with endurance* the race that is set before us" (Hebrews 12:1, emphasis added). "Endurance" (the Greek word is *hupomone*) means a steady determination to keep going. The word combines the verb translated "to bear up" with the prefix translated "under." It literally means "to bear up under," as bearing up under a heavy load or difficulty. It means to bear up patiently while running under the constant stress and demand of a marathon.

We are talking about perseverance to keep running even when you want to stop. This is the steadfastness to never give up. This is the persistence to refuse to quit.

The Christian life is a long obedience in the same direction. It requires hanging tough through the daily grind. Day after day. It will push us to the very limit of what we can endure. Remember, this is a marathon—twenty-six-plus grueling miles—not a short sprint.

The First Marathon

Do you know the origin and significance of the term *marathon*? The year was 490 BC. On the open plains near the small town of Marathon, the ancient Greeks met the invading Persian army in a strategic battle. If the Persians won, the Greek Empire would surely topple.

Against impossible odds, the Greeks charged into the Persian camp, catching their enemy by surprise, and overcame the mighty Persians, thus saving the Grecian Empire from defeat.

As legend has it, a Greek soldier—Pheidippedes—was then dispatched to run to headquarters in Athens, about twenty-five miles away, to announce the good news of victory. With unwavering determination and resolve, Pheidippedes ran through the night all the way from Marathon to Athens.

Upon entering the city of Athens, he sprinted to his superiors. "Rejoice," Pheidippedes gasped, "we have conquered!" As he delivered the message, he fell to the ground dead.

Pheidippedes became a Greek hero. A symbol of endurance and determination. As a tribute to this faithful soldier who ran so bravely through the night, the marathon race was born. Runners in the Greek

Empire would soon attempt to duplicate his courageous feat, calling up the same endurance.

The Distance

How then did it become twenty-six miles and 385 yards?

The precise distance of the marathon was not fixed until more recent days. The distance that Pheidippedes ran from Marathon to Athens was roughly twenty-five miles. In 1908, the Olympics were held in London, and the marathon was extended to twenty-six miles, 385 yards. Why such an unusual distance? That year, the Olympic race would begin at Windsor Castle and end in front of the royal box at the new White City Stadium. To accommodate those plans, the length of the race would have to be extended.

This new distance was measured to be exactly twenty-six miles and 385 yards. Longer than any of the previous marathons, this distance went on to become the standard length for all marathons.

The Long Haul

What is the significance of this background information? When we compare the Christian life to a marathon, we are talking about a long-distance race. The Christian life is a long-distance haul. It is no short sprint. We do not run a while and stop, then run again. A marathon requires perseverance and sustained effort.

I fear there are too many "100-yard dash" Christians. They begin well as they come sprinting out of the starting blocks. They are at church every time the door is opened. They read their Bibles and their enthusiasm is obvious to all. But eventually they burn out and drop by the wayside. They go up like a rocket, but come down like a rock. In the day-to-day grind of the race, they eventually weaken, waver, and lose heart.

Now, suppose *you* are running a marathon. For the first mile, you are leading the pack. At the halfway mark, you are farther ahead than you have ever been. At twenty miles, you are way ahead. Everybody is behind you.

But at the twenty-five-mile mark, the "bear" jumps on your back. You want to quit. The blisters on your feet are killing you. Your lungs are gasping for air. Your knees are wobbling. You do not want to keep going any longer. Your body is screaming at you: "Stop! I cannot take it any longer. There has got to be an easier way."

What do you do? Give in? Quit trying? Stop running? Do you just pull over to the side and sit down? That would be the easy way out.

No, you choose to endure. You choose the hard way. Because you know in your heart that no matter how *fast* you have run, no matter how *far* you have run, no matter how *far ahead* you are, if you quit now, you will lose the prize.

Perhaps right now, you are in danger of quitting.

Listen: It is always too soon to quit!

Maybe you feel like quitting on your marriage. You want to take the easy way out. It matters little that you began your marriage well. What matters to God is that you *finish* well. You must finish your race with your spouse who is still with you.

Or maybe you are weakening to the lure of the world. You are about to replace your passion for Christ with the lust of the world. Do not let it happen. Again, that is the easy route. You must persevere in your love for Christ.

What Does Endurance Look Like?

In order to run with endurance, we must have a realistic idea of what it involves. There are four basic components:

A Long-Term Commitment

First, if we are to run God's race with endurance, we must have a long-haul commitment to Christ. We must see our involvement as life-long, not a ninety-day option.

Walter Alston managed the Brooklyn and Los Angeles Dodgers for twenty-four consecutive years. At the beginning of each year, he would sign a one-year contract. He signed twenty-four one-year contracts. His commitment was for only one year at a time.

Some people live the Christian life this way. Just making short-term commitments each year, to be reconsidered and renegotiated annually.

It cannot be this way. We make one long-term commitment to Christ at the beginning of the race. It is not subject to renegotiation annually, to be renewed at our whim.

I began God's race with the commitment that I would follow Him the rest of my life. Wherever He leads, I will go. Whatever He requires, I will give. I *will* run with endurance to the finish line. That is my front-end commitment. Jesus says, "No one, after putting his hand to the plow and looking back, is fit for the kingdom of God" (Luke 9:62).

Maybe you have never stopped to consider that this is not a 100-yard dash, but a marathon. You were once running in a dead sprint, but now you are dead tired because you eventually discovered this is a marathon.

No runner would ever finish a marathon if he entered thinking he was running a 100-yard dash. Never. He would never "just happen" to run twenty-six-plus miles. The only way he could finish is if he knew on the front end that it was a marathon, and he had resolved, "I am going all the way to the end."

Running the Christian race with endurance requires making a lifelong commitment to go all the way with Christ. We must purpose to finish strong, no matter what. We must resolve to live every day for Christ. We must be determined for the rest of our lives.

Pain and Agony

Second, we must recognize that running a marathon involves pain and agony. This is not a Sunday stroll in the park. This is an agonizing marathon. Therefore it involves discomfort and suffering. Those who are in it to win it have counted the cost and know that without pain there is no gain.

Jesus said, "In the world you have tribulation" (John 16:33). His race involved a cross. And so will ours. Jesus said to His disciples, "If anyone wishes to come after Me, he must deny himself, and take up his cross and follow Me" (Matthew 16:24).

The Greek word translated "race" (*agon*) is the very word from which we get the English word *agony*. Literally, Hebrews 12:1 says, "Let us run with endurance the agony set before us." God's race is agonizing. Did you hear that? Agonizing. A blessed agony, yes. But agony nevertheless—grueling, demanding, draining, stressful, taxing, tiring, torturing. Do not let anyone tell you otherwise.

We will experience the pain of self-denial and cross bearing and persecution and rejection and misunderstanding and satanic attack and thorns in the flesh. We must undergo trials and mortification of the flesh and long hours and the storms of life and the squeeze of this world and even God's discipline. The agony of repentance and the deep conviction of our sin and mourning over our wrongs will assail us. This is all par for the course. It is all hard work and sacrifice. God's marathon is painful and agonizing.

Paul shares his spiritual diary in 2 Corinthians 4:8-10: "We are afflicted in every way, but not crushed; perplexed, but not despairing; persecuted, but not forsaken; struck down, but not destroyed; always carrying about in the body the dying of Jesus, so that the life of Jesus also may be manifested in our body."

A Major Gut Check

The apostle said he ran with endurance "in afflictions, in hardships, in distresses, in beatings, in imprisonments, in tumults, in labors, in sleeplessness, in hunger" (2 Corinthians 6:4-5).

His marathon concluded, Paul then cataloged some of his trials, which included the following:

> Five times I received from the Jews thirty-nine lashes. Three times I was beaten with rods, once I was stoned, three times I was shipwrecked, a night and day I have spent in the deep. I have been on frequent journeys, in dangers from rivers, dangers from robbers, dangers from my countrymen, dangers from the Gentiles, dangers in the city, dangers in the wilderness, dangers on the sea, dangers among false brethren; I have been in labor and hardship, through many sleepless nights, in hunger and thirst, often without food, in cold and exposure (2 Corinthians 11:24-27).

The Christian life is a serious marathon. It is one major gut check. It clearly was for Paul. And it will be for you and me too. We are exposed to all kinds of difficulties as we run God's race.

Too often, when we get tired, we seek the easy way out. I have men come to my office and whine, "Pastor, I want out of my marriage. I am just not happy." They want to quit running. Quit their spouse. Quit their marriage. Quit their children. They want the easy way out.

I will say, "God wants you to remain faithful in your vow to your wife." Too often I hear in response—and it breaks my heart—"But God would not want me to be unhappy. I have met somebody else who really turns me on."

What I want to do is jerk them up by the lapels, pull them up close, and say, "Listen, suck it up! Gut it out, man! This is a marathon. If you are just trying to feel good, you are in the wrong race. Buck up!" Mind you, I do not say that. At least not in those exact words. But I want to.

However, I do say, "I want to help you honor your marriage vows. Run with endurance. Hey, it is *only* another forty years. That is nothing compared with eternity. You can endure another forty years."

Becoming a Christian does not mean the subtraction of problems from life, but the addition of power to endure them. What about you? Are you looking for the easy way out? There is no painless path. Not in God's marathon.

An Aggressive Effort

Third, running with endurance requires our aggressive effort. We must go all-out.

When the Bible says, "Let us run with endurance" (Hebrews 12:2), it is calling us to action. We must assume the responsibility to endure. This is not something we just sit back and let God do.

Now, do not get me wrong. I believe God gives us the power we need in order to run. And I believe that He is at work within us (Philippians 2:13). But we must pick up one aching foot and put it before the other. We must keep running. We bear that personal responsibility for our Christian life.

When I hear someone express a passive view of the Christian life and say, "Let go and let God," I get the clear picture that this person wants to shift into autopilot and stop running. This view of the Christian life urges one to just let God do everything while we do nothing. This mind-set is dangerous because it goes against the Bible's call for us to put forth effort. Yes, God will take over, but only as long as we assume our responsibility to run with endurance.

I want to point out another danger to our aggressive effort—an overemphasis of God's sovereignty to the exclusion of our human responsibility. Now, I believe in God's sovereignty, absolutely, totally, and unequivocally. But a constant focus upon divine sovereignty to the neglect of our human responsibility is paralyzing. Our race demands endurance, and endurance demands our effort. We cannot sit around and speculate, "I wonder if I am predestined to keep enduring." That is crazy. God says, "Run with endurance." Just do it!

We must step out by faith, trusting in His grace, and run with perseverance. We are responsible before God to endure. He will enable us, but we must endure. We must pursue holiness. We must pursue obedience.

Paul wrote, "I press on so that I may lay hold of that for which also I was laid hold of by Christ Jesus…One thing I do: forgetting what lies behind and reaching forward to what lies ahead, I press on toward the goal for the prize of the upward call of God in Christ Jesus" (Philippians 3:12-14).

These verses picture a runner pushing toward the finish line with aggressive, energetic endurance. He is straining every muscle to win. He is "reaching forward," giving his all to press to the end. In like manner, so must we live the Christian life.

A Strong Finish

Fourth, we must finish strong if we are to run with endurance. The last 100 yards are more demanding than the first 100 yards. It is not enough to start strong. We must finish strong.

Maybe you are thinking, *I am retired. I am going to drop out for a while. I have done my turn. Now it is time for those younger people to get involved.*

Excuse me, but the devil told you that. Not God.

You may be retired from your career, but you never retire from Jesus. All your retirement does is give you more time to serve God. Do not stop running!

I have some great prayer warriors in my church. They are older folks who are world-class runners in God's race. They are not retired. To the contrary, they are refired. In fact, I think they are just now hitting their full stride. Instead of slowing down, they are picking up their pace. The closer they draw to the finish line, the faster they are running. May their tribe increase.

Each one of us must finish well. This requires endurance. There has never been an athlete who has ever won who did not endure.

Never, never, never quit.

It is always too soon to quit!

The Slowest Marathon, the Greatest Victory

Almost 20,000 runners entered in the 1986 New York City Marathon. What is memorable about this famous race is not who won, but who finished last. His name is Bob Wieland. This unknown runner finished 19,413th. Dead last. Bob completed the New York Marathon in—are you ready for this?—four days, two hours, forty-eight minutes, seventeen seconds. This was unquestionably the slowest marathon in history. Ever.

What makes Wieland's story so special?

Bob ran with his arms.

Seventeen years earlier, when he was a soldier serving in Vietnam, Bob's legs were blown off in battle. When he runs, Wieland sits on a fifteen-pound "saddle" and covers his fists with pads. He "runs" with his arms.

At his swiftest, Bob can run about a mile an hour, using his muscular arms to catapult his torso forward. He advances one "step" at a time.

Bob Wieland finished four *days* after the start. What did it matter? Why bother to finish? There is a victory to be experienced in just finishing the course. Bob Wieland ran with endurance. In my estimation, he won because he ran with the greatest endurance, overcoming the greatest adversity.

The Christian life is much like this. The Bible says, "Many who are first will be last; and the last, first" (Matthew 19:30). It will take another world to determine who the real winners are in this life.

You may believe you are so far behind that it is no use to even try to finish. That is where you are wrong. Endure and finish the course. Leave the evaluation to God. Remember, it is the last 100 yards that count the most.

Champions like Bob Wieland, who finished last down here, will be crowned winners up there.

Paul and Jesus Finished Well

Paul finished well.

He ran God's marathon, beginning on a Damascus road and enduring all the way to his death just outside of Rome. He sprinted to the finish. Shortly before his death, Paul wrote, "I am already being poured out as a drink offering, and the time of my departure has come. I have fought the good fight, I have finished the course, I have kept the faith" (2 Timothy 4:6-7).

As Paul approached the finish line, he did not slow down. With head held high and eyes on the goal, the apostle pushed to the tape. He widened his stride. He picked up his pace. He sprinted to the finish.

Jesus finished well.

He ran God's marathon for His life, beginning in a stable in Bethlehem, and He endured all the way to the cross. He did not pull up short. The night before He was crucified, Jesus prayed to the Father, "I glorified You on the earth, having accomplished the work which You have given Me to do" (John 17:4). Talk about finishing the course!

When Jesus died on the cross, He cried out, "It is finished!" (John 19:30). He had finished the race God had set before Him. Redemption was accomplished! Jesus sprinted all the way to the finish line and burst the tape with His chest out and head erect.

I am reminded of a poster depicting a young football player, sitting dejected, battered, and beaten, with the caption "I quit." In the background is the shadow of the cross on Calvary with the caption "…but I did not."

No, Jesus did not quit. He finished the race.

How will it be with you? Will you sprint to the finish? Are you running with endurance?

"Winners never quit. Quitters never win."

Keys to Endurance

We have defined endurance. We have described it. Now let us get intensely practical. I want to talk about some specific areas in which you and I must endure.

Certainly, I could say we must endure in every area of the Christian life, and I would be right. But time and space do not allow me to pursue *every* area. Such a pursuit would be a marathon in and of itself.

In the Bible, there are some specific areas mentioned in which we are encouraged to endure and not lose heart. It is on four of these areas that I want to focus our attention.

In each of these key areas, we have a natural tendency to quit and stop running. I know I sure do. We need the prodding of the Holy Spirit to spur us onward—with patience and perseverance.

I am talking about areas like prayer and witnessing. Areas like love and good works. It is in these areas that we often grow weary and lose heart.

Let these next pages be an encouragement for us to pick up the pace, to widen our stride, and to sprint to the finish.

Relentless in Prayer

The first specific is prayer. I find it interesting that the only area in which Jesus instructs us not to lose heart is in the area of prayer. That tells us two things. One, we must have a real tendency to lose heart and grow weak in the area of prayer. Two, prayer must be especially important if Jesus singles it out.

When Jesus told the parable of the relentless widow, He taught His disciples that "they ought to pray and not to lose heart" (Luke 18:1). We must not lose heart in prayer. We must never give up in intercession.

Why would we be tempted to lose heart in prayer? Because when we pray, we do not usually receive the answer to our prayer immediately. So often, there is only silence. No response. No answer.

We pray, but the illness remains. The needed job is still unoffered.

The loved one is still lost. The injustice is not righted. Pray as you might, God has not yet answered.

So we lose heart and become discouraged. We live in a society that expects instant results, and when we do not get an immediate answer from God, we stop praying. We quit running in prayer. We get up from our knees and reason, *It is just not going to happen. God is not going to change it.* And endurance goes out the window.

Jesus knew we have this inherent weakness. So He told the following parable to encourage us to endure in prayer:

> In a certain city there was a judge who did not fear God and did not respect man. There was a widow in that city, and she kept coming to him, saying, "Give me legal protection from my opponent." For a while he was unwilling; but afterward he said to himself, "Even though I do not fear God nor respect man, yet because this widow bothers me, I will give her legal protection, otherwise by continually coming she will wear me out."…Hear what the unrighteous judge said; now will not God bring about justice for His elect who cry to Him day and night, and will He delay long over them? I tell you that He will bring about justice for them quickly. However, when the Son of Man comes, will He find faith on the earth? (Luke 18:2-8).

Our Lord is teaching that we must endure in prayer. We must continually come before God's throne with our requests, over and over.

In another place, Jesus explained prayer this way: "Ask, and it will be given to you; seek, and you will find; knock, and it will be opened to you" (Matthew 7:7). Do you see the increasing intensity of this prayer thrust? From asking to seeking to knocking. It pictures an aggressive pursuit of God in prayer.

These verbs are in the present tense. They are most properly translated, "*Keep on* asking…*keep on* seeking…*keep on* knocking." In other words, pray with endurance. Do not give up so easily. Be relentless. Do not quit.

Have you slowed down in your prayer life? Have you stopped altogether? Jesus said, "Pray and do not lose heart." You can start again, right now.

Relentless in Evangelism

A second area in which we must endure is witnessing. I believe we have a tendency to easily lose heart in our personal evangelism. Why is that? Again, there are two primary reasons. One, much like in prayer, when we do not see immediate results, we get discouraged and stop witnessing. Two, sharing our faith with others opens us to persecution and ridicule from others, causing us to want to quit.

But consider Paul's example when it comes to enduring in the face of adversity: "I suffer hardship even to imprisonment as a criminal, but the word of God is not imprisoned. For this reason I endure all things for the sake of those who are chosen, so that they also may obtain the salvation which is in Christ Jesus" (2 Timothy 2:9-10).

Paul wrote these words from a Roman prison cell shortly before he was put to death. It would have been easy for him to become discouraged and stop witnessing when he was put into jail.

But did Paul quit speaking Christ's name? No, quite the contrary. He endured because he was confident of the sovereign working of God in the hearts of the lost. He knew that his witnessing would not be in vain because God has His people who will believe. So he pressed on in the face of great persecution, knowing that the Word of God could not be imprisoned.

Each one of us needs to be reminded of this great truth. God has a chosen people who will surely come to faith in Christ. When others refuse our offer of the gospel, we need not lose heart because we know the sovereign purposes of God will still move forward. If one refuses Christ, another will receive Him. So let us endure in our witnessing.

To whom have you witnessed and received a cold shoulder? A boss? A loved one? A neighbor? Do not quit. Run with endurance. Stay after them. God can pry open even the hardest heart. Be encouraged.

Relentless in Love

Third, we must endure in loving others. Here is another area in which we can easily stop running with endurance. People can disappoint us, can they not? Hurt us. Even offend us. It can become very difficult to love some folks. Yet Paul says that love "bears all things, believes all things, hopes all things, endures all things" (1 Corinthians 13:7).

It is the nature of love to endure. Love refuses to quit reaching out, even in the face of rejection and opposition. It will not give up on someone, even when everyone else has given up.

Such enduring love is certainly the nature of God's love toward us. Despite our rejection of Him, He continued to reach out to us and to bring us to Himself. The story of the prodigal son verifies this. Really, it is the story of the forgiving father and his enduring love. It is found in Luke 15:11-24.

The son demanded his inheritance immediately, which is tantamount to telling his father, "I wish you were dead." A father's inheritance was not distributed until the time of the father's death.

Once he received it, the son crassly and coldly took the money and ran. He turned his back on his father and went to a far country. He just wanted to get as far away from his father as possible.

But he soon blew all his money and then decided to come crawling back home. He came back on his hands and knees, begging to be received back.

How did the father respond? Did he fold his arms, furrow his brow, and give his son a lecture? No way! The father endured in love, despite his son's rejection, and never ceased loving his boy.

When the father saw his son coming, his heart burst with love. He took off running down the road to meet his prodigal. He embraced him, smothered him with kisses, and called for a feast.

He had never stopped loving that boy.

That is precisely how we are to love others. Though others mistreat or belittle us, we are to endure in our love toward them. We must never quit reaching out to them.

Toward whom have you grown cold in your love? Your spouse? A once-close friend? An overbearing boss? An unkind family member? Run with endurance. Love endures all things.

Relentless in Good Works

I want us to consider one final area, and that is good works. We must not grow weary in serving one another.

The Bible says, "Let us not lose heart in doing good, for in due time we will reap if we do not grow weary. So then, while we have opportunity, let us do good to all people, and especially to those who are of the household of the faith" (Galatians 6:9-10).

As we run God's race, we can become so tired that we weaken in our service to others. Losing heart and growing weary carries the idea of becoming exhausted and giving up in the race. We all face that danger while running the marathon.

In 1 Corinthians 15:58, Paul wrote, "My beloved brethren, be steadfast, immovable, always abounding in the work of the Lord, knowing that your toil is not in vain in the Lord."

You must exert energy to get energy.

Stick It in the End Zone!

Yes, it is still there. The sign "WINNERS NEVER QUIT. QUITTERS NEVER WIN." This slogan became my creed in my senior year in high school. It was only then that it came off the wall to lay hold of my heart.

The scene was Jackson, Tennessee. Our opponent was the Jackson High Golden Bears. They were undefeated and ranked number three in the state. We, the White Station Spartans, were also undefeated and ranked in the top ten. The entire city was abuzz as two undefeated titans prepared to clash for western Tennessee bragging rights.

The game lived up to its advance billing. It was a bone-crushing standoff from the kickoff to the final gun. With three minutes left in the game, the score was 7-6. The Golden Bears were clinging to a thin lead. We took the ball on our own thirteen-yard line. Eighty-seven yards to pay dirt lay before us. It looked like eighty-seven miles. We barely had eighty-seven yards total offense all night. This would be our last shot at winning. It was do or die. Now or never.

As our quarterback, I huddled our team together and gave my best Knute Rockne speech: "I am calling on each one of you to give everything you have got left within you. We have played together for the last five years. We have practiced together. Run together. Bled together. Sweated together. Now, let us win together.

"We will remember this drive for the rest of our lives. Forty years from now, when I see you at a class reunion, we will remember whether or not we stuck it in the end zone. Let us give it everything we have got and win this game."

With deep resolve, we broke the huddle as men on a mission. We were determined to stick it in the end zone. With every tick of the clock, every yard of advancement became more and more precious.

We moved the ball to midfield. I encouraged the guys, "Only fifty yards to go!" Two fourth-down situations left us no choice but to go for broke. This was no time to punt. Our backs were against the wall.

We converted both "suicide" fourth downs.

The clock continued to tick.

With each first down, we gained new confidence. Finally, we marched down to Jackson's five-yard line. With eighty-two yards behind us, we knew the last five would be the toughest. We had to score to win. The five-yard line is not sticking it in the end zone.

It was third down. Only fifteen seconds remained. We had two downs to score, but we wanted the touchdown on third down. If we did not get it, we would be forced to kick a field goal, and that would spell big trouble. I was the placekicker.

One of our running backs brought the play in. "Power Sweep Right." This was the proverbial "Student Body Right." We lined up in strong formation right, which told the Golden Bears, "We are coming this way. Right at you." They answered with a stacked defense, ready for the challenge.

The line was drawn in the sand.

Both grandstands were on their feet screaming.

On the snap of the ball, I pivoted and pitched the ball to our fullback, sweeping right end.

Jackson High blitzed everyone. Everybody shot the gaps. I was immediately hit and driven facedown into the turf, unable to see the outcome of the play. I just lay there waiting to hear which grandstands would explode.

Would it be theirs or ours?

Then I heard it.

Our stands erupted! We had scored and won the game! We did it. Eighty-seven yards of glory. We had stuck it in the end zone. We had won.

You Can Stick It in the End Zone Too

This is the kind of endurance we need in the Christian life. A deep resolve to run all the way to the finish line. A commitment to persevere, no matter what.

Some of you may be eighty-seven yards away in your marriage. You are wanting to throw in the towel. Do not do it. Hang tough.

Others of you may be fourth and five in your prayer life. Do not punt. Go for it. Reintensify your commitment in prayer.

Still others of you may be running out of time to reconcile a broken relationship. Do not settle for anything less than complete restoration.

Endure. You can do it! With renewed resolve, you must determine to hang in there. Do not pull up short. Stick it in the end zone for the glory of God.

You say, "I want to do that. But how do I endure? I feel so weak. How can I hang in there?"

I have good news for you. In your weakness, God's strength is perfected. When you are weak, you are ready to experience the supernatural power of God to endure. I am going to tell you how to endure in the next chapter. So stay tuned.

Let me conclude this chapter by saying it is always too soon to quit. Do not give up. You can do it, by God's help and strength. Do not lose heart.

Endure.

10

Keep Your Eyes on the Prize!

I hope you have taken to heart what we learned in the last chapter about how winners never quit, and quitters never win. We are called to run with endurance. So how do we hang in there and persevere? Where do we get the strength to run God's race and win the ultimate prize? That is what we will focus on in this chapter.

Worst to First

The 1991 World Series will long be remembered as one of the greatest ever played. Perhaps the greatest. It was a Cinderella story come true for the Atlanta Braves and the Minnesota Twins. Both teams, in the span of one year, went from worst to first in their divisions to reach the World Series. In the Series itself there were five one-run games. Four were won on the game's final play; three went into extra innings. It had all the makings of a true classic.

The entire Series all came down to the seventh and deciding game. For all the marbles. There would be no tomorrow. More than 55,000 frenzied Twins fans were rocking Minnesota's Metrodome. Homer hankies were everywhere, cheering the home team on.

The workhorse of the Twins' pitching staff, Jack Morris, was sent to the mound on a mission. There was one thing and one thing only on his mind—to win it all. The outcome of the game, the World Series, and the entire 1991 season all rested squarely on his broad shoulders.

Picture this. After eight pressure-packed innings, the score is still knotted 0-0. This is baseball's answer to the arms race, a real pitchers' duel. Mounting a serious rally, the Braves load the bases with only one out. Morris never blinks. He has waited a lifetime for this moment. Every ounce of concentration is riveted on the business at hand.

The three Braves runners pose a serious threat to the Twins' place in history. One mistake from Morris and the score is 4-0, Atlanta. Sid Bream, the Braves' lefty batter, digs into the batter's box and begins waving his dangerous bat. A global television audience is glued to this epic moment in baseball history. Both dugouts are deathly still. The deafening roar escalates from the partisan crowd. This is one of those moments you feel in the pit of your stomach. But Morris is numb to it. All he can see is the heart of Brian Harper's catcher's mitt.

As Morris stares at Harper's signal, he blocks out every distraction in this den of noise. His face is expressionless. He is entirely deadpan. His eyes bore a hole in his catcher's mitt, which is positioned low and inside in the strike zone. He toes the rubber, pauses after a slow stretch, glances at the runner on third, and then zeroes in on the catcher's mitt.

For one split second, Morris is absolutely frozen on the mound. He kicks his leg toward the plate and hurls a rocket low in the strike zone. Bream swings and makes contact. At the crack of the bat, all three Braves runners break. A sharp grounder bounces high off the synthetic turf to the Twins' first baseman, Kent Hrbek, who smothers the ball and fires a strike to home plate for out one. The catcher, standing on the plate, fires back to Hrbek at first for out two. A 3-2-3 double play! And the Twins are out of the inning. The bullet is dodged.

Jack Morris dances off the mound with a glazed stare, oblivious to the pandemonium that has just erupted around him.

Winners Block Out the Distractions

Winners must be able to focus. And block out all distractions. And zero in on the goal.

Jump with me from the diamond to the hardwood. Michael Jordan, who was the greatest basketball player on this planet, is at the free-throw line shooting a one-and-one. The Detroit Pistons' defense has been clinging to this human highlight film like a cheap sweater. But nobody can shut him down. How do you contain the wind?

The Pistons' Dennis Rodman has been given the impossible task of stopping Jordan. In Jordan's face all night, Rodman still cannot contain him. So Jordan is back on the line to shoot the one-and-one.

As Jordan eyes the basket, the Pistons' rowdy crowd rises to its feet to distract the Bulls' scoring machine. Behind the backboard, Detroit diehards are stomping their feet, waving their hands, shaking their programs. Anything to distract Jordan.

But Jordan does not even blink. His eyes are glued on the goal. Instinctively, he dribbles twice, sticks out his famous tongue, and with ice water in his veins, calmly converts both free throws.

Michael does not even see the intimidating crowd and their diversion tactics. He blocks out 18,000 screaming fans and goes about his business. Just another day at the office.

Winners like Michael Jordan must block out distractions.

Winners Must Focus

I want you to go back in time with me to the 1950s. Ted Williams is in the batting cage taking his cuts at Boston's Fenway Park. Unequivocally, the Splendid Splinter is one of the greatest hitters of all time. Arguably the purest hitter in the game's history. Williams remains baseball's last .400 hitter, and when Ted called it quits, he retired with 521 lifetime home runs and a .344 career batting average.

What made Ted such a great hitter? Great eyesight? Perfect hand-eye coordination? Being a student of hitting? Yes, all of these things, but most of all, a rare ability to concentrate on the pitch. Teddy Ballgame could block out all distractions and focus.

As the story goes, his Red Sox teammates decided to test his notorious concentration skills by playing a prank on Williams. While Ted was hitting in the batting cage, his teammates quietly lit some firecrackers and tossed them at his feet.

Boom! Boom! Boom!

Guess what? Ted was so focused he did not even blink. As the firecrackers went off, his eyes remained riveted on the pitch. He was so intense that he could block out every distraction. Even exploding firecrackers.

Winners like Ted Williams must be focused.

What do these three champions—Jack Morris, Michael Jordan, Ted Williams—have in common? Among many things, the ability to focus on a goal, whether it be a catcher's mitt, a basketball rim, or a pitched ball. The capacity to block out all other distractions and remain intent on the goal was their common strength.

Champions compete as if wearing blinders. They are single-minded. Myopic. Intent. Focused.

Do you think a major league pitcher could throw strikes if he were looking at the base runners? Do you think an NBA star could convert free throws if he were watching the antics of the crowd? No way. To win, one must be focused on the task at hand.

Winners like you and me must be focused.

The Bible says,

> Therefore, since we have so great a cloud of witnesses surrounding us…let us run with endurance the race that is set before us, *fixing our eyes on Jesus*, the author and perfecter of faith, who for the joy set before Him endured the cross, despising the shame, and has sat down at the right hand of the throne of God. For consider Him who has endured such hostility by sinners against Himself, so that you will not grow weary and lose heart (Hebrews 12:1-3, emphasis added).

Do you want to run with endurance and win the prize? Then fix your eyes on Jesus. That is what this chapter is all about—running with your eyes focused on Christ and being single-minded on Him.

When we concluded the last chapter, I promised we would learn how to obtain the strength to run God's marathon with endurance. That will be our aim here. We will discover that fixing our eyes on Jesus produces the power we need to persevere. Like the seventh game of the World Series, this chapter is critically important. So read it carefully because here is how you will find the endurance to press on.

Fix Your Eyes on Jesus

What a runner focuses on during a race is critically important. As he comes down the straightaway, he must look directly ahead to the goal before him. He must not become distracted and glance into the stands to see who is cheering. Nor can he become fixed on the other runners. Such distractions would cause him to lose his balance, sacrifice his speed, or stray off track.

This principle holds true in the Christian life as well. What we focus our eyes upon during the race will play a major factor in how we run the race. That is why the Bible urges us, "Let us run with endurance the race that is set before us, *fixing our eyes on Jesus*" (Hebrews 12:1-2, emphasis added). As we run God's race, we must be riveted on Christ. We must be preoccupied with Him. Our heart and mind must be fixed on Him.

In order to understand what it means to be focused on Jesus, we first need to determine what it does *not* mean. As we run God's race, we must not allow ourselves to become preoccupied with anything else, such as circumstances, self, Satan, other people, or even the Holy Spirit.

Not on Circumstances

First, our circumstances can become a dangerous distraction, stealing away the focus of our heart while we run. Too often we allow our eyes to become fixed on our successes and failures, our good times and trials. Unfortunately, our circumstances are constantly changing—up and down, up and down. Therefore, our emotions and faith become like a roller coaster—up and down, up and down.

Whatever we focus upon controls our life. We come under the grip of our circumstances when we focus upon them.

Certainly, focusing on our circumstances is a very natural thing. But that is the problem. It is the natural thing to do, not the supernatural thing. Eyes of faith focus upon Christ, while eyes of fear peer at circumstances.

The apostle Peter had this problem. One night the twelve disciples were on the Sea of Galilee when a strong wind blew up. In the midst of the storm, Jesus came walking on the water toward their fishing boat (Matthew 14:22-33).

The disciples were terrified. They cried out in fear, "It is a ghost!" Jesus spoke, "Take courage, it is I; do not be afraid."

Peter was overwhelmed at the sight of Christ walking on the water. In typical, impetus fashion, he wanted to walk toward Jesus. "Lord, if it is You, command me to come to You on the water," he said.

Jesus said, "Come!"

Peter hopped out of the boat and started walking on the water! First one step. Then another. Soon he was cruising.

Then something disastrous happened. Peter took his eyes off the Lord and began looking around at the crashing waves. Fear gripped his heart. And Peter started to sink.

"Lord, save me!" he cried.

Immediately Jesus reached out His hand, lifted Peter up, and led him back into the boat.

Now, before we get too hard on Peter, remember that he at least had enough faith to get out of the boat.

What do we learn from this? As long as Peter's eyes were fixed on Christ, he did the impossible and remained above his circumstances. But when he became distracted by the waves, he started to sink. And Peter was soon under his circumstances.

The same principle is true as we run God's race. If we are to live above our circumstances, we must stay focused on Christ. As long as we do that, we can "run on water." But the moment we take our eyes off the Lord, we will surely sink. Before we know it, we are in over our heads.

Are you so focused on a problem that you have lost sight of the Lord? Maybe you are preoccupied with a career path now blocked. Or perhaps financial adversity. The greatest encouragement I can give you is to focus on the Lord.

We tend to sprint when things are going our way. But we slow to a walk when things are against us. That produces a "sprint, walk, sprint, walk" Christian life. Such living is inconsistent, erratic, and immature.

Not on Self

At other times we are preoccupied with looking to ourselves. The result is the paralysis of analysis. We begin to overanalyze our motives.

Or replay our past failures. We end up expending more energy questioning our motives than we do accomplishing the task. The apostle Paul wrote, "Forgetting what lies behind and reaching forward to what lies ahead, I press on toward the goal for the prize of the upward call of God in Christ Jesus" (Philippians 3:13-14). Rather than looking straight ahead at the goal, we are like a runner who is running with his head down, looking at his own feet or arm movements. No wonder we are slowed down and passed up by others.

Some of you may be victims of guilt. Satan is a grave digger, constantly shoveling up your past failures and faults. These are devilish distractions that impede any Christian's progress in pursuing the ultimate prize. Guilt should not be discounted. Often, it is a warning signal that something is wrong. But it should sharpen our focus upon Christ and require that we no longer dwell on our failures, but on His grace and forgiveness.

Certainly, we must watch over our hearts (Proverbs 4:23) and examine ourselves (2 Corinthians 13:5). But we must never allow ourselves to become preoccupied with ourselves.

Paul said, "If then you have been raised up with Christ, keep seeking the things above, where Christ is, seated at the right hand of God. Set your mind on the things above, not on the things that are on earth" (Colossians 3:1-2).

Only glance at self. Gaze upon Christ.

Not on Satan

Some Christians are, strange as it sounds, fixing their eyes on Satan. They have developed an unhealthy preoccupation with the evil one. It is easy to wonder if they fear Satan more than they fear God. They live as if there is a demon behind every bush, and they blame everything on the devil.

But our eyes must not be focused on the opposition. We cannot win looking at the other team. If we do, doubts will arise and we will become defensive. Ultimately, we will lose.

Let me illustrate. Years ago, I coached my twin boys' Little League baseball team. One of the first principles I taught the boys was, "After you hit the ball, do not watch the other team field the ball. Just drop the bat and run to first base as fast as you can. Do not—I repeat, do not—watch the other team!"

Guess what? My little sluggers would smack a line drive and then—you guessed it—just stand frozen in the batter's box and watch the other team field the ball. Only after watching them throw the ball to first base would they start to run. And all the while they were running to first base, they would be looking at the ball.

I would yell, "Run, run! Stop looking at the ball! Run!" Then they would run looking at me yelling at them.

Many a time they would be thrown out at first base by just a step. All because they watched the other team in the field rather than running focused upon the goal—first base.

There are a lot of Christians who live their lives just like that. They focus on the other team—Satan and his demonic host—rather than fixing their eyes on Christ. I agree we are not to be ignorant of Satan and his devices (Ephesians 6:10-17), but we must not be preoccupied with Satan. We must dwell on Christ, not the devil.

Not on Other People

Some Christian runners are preoccupied with other people. They are looking at the other runners, or at the spectators in the stands in the hopes of gaining their approval. But this misdirected focus causes them to stumble. Why? Because they have lost sight of the goal, Jesus Christ.

Be sure, we are headed for a fall if we are focused on others. Even our spiritual leaders may disappoint us. Maybe they do not keep their word. They may not practice what they preach. If we are riveted on them and they fall into sin, it can cause us to stumble.

We need to face that our expectations of spiritual leaders are sometimes unrealistic. We put them on too high a pedestal. And when they fall, it can cause our whole Christian life to go into a tailspin. This will happen every time we focus on the man of God rather than the God of the man.

All this can lead to is disappointment, disillusionment, and despair.

Let us consider again our race analogy. If we are way ahead of another runner, our tendency can be to relax and slow down. But remember, we do not compete against each other. God is measuring us against Christ, not the other runners. He may be expecting far more from us than from them.

Conversely, when others are far ahead of us, we may become discouraged and lose heart, backslide, and come to a standstill. That would be tragic because God may be expecting far more from the front-runners than He is from us.

I must confess to you the constant danger I face. I love to hear great preaching, just as I love to preach. Sometimes, the former is the enemy of the latter. For example, there are certain longtime preachers whom I enjoy listening to. But sometimes when I hear them preach, rather than be encouraged, I get discouraged. Why? Because I realize they are way ahead of me. I feel there is no way I can measure up to them.

Instead, I must remain focused on Christ. Yes, I can benefit greatly from these godly men. But I must not become preoccupied with them. I must look intently at Christ. When I look to Him, I am always encouraged because I feel privileged to have the opportunity to preach His Word.

Not on the Holy Spirit

I have purposefully saved this distraction—the Holy Spirit—for last. You may be saying, "Wait a minute! Time out! What is wrong with fixing my eyes on the Holy Spirit?"

Please notice that Hebrews 12:2 does not say "fixing our eyes on the Holy Spirit." Some Christian runners have a preoccupation with the third member of the Godhead—the Holy Spirit. But the Holy Spirit's preoccupation is to make us preoccupied with Jesus.

Jesus Himself said,

> When He, the Spirit of truth, comes, He will guide you into all the truth; for He will not speak on His own initiative, but whatever He hears, He will speak; and He will disclose to you what is to come. He will glorify Me; for He will take of Mine and will disclose it to you. All things that the Father has are Mine; therefore I said that He takes of Mine and will disclose it to you (John 16:13-15).

The Holy Spirit's desire is that we be intensely focused on Jesus Christ, not Himself. That is the Spirit's chief ministry. He points us to Jesus and brings Him more clearly into focus.

When the Holy Spirit becomes an end in Himself, then we have misunderstood His ministry. The Spirit's ministry is a means to an end—to focus on Christ.

Adrian Rogers has well said, "Whenever we see a parade with the Holy Spirit out in front, something is wrong. Jesus is always to be the One out front and the Holy Spirit is standing on the sidelines pointing us to Jesus."[1]

But on Jesus Christ

Okay, enough of the negative. Now to the positive. On whom must we fix our eyes? Jesus Christ. We must be "fixing our eyes on Jesus, the author and perfecter of faith" (Hebrews 12:2).

The word "fixing" (Greek, *aphorao*) means looking away to, focusing attention on, gazing intently upon. To fix our eyes on Jesus means to look to Him with the eyes of faith. It means to be preoccupied with Him. To trust Him. To love Him. To seek Him. To meditate upon Him. It is, quite simply, a Christ-centered life. Jesus only. Jesus always. No divided attention.

We are to run with eyes for nothing and no one except Jesus. Just as a runner concentrates on the finish line, so we must be singularly focused on Jesus Christ, who is the goal and object of our faith. Our eyes must be trained on Him without yielding to distractions.

Looking to Jesus is a life of faith. It is a looking with a heart that trusts Christ completely. As the dying Old Testament Jews looked to the uplifted serpent in the wilderness and were healed, so we are to look to Jesus with a heart of faith (Numbers 21:4-9; John 3:14-16).

God says, "Turn to Me and be saved, all the ends of the earth; for I am God, and there is no other" (Isaiah 45:22). There is no one else to look to for salvation and strength.

We must be *constantly* looking to Jesus. The same act of faith required for salvation must become a part of our daily lives. Paul instructed us, "As you have received Christ Jesus the Lord, so walk in

Him" (Colossians 2:6). More than an initial act of faith, we must maintain an ongoing life of faith. "Fixing" is a present participle and could be translated "*always* fixing our eyes on Jesus." Throughout the entire race, we must always look to Jesus. Not just on Sundays. But every day, all day, never allowing distractions to steal the focus of our faith.

We must look intently to Jesus. Not as in a daydream. But with alertness of mind. We must be totally absorbed with Christ. Our gaze must be resolutely fixed on Him who is both our goal and the prize.

Too many Christians are running with their eyes fixed on the grandstands. They are much too concerned with what others are thinking. They are so preoccupied with the approval of others that they lose sight of Christ's approval. What do my parents think? Is my boss watching? Do my friends approve?

Where Is Your Camera Aimed?

Some time ago I saw a television report from Texas A&M. During football spring training, the Aggies coaches mounted a small video camera on the helmet of their quarterback. They then put a special set of goggles on his face mask with an infrared light that followed the focus of his eyeballs. This caused the camera to videotape whatever the quarterback was focused on.

As the Aggies went through their passing offense, the coaches were able to monitor their quarterback's eye motions. At the end of practice, the coaches sat down and watched the video. On the screen, they would see exactly where their quarterback was looking during each play.

Was the quarterback distracted by the defensive linemens' rush? When did he visually pick up his primary receiver? Did he quickly read the free safety? When did he pick up his secondary receiver? When did he look for his safety valve? All of this is critically important information for assessing a quarterback's actions and skills.

A successful quarterback must focus on the right keys. His eyes must be fixed on the right object at the right time. A successfully executed play would hinge on where the quarterback was fixing his eyes. Ultimately, the outcome of the game would hinge on the quarterback's eyes.

The same is true spiritually. We must fix our eyes on Jesus. And keep them there.

If God were to mount a camera on your eyes and heart, what would it record? If God were to video the focus of your heart today, what would it reveal?

Consider Jesus' Example

As we run with our eyes fixed on Jesus, we must also "consider Him." Our minds must be engaged in a careful study of Jesus Christ. The Bible admonishes us, "Consider Him who has endured such hostility by sinners against Himself, so that you may not grow weary and lose heart" (Hebrews 12:3). As we run, we must consider Him.

The word "consider" (Greek, *analogizomai*) means to reckon, compare, weigh, think over. It is a mathematical term signifying "to compute by comparing things together." It means to take a hard, analytical look and come to a conclusive decision. Even so, we must take full note of Christ and run our race accordingly.

We must consider Jesus, who is "the author and perfecter of faith" (Hebrews 12:2). The word "author" (Greek, *archegon*) means leader, founder, pioneer. It portrays one who takes the lead, one who blazes the trail for those who follow. In running God's race, Jesus Christ is our Leader, the One who must be followed. He set the course, and we are to follow hard after Him.

Jesus is also the "finisher" (Greek, *teleioten*) of faith, the One who perfectly completed God's race which we run. He ran the race of faith to its triumphant finish. Having finished His race, Jesus shouts words of encouragement to us to follow His example and run with endurance. By His words and life, He shows us how to run victoriously.

More specifically, let us consider three things we can learn from the life of Christ: His endurance, His focus, and His reward.

His Endurance

First, we should consider Christ's endurance as He ran God's marathon. What a world champion Jesus is! As He came down the homestretch of His race, He endured the hostility of sinners and the cross.

Jesus is the epitome of endurance, the ultimate role model, the perfect example.

In the Garden of Gethsemane, Jesus sweated drops of blood as He agonized in prayer under the shadow of the cross and poured out His heart to God: "My soul is deeply grieved, to the point of death… Father, if it is possible, let this cup pass from Me; yet not as I will, but as You will" (Matthew 26:38-39). Shortly afterward, Jesus, engulfed in sorrow, turned Himself over to His betrayer and was arrested by the Roman cohort.

Yet He endured.

Then Jesus suffered a mockery of justice and underwent an attack on His personage. Through the night and early morning hours, He endured six trials—three Jewish, three Roman—during which He was interrogated, falsely accused, ridiculed, mocked, and spit upon. Before Pilate, He was scourged with a whip. His back was lacerated. He was crowned with thorns. His skull was pierced. His dignity was attacked. He was robed in purple and beaten with a rod. His beard was plucked from His face, marring His appearance.

Yet He endured.

He was presented to the mob outside the Praetorium. Pilate said, "Behold, the Man!" But the crowd—aroused by the sight of His blood like hungry sharks at feeding time—wanted more blood. They cried out, "Crucify, crucify!" (John 19:1-6).

Yet He endured.

Sentenced to die as a condemned criminal, Jesus was forced to carry His cross through the jeering crowds on the streets of Jerusalem. This was a sign of guilt and shame. He staggered under the heavy weight of his load. Finally, a Cyrenian helped Him carry His cross, which served as a torture chamber, to the execution sight.

Yet He endured.

At Golgotha, the Roman soldiers stripped this blameless "criminal" and nailed Him to a wooden cross. A large spike was driven through each wrist. Another spike was sent through His crossed legs. With the victim now attached, the cross was hoisted up and dropped into a hole in the ground.

Jesus was suspended between heaven and earth, suffering the cruelest death imaginable. Those passing by hurled abuse at Him. It was not enough that He be put to death. He must be abused and shamed as well. He struggled for every breath, pulling Himself up with His weary arms so He could exhale.

Yet He endured.

At high noon, the sky became mysteriously dark, as at midnight. The sins of all who would believe upon Him were being laid upon His back. Even the Father forsook Him. He was all alone. His holy body became the repository for all the filthy depravity of man. The wrath of God thundered as Jesus was engulfed by His fierce judgment. Only the damned already in hell can faintly begin to know His agony.

Yet He endured.

The finish line was now in sight. His blood had been shed, making the perfect atonement for sins. Redemption was secured! As His lungs gasped for air, He sprinted through the finish line. Triumphantly He cried out, "It is finished!" Then the Victor bowed His head and gave up His spirit.

Never has anyone endured such hostility, such pain, such suffering. He died bearing the sins of His people. He died absorbing the hellish wrath of God. He died rejected by God and men. He endured faithfully to the end of His race—the Jerusalem Marathon.

Consider Jesus, our Champion in God's race. By His life, He marked the course that each one of us will travel. It is a race that involves a cross, self-denial, and death. The apostle Peter corroborates this: "For you have been called for this purpose, since Christ also suffered for you, leaving you an example for you to follow in His steps" (1 Peter 2:21). God's race involves a cross for every believer.

When is the last time you considered His sufferings? As we run with endurance, we must consider Him. If He endured His cross, so must we endure ours. Is a slave greater than his Master?

His Faith

Second, consider Jesus' faith. Throughout His marathon, He kept entrusting Himself to God and looking to the promised "joy set before

Him" (Hebrews 12:2). This is how Jesus received the strength to endure. He pressed on by faith. He kept trusting God. He endured by fixing His eyes on the joy set before Him.

Jesus endured the cross because of His complete dependence upon God. During His earthly ministry, He did not use His divine power to meet His personal needs. That was reserved for others. Jesus resisted Satan's temptation through faith in God, not by snapping His fingers.

Amidst the suffering of the cross, Jesus endured by looking to the joy set before Him. Psalm 16 is a messianic psalm that speaks about the "fullness of joy" Christ would experience in the presence of the Father. Jesus knew God would keep His word. After His death, He would surely come out of the tomb alive, be exalted to heaven, and ushered into the "fullness of joy" (verse 11). Just as God's Word said.

Jesus endured the cross by focusing on His future joy. He looked beyond the pain to the prize. He kept His eyes on the goal and never blinked.

Have you considered Jesus' faith? This is exactly how we are to run with endurance. By faith, we are to look to the joy set before us. We must fix our eyes on Jesus and keep our focus on the prize.

No, we are not Jesus. But we do have access to the power of Jesus through His Spirit. Maybe you are focusing on circumstances that scream, "You are losing." Maybe you are listening to the world that ridicules, "You are a loser." Maybe you believe your pain that says, "You have lost. It is over. Just sit down and quit. What is the use?" But with the eyes of faith, you have a future of hope that says, "You are winning!"

By faith, Paul ran with endurance, fixing his eyes on future glory: "I consider that the sufferings of this present time are not worthy to be compared with the glory that is to be revealed to us" (Romans 8:18).

We must consider what joy awaits us in glory. We must keep our eyes on the prize. We will see God. We will behold Christ's glory. We will fellowship with Him, serve Him, and enjoy His glory with Him. We will receive the prize and reign with Him forever. We will enjoy everlasting light, inexpressible joy, and eternal rest. We will possess treasure in heaven, bear an eternal weight of glory, and drink from the stream of life.

His Reward

Third, consider Christ's reward. After Jesus endured the cross, He "sat down at the right hand of the throne of God" (Hebrews 12:2). After Jesus died for our sins, He was raised. He ascended and was seated at the right hand of God. And God richly rewarded His endurance.

The right hand of God is the place of supreme sovereignty and absolute authority. That is where Jesus sat, signifying that His work of salvation was finished. No more sacrifice for sins is needed. It is finished! Jesus is seated in glory, resting and reigning.

Because Jesus wore a crown of thorns, He was given a crown of glory.

The Bible says,

> He humbled Himself by becoming obedient to the point of death, even death on a cross. For this reason also, God highly exalted Him, and bestowed on Him the name which is above every name, so that at the name of Jesus every knee will bow, of those who are in heaven and on earth and under the earth, and that every tongue will confess that Jesus Christ is Lord, to the glory of God the Father (Philippians 2:8-11).

Consider Jesus' reward. Faith honors God, and God honors faith. Jesus obeyed God by faith, and God rewarded Him with a crown. The same is true in our lives. We will wear a crown only after we have carried a cross. There is no coronation without a crucifixion. No exaltation without humiliation. No reward without reproach.

Consider Jesus. Consider His endurance. Consider His faith. Consider His reward. He is the Leader of God's race. He endured faithfully to the end. He is the embodiment of endurance. He marked the course we run. If we will follow His steps, we will receive His prize.

His Strength Is Our Strength

Let me relate one last truth. We need more than an example—even One who is a perfect example. We need God's power to follow that example and run God's race. We need the strength to endure. And what we so desperately need, God provides.

Here is what I want you to grasp: As we fix our eyes on Christ, God strengthens our faith to endure in the midst of difficulty. Looking to Jesus puts steel in our faith. Considering Him bolsters our weakening legs and enables us to keep running, "fixing our eyes on Jesus, the author and perfecter of faith" (Hebrews 12:2). As we focus on Him, He perfects our faith.

So, not only is Jesus before us as our example, He is also within us as our enabler. Throughout the race, He is strengthening our legs and lifts our hearts to endure.

Where did this faith to trust Christ originate? Certainly not within our depraved hearts, which were once dead in sin. A dead heart is lifeless and unable to do anything toward God. Faith comes from above; it is the gift of God (Ephesians 2:8). It is given to us to believe (Philippians 1:29). Jesus is "the author and perfecter of faith." From within, no one can take a step of faith and come to Christ (John 6:44). So Jesus must be the author of faith within spiritually dead hearts. We first believed in Him because He first drew us to Himself.

He Brings Faith to Completion

This One who authored our faith is also the "perfecter of faith." As the perfecter of faith, He keeps our faith alive and brings it to completion. When we are most prone to falter and waver, He works within our hearts to sustain our faith. God is working within our hearts, maturing, strengthening, and deepening our faith, enabling us to endure.

The further we go in God's race, the more intense the pain becomes. And the more the temptations intensify. We begin to weaken. The desire to quit begins to override the desire to endure. Just when we want to pull over to the side, God strengthens our weakening faith. He enables us to endure to the end.

God gives us the faith to press on. We run in His strength. The Bible says, "Work out your salvation with fear and trembling; for it is God who is at work in you, both to will and work for His good pleasure" (Philippians 2:12-13).

Paul wrote, "I labor, striving according to His power, which mightily works within me" (Colossians 1:29). As Paul ran God's race, he overcame the pain and resisted the temptation to quit. How? Through

God's power mightily working within him. So too should we be encouraged to endure.

You may be saying, "Time out! That is great for Paul, but I am so weak, I do not think I can run another step." Be encouraged! I have good news. It is only in our weakness that God's power works. God told Paul, "My grace is sufficient for you, for power is perfected in weakness." The apostle concluded, "Most gladly, therefore, I will rather boast about my weaknesses, that the power of Christ may dwell in me. Therefore I am well content with weaknesses, with insults, with distresses, with persecutions, with difficulties, for Christ's sake; for when I am weak, then I am strong" (2 Corinthians 12:9-10). It was only when Paul was weak that he experienced God's supernatural power.

Did you get that?

When you are weak, then you are strong. Only then does the power of Christ work within you. When you cannot, He can. And He will. When the marathon is the most grueling, you most fully experience His power to endure. No wonder Paul bragged about his weakness. Because that is when Christ most strengthened Paul's faith and released His power.

Do you feel qualified to experience God's power? All you need to feel is your weakness and your need of Him. When you are feeling tired, just gaze into His glorious face. Sit at His feet. Take in His Word. Trust Him. Abide in Him. Rely upon Him. Rest in Him. And He will strengthen you mightily.

The Marathon of Life

Let me illustrate how Jesus strengthens us.

At the finish line stands the Judge, a far different Judge than you are accustomed to. He is not to be feared, but trusted. He has earned the right to officiate the race because He is the greatest Champion these games have ever produced. He is calling for you and me to share in His victory. Strategically positioned at the finish line, He patiently waits, looking for the approaching runners.

This Judge has placed the cherished victor's crown at the finish line. He knows that the sight of this crown will inspire weary runners to endure. Those who finish will have this wreath bestowed on their heads by this Judge.

The long marathon of life now winds its way back into the stadium. As the first runner makes his dramatic entrance, the crowd jumps up to its feet.

This runner is so tired he doubts he has the strength to finish. Every fiber of his being wants to stop. His legs are cramping. His feet are blistered. His lungs are gasping for air. His mouth is wide open, desperately sucking oxygen like a drowning man does air. His arms are so heavy he cannot move them. He tries to convince his mind that he can live with the pain. But that argument is short-lived.

The Finish Line in Sight!

He is scarcely able to muster enough strength to look up. With blurred vision, he sees the most inspiring sight he has ever seen. There, just ahead, he can see the finish line. And he can see the victor's crown. And most of all, he can see this esteemed Judge. He has dreamed about that crown for years. Now, here it is, just 100 yards away.

But as much as he wants to sprint to the finish, he cannot. His heart screams, "Sprint!" But his legs are deaf. He collapses hard.

He looks up in desperation to the Judge. His face tells it all. It tells the story of his heart. "I cannot go any farther."

His coach yells at him, "Get up, you loser! I knew you would never make it. On second thought, just stay down." His words cut deeply.

The runner gets up on his knees, but collapses back to the cinder track.

Then something extraordinary happens. It is unheard of in the long history of the games. This has never before been witnessed.

The Judge, standing at the finish line, strips off His coat, and sprints to the collapsed runner. What will He do? Drag him off the track? Lecture him on overcoming fatigue? Disqualify him?

The Judge's Sudden Move

The Judge, Himself a championship runner who once won this very race, makes His way to the runner. He then stoops down and, with arms muscular and strong, lifts the fallen runner to his feet.

The crowd is stunned into silence. Then a murmur of wonder ripples through the grandstands. To the spectators, this is unprecedented. They have never seen this happen before.

The Judge swings the runner's arm over His shoulder and bodily carries this runner—exhausted, defeated, drained—toward the finish line.

Fifty yards. Forty. Thirty. Only twenty now. Ten yards. Together, they lunge across the finish line ahead of the other runners. But what will be the ruling? Will such aid be allowed? Will the victory count?

Without hesitating, the Judge victoriously holds up one of the runner's arms. He emphatically declares him to be the winner. The bewildered crowd bursts into applause.

The Judge then goes back to His seat, reaches for the winner's wreath, and places it upon the marathoner's head. The exhilarated runner looks into the face of the Judge. Never has he seen such compassion. Such strength. Such understanding.

Then, placing His hands on the runner's shoulders, the Judge affirms, "Well done, My good and faithful runner."

The crowd chants the runner's name over and over. But what rings true in this champion's ears are the Judge's words: "Well done, My good and faithful runner."

The Victory Goes to...

Nevertheless, the runner knows the truth. So does everyone else present that day. He never could have won without the Judge's strength. His victory is, in reality, the Judge's victory. He would never have finished, much less won, without the Judge. In humility, he removes the crown from his head, knowing it is not really his. He places it back at the feet of its true owner—this strong and compassionate Judge.

This runner's story can be our story. If we will look to Christ, this scene can be repeated at the end of our race. Sure, we stumble and fall. Yes, we grow weary and tired during our race of faith. And if we focus on our failures and shortcomings, we will never win.

But if we fix our eyes on Jesus, the One who marked the course and ran victoriously, He will empower us to finish the race. His strength will become our strength. If we will look to Jesus, we will find the needed power to endure and win the cherished crown. Then, in that last day, we will cast our crown back at His feet. We will know that our victory is really His victory.

One day, we can hear Him say, "Well done, My good and faithful runner." All our pain will be quickly forgotten when we receive the prize.

Maybe you think you cannot run any longer. Maybe you think you do not have the strength to go another step. Let me assure you, if you will look to Christ, He will inwardly enable you to cross the finish line victoriously.

If you are down, look up to Him. Keep your eyes on the prize. And Jesus will empower you. To be sure, you can endure in His strength.

11

Benched, Booted, and Disqualified

Like a bone-jarring fullback, some subjects are hard to tackle. This chapter addresses one of those subjects. Hard-hitting. Powerful. It could run you over. But it must be stopped—dead in its tracks.

I do not want to just tackle this subject. I want to play smashmouth and hit it so hard that it never scores another advantage in our lives again.

Honestly, I wish I did not have to write this chapter at all. I would much prefer to simply wrap up this book with a positive fire-you-up chapter. But I would be less than honest with you—and, most importantly, with the Word of God—if I failed to warn you about a potential danger that has overtaken many a runner.

So I am going to put it on the line. As we run God's race, the Bible warns us about the ever-lurking danger of disqualification. The danger of being put out of the race. The danger of being sent to the sidelines and benched. The danger of being stripped of the prize.

This subject is as serious as a heart attack. Buckle your seat belts. This will jar you. It jolts me just to have to deal with it.

Disqualification.

It is an ever-present peril for every runner.

A Long-Awaited Duel

Come with me to the 1988 Olympic games in Seoul, Korea, where the world's finest athletes were gathered to go head-to-head to determine the fastest human on the planet in the 100-meter run. The race would go on to become the most publicized ever in Olympic history. Headlining the star-studded field were the two marquee names in sprinting—Ben Johnson, the Canadian speedster, and Carl Lewis, the great American hope.

The Race for Global Bragging Rights

For years, Johnson and Lewis had been battling head-to-head for global bragging rights. This race would officially settle the matter once and for all.

Before a crowd of 70,000 in Olympic Stadium, and a global audience of two billion viewers via satellite hookup, Johnson and Lewis got ready for their long-awaited duel.

In the starting blocks, Johnson's expression was one of angry, vengeful determination. Lewis appeared loose, confident, nonthreatened.

As the field of finely honed athletes crouched into position, the rise of the starter's gun brought the crowd to its feet. At the crack of the pistol, the runners simultaneously exploded out of the starting blocks.

At thirty meters, Johnson was a half-stride ahead of Lewis. No problem. Lewis was a known strong finisher, Johnson a fader.

"Then," as Johnson said after the race, "I blew it out."

His face a mask of ferocity, Johnson continued to propel into the lead. At fifty meters he had a full meter lead. By the eighty-meter mark, he had extended it to two meters. By this time, Lewis could not close the gap. It was over.

Two meters from the finish, Johnson knew he had won. He cruised through the finish tape, his right arm raised victoriously, and his eyes glaring audaciously back at Lewis. In your face!

The World's Fastest Human?

The timekeepers were stunned. They could hardly believe their eyes—9.79 seconds. A world record! The Canadian had just eclipsed all previous standards, breaking his own world record.

Lewis finished a distant second at 9.92, still his personal best and the American record.

Carl Lewis walked over to Johnson, who was standing at the edge of the track, and shook his hand. He had been blown away in the fastest sprint in human history.

On the victory stand, Ben Johnson was presented the Olympic gold medal and was officially recognized as the world's fastest human ever. He alone stood atop the athletic world. No one faster. No one stronger. No one greater.

Behind the scenes, a mere formality was being undertaken by the Olympic doping control laboratory. All runners are routinely tested for banned substances.

Four hours after the race, the urine samples were analyzed by Dr. Park Jong Sei. One sample showed an illegal anabolic steroid. Not knowing to whom the numbered sample belonged, Park tested it once more.

The same result. Positive.

Then Park and two Canadian officials tested it and again found stanozolol in the specimen. Wanting to be certain, Park tested this sample twice more.

Each time, the result was the same—positive.

A deceiver had been unmasked. Ben Johnson!

The sinister plot among Johnson and his sponsors to cheat the athletic world had been foiled. With news that would send shock waves around the world, the International Olympic Committee (IOC) was promptly notified that Ben Johnson—the newly crowned world's fastest human—had an anabolic steroid in his system. A drug designed to beef up the muscles. A drug that gives bursts of power. A drug that disqualifies.

The Agony of Disgrace

A long night of deliberation followed for the IOC executive board. Clearly, Johnson was guilty. Unquestionably, he had violated the rules against using performance-enhancing drugs. Left with no other alternative, the IOC declared Johnson's race null and void. He was stripped of his gold medal, and the next day it was awarded to its rightful owner, Carl Lewis. Johnson was suspended from all international meets for two full years. Jean Charest, sports minister of Canada, announced that Johnson would be banned from Canada's national team for life. Johnson had made history, all right. The wrong kind.

All this would cause Johnson to lose millions of dollars in appearance fees and endorsements. In two short days, he went from the pinnacle to the pits. The record that Johnson so brazenly predicted would last for over fifty years did not even stand for fifty hours. In an international tragedy, Ben Johnson was buried in a grave of disgrace.

Busted, he was a loser with shame.

There is a poignant, powerful lesson to be learned from this Ben Johnson tragedy. Painted in painful colors, we see illustrated before our eyes the truth of God's Word. The apostle Paul wrote, "I discipline my body and make it my slave, so that, after I have preached to others, I myself will not be disqualified" (1 Corinthians 9:27).

Disqualified. Few words contain such stinging regret.

As we run God's race, we must guard against the constant threat of disqualification. No matter how successfully we have run in the past, one wrong step can affect the rest of our life. Our race can be so quickly jeopardized. Wiped out. Cancelled. Disgraced. Benched. Booted. Disqualified.

In this chapter, I want to answer the following questions: What sin disqualifies? What does disqualification involve? How can I avoid it? May I reenter the race?

These are critical questions that deserve careful answers. I want us to look into the Word of God and discover what God says. The truth we will learn must be heeded. Seriously.

The Danger of Sexual Sin

One of the greatest dangers facing us today as we run God's race is that of sexual sin. Lustful thoughts. Immorality. Adultery. Sexual addictions. And all kinds of sexual perversions. Whatever you want to call it, God calls it sin. Sexual sin disqualifies us from the race.

Speaking like a world-class athlete, Paul said, "I discipline my body and make it my slave" (1 Corinthians 9:27). Mixing metaphors, Paul then moved from the track to the boxing ring. Literally, "discipline"

(Greek, *hupopiazo*) means to land a knockout punch under an opponent's eye and give him a black eye.

The ancient Greeks were so fond of boxing that it became a part of the ancient games. Wearing no gloves, the participants wrapped their hands with leather strips. Fighters were not matched according to weight. Nor did they have timed rounds or a confined boxing ring. They simply slugged it out until one participant could no longer stand.

If the match went too long, the judges would call a halt and instruct the bloody participants to really get serious. They would attach rigid leather thongs studded with metal—yesterday's version of brass knuckles—to the fighters' fists. Then these fighters would battle until the match ended in permanent injury or death. It was the Greek version of sudden death.

The picture is graphic—ancient boxers fighting one another with knuckles bound with leather thongs, leaving their opponents black and blue.

A Knockout Punch

This boxing scene is the background of this verse. Figuratively, Paul is saying he beats his own body black and blue, knocking it out, if necessary, to win the race. The apostle says he makes it his "slave" (Greek, *doulagogeo*), bringing it into subjection, as a slave to his master—Jesus Christ. We must present our entire body to His lordship and obey His will.

The "body" refers to one's fleshly desires, the lusts of the flesh. While Paul could be referring to any number of sins, I believe that at the heart of his warning is sexual sin. Other sins may be worse, but no other sin quite so uniquely disqualifies us as sexual sin.

Paul uses a word here for "body"—the Greek word *soma*—that refers to the physical body. Paul is saying he buffets his physical body, which is in danger of sinful activity, lest he be disqualified.

How has Paul been using the term "body"? In 1 Corinthians 6:18, we discover that a sin against the body (Greek, *soma*) is sexual sin. Writing on this verse, John MacArthur comments, "In referring to the body, Paul obviously had sexual immorality in view. In 1 Corinthians 6:18, he describes it as a sin against one's own body. It was almost as if he put sexual sin in a category of its own. Certainly, it disqualifies a man from church leadership. First Timothy 3:1 demands that elders be a 'one-woman man.'"[1]

Let us look at 1 Corinthians 6:18 and see what it says. Earlier in 1 Corinthians, Paul had been teaching that sexual immorality is a sin against one's own body. He then wrote, "Every other sin that a man commits is outside the body, but the immoral man sins against his own body" (1 Corinthians 6:18). The word "immoral" (Greek, *porneia*) refers to any sexual perversion—whether premarital sex (before marriage), adultery (during marriage), homosexuality, lesbianism, or bestiality.

Paul is putting sexual sin in a category all its own. All the sins in the world are put in one column. And sexual sin is put in another. All sins are outside the body except sexual infidelity, which alone is against one's own body.

Destruction Like No Other

Immorality is not necessarily the worst sin. Unbelief and blasphemy against the Holy Spirit fit that bill. Nevertheless, sexual sin is unique in its character. Like a malignant cancer to the body, immorality internally destroys the soul like no other sin. Why is this?

Because sexual intercourse is the most intimate uniting of two persons, it causes a man to become one with the other person. Physically. Mystically. Emotionally. Paul puts it this way: "Do you not know that the one who joins himself to a prostitute is one body with her? For He says, 'The two shall become one flesh'" (1 Corinthians 6:16). Consequently, its misuse corrupts at the deepest human level, arguably far more destructively than worldliness, drugs, or alcohol.

A man's sexual drive arises from within his body, bent on personal gratification. It drives like no other impulse. When unlawfully fulfilled, it destroys the soul like no other sin.

So, Paul says, we must master our sexual drive and make it our slave, bringing it into submission to Jesus Christ. When aroused toward anyone other than our spouse, it must be dealt with severely and beaten black and blue, not pampered or caressed.

Concerning the flames of illicit lust, Solomon said, "Can a man take a fire in his bosom and his clothes not be burned?" (Proverbs 6:27). That is, the warm heat of passion will destroy your life. You will become like one inflamed, as though your clothes are on fire. You will be burning in lust, engulfed in a prison of fire, unable to escape.

In the Sermon on the Mount, Jesus Himself taught the necessity of a pure heart. He quoted the sixth commandment, saying, "You shall not commit adultery" (Matthew 5:27), and then gave its deepest interpretation. He asserted, "But I say to you that everyone who looks at a woman with lust for her has already committed adultery with her in his heart" (verse 28). There, Jesus went to the heart of the problem—the problem of the human heart. He pinpointed the inner person, where actions find their root. "Do not lust after and mentally undress a woman," Jesus was saying. "Lust equals adultery."

Then Jesus delivered the knockout punch: "If your right eye makes you stumble, tear it out and throw it from you; for it is better for you to lose one of the parts of your body, than for your whole body to be thrown into hell. If your right hand makes you stumble, cut it off and throw it from you; for it is better for you to lose one of the parts of your body, than for your whole body to go into hell" (Matthew 5:29-30).

This is a call for serious buffeting of our body!

At first glance, it appears that Jesus is calling for a literal mutilation of our body. "If you lust, just desocket your eye. If you fondle, amputate your hand." Should we take what He is saying here literally? If so, this book would be the blind leading the blind.

Actually, Jesus is speaking figuratively, employing a figure of speech called *hyperbole*, which makes a point through an exaggerated statement. The right eye represents our clearest vision, and the right hand our first advance. Our Lord is saying, "Deal radically with sexual passion. Take whatever drastic steps are necessary to keep your eyes, hands, and whatever else pure. Go to extreme measures—anything short of plucking out your eyes or chopping off your hand—to mortify your fleshly impulses." Do not gaze. Do not fondle.

Simply put, it would be better to go to heaven blind than to go to hell with 20/20 vision. Jesus calls us to take whatever drastic steps are

necessary to remain holy in heart and deed. He demands that we control where we go, what we do, what we watch, and the company we
keep.

The Disqualification of Sexual Sin

Disqualification. The very word has a sobering, unsettling ring
about it. It sends a chill up the spine. Hear Paul again: "I discipline my
body and make it my slave, so that, after I have preached to others, I
myself will not be *disqualified*" (1 Corinthians 9:27, emphasis added).
The apostle was warning us that there are serious consequences to sin.
This is especially true with sexual sin.

The word "disqualified" (Greek, *adokimos*) was known to all who
attended the ancient Isthmian Games. It meant to be put out of the
games for infracting a rule. It meant to be stripped of one's prize. Before
the race, a herald stood at the starting line and announced the rules
of the contest, along with the names of the competing runners. After
the race, he announced the names of the winner and the top finishers.
Likewise, the names of any runners who were disqualified would be
called out by this herald.

When Paul said, "I have preached to others," he represented himself as a herald who preached God's truth and announced the rules of
the Christian life. At the same time, Paul was also a runner—a fellow
Christian—who competed in the same race. His deep concern was
to not become so busy preaching to others that he himself ignored
the rules by failing to discipline his own body. If he failed to do so, he
would suffer the embarrassment of proclaiming the rules, but then
being disqualified by them.

What is disqualification? At first glance, you might think that it
is losing one's salvation, a falling from grace. But all the Bible—from
Genesis through Revelation—teaches that all believers in Christ are
eternally secure in Christ. Once saved by God's grace, we are kept
by His grace. The Good Shepherd loses not one of His sheep (John
10:27-29).

In reality, disqualification means a loss of reward at the end of the
race. Once a believer reaches heaven, it is possible to be stripped of

God's reward, but not of God's redemption. I will go one step further: Disqualification also may mean being put out of the race while it is still in progress.

Let us to look now at both of these aspects of disqualification—one *after* the race, one *during* it.

After the Race—Stripped of Future Reward

It is possible for a runner to come to the finish line, apparently winning the race, only to be stripped of the reward. Just ask Ben Johnson. In this instance, disqualification means a loss of heavenly reward. A failure to discipline one's body will forfeit God's reward at the end of the race.

The historical background of the Isthmian Games supports this. A disqualified Greek athlete did not lose his citizenship, only his right to the crown. The whole emphasis of this context is upon the reward at the end of the race. The preceding verses (1 Corinthians 9:24-25) call us to run the race to win the crown. If we fail to do so, we will forfeit the crown and lose the reward in the end.

Turn back a few pages in 1 Corinthians to chapter 3. Paul is discussing the judgment seat of Christ—the *bema*. This is the same word he uses in 2 Corinthians 5:10 to describe the judge's stand at the Isthmian Games outside Corinth. Although the imagery in 1 Corinthians 3 shifts from the athletic field to the construction business, the spiritual truth remains the same: unfaithfulness brings disqualification.

Paul wrote,

> According to the grace of God which was given to me, like a wise master builder I laid a foundation, and another is building on it...For no man can lay a foundation other than the one which is laid, which is Jesus Christ. Now if any man builds on the foundation with gold, silver, precious stones, wood, hay, straw, each man's work will become evident; for the day will show it because it is to be revealed with fire, and the fire itself will test the quality of each man's work. If any man's work which he has built on it remains, he will receive a reward. If any man's work is

> burned up, he will suffer loss; but he himself will be saved,
> yet so as through fire (1 Corinthians 3:10-15).

For believers, the purpose of the final judgment is to test their lives in order to determine not salvation or loss of salvation, but reward or loss of reward.

On the last day, the fire of divine judgment will reveal whether one's works are eternal (gold, silver, precious stones) or temporal and worthless (wood, hay, straw). Believers who build their lives with gold, silver, and precious stones will be rewarded. But those who build with wood, hay, and stubble will suffer loss. Not loss of salvation, but loss of reward.

To be "saved, yet so as through fire" pictures a person who runs through the flames personally unharmed but with the smell of smoke on him. He escapes the fire, but his entire life's work will go up in smoke. It will be destroyed, and he will be disqualified.

We must be careful how we run the race set before us as Christians. There is the ever-present danger of being disqualified and losing our reward at the end.

The Bible teaches we can run well and be positioned with a lead to win a crown, only to later stumble and lose what reward would have been ours. The apostle John wrote, "Watch yourselves, that you do not lose what we have accomplished, but that you may receive a full reward" (2 John 8).

We must hold on to what reward we would have received. Jesus said, "I am coming quickly; hold fast what you have, so that no one will take your crown" (Revelation 3:11). Our Lord concurs that it is possible to have earned a crown through a strong start, but then later lose it through unfaithfulness.

During the Race—Forfeit Your Spiritual Influence

We are all responsible for spiritual leadership in one form or another—either as a spouse, a parent, a church leader, a Bible teacher, a pastor, or a ministry worker. As a result, we can all experience disqualification.

Disqualification also brings a present loss. It puts a runner on the sidelines while the race is still in progress. After spotting the infraction, the judge signals, "You are out of the race!" He then boots the runner out and escorts him to the bench.

Picture a runner who, in the midst of the race, breaks in front of another runner, cutting him off illegally. Or he takes a shortcut in an attempt to move ahead of the other runners. The watchful judge who detects this infraction will blow his whistle and put him out of the race. The runner will be told to sit down. Immediately. Stop—do not continue running.

One's spiritual influence is always directly related to one's personal integrity. A spiritual leader cannot live however he desires. If he wants followers, his life must be worthy of following. His walk must be consistent with his talk.

Sexual sin uniquely disqualifies a runner in God's race. Whether one is a pastor, a church leader, a parachurch worker, a Sunday school teacher, a small-group Bible leader, a soloist, or a choir member, sexual sin disqualifies.

Falling into sexual sin forfeits the right to lead. The leader sacrifices the integrity of his life and ministry. According to the biblical standard of leadership, one is no longer qualified (1 Timothy 3:1-11). No longer above reproach. No longer a one-woman man. No longer managing his household well. No longer possessing a good reputation outside the church. Once qualified, he is now no longer qualified.

Disqualified.

It takes only one rock to break a glass window. Even so, once purity is sacrificed, the ability to lead is gone.

Take the life of King David. Although a man of God, David fell into serious sexual sin with a bathing beauty named Bathsheba. He tried to cover up his sin through another sin—the sin of murder—as he put Bathsheba's husband to death.

David eventually was brought to confession before God through the convicting confrontation of Nathan the prophet. Nathan pointed a finger in David's face and said, "You are the man." David, a year after his adultery, finally confessed his sin to God. The result? David was forgiven. But his service for God went downhill from there.

No longer spiritually qualified to sit on the throne, David was chased from his kingdom by his two sons. There were serious consequences to his sin.

Nearly every verse of Psalm 51 records the monstrous effects of sexual sin in a believer's life. As so painfully revealed in David's life, we see that immorality soils the soul (verses 1-2,7,10), saturates the mind (verse 3), stings the conscience (verses 4,9), shames the character (verses 5-6), saddens the heart (verses 8,12), sickens the body (verse 8), sours the spirit (verse 10), severs fellowship (verse 11), steals power (verse 11), stiffens the will (verse 12), and stifles the tongue (verses 13-15). One's entire life and ministry suffers!

After David confessed his sin—a year after he committed it, and then only because he was caught and confronted with it—he was forgiven, but also fallen. Yes, he was forgiven of all his sin. But no, he was no longer fit for the throne of Israel. The disciplining hand of God drove David from the throne, and his immediate ministry went on a downhill slide from that point onward.

This discussion, though, must raise the question of forgiveness. Should we be eager to restore our fallen brethren? To fellowship, yes. But to leadership? No. At least, not for a long while. This does not mean we "shoot our own wounded." By all means, we should be forgiving, accepting, and restoring. We must be. This is the very character of Christ Jesus and the gospel. We should help repair the broken pieces of those who have sinned.

But that does not mean such a person remains qualified for leadership. That right to lead is forfeited. True repentance leads to the rebuilding of one's character and a regained sense of trust in the body of Christ. This process must occur before any restoration to leadership can ever occur. And it takes a long time.

Imagine building credibility for over a period of twenty years only to squander it in a moment of passion. How deceitful is sin.

The same tragedy can wreck our lives. We can lose the influence of our spiritual leadership, as well as forfeit God's power through infidelity.

The evangelical landscape is strewn with the wreckage of those who have fallen into sexual sin. Their lives have been ruined. Their marriages have been destroyed. Their ministries have been stripped. All because of sexual immorality. It has hit pastors and television evangelists hard, causing many to be disqualified. And it has also hit those in the pew just as hard, knocking many out of the race and onto the sidelines.

Three Important Places You Are Sidelined

Such a benching affects three key areas of one's life. First, one's public ministry is sidelined. A teacher of God's Word—whether in the pulpit, Sunday school, or a small Bible-study class—who falls into sexual sin must step down. James wrote, "Let not many of you become teachers, my brethren, knowing that as such we will incur a stricter judgment" (James 3:1). The same strict requirement is placed upon a church officer—an elder or deacon—or ministry leader outside the church. He should step down from his place of responsibility. Or be asked to step down.

Second, one's family life is sidelined. An enormous breach of trust occurs with one's spouse, who will suffer damaged emotions. In most cases, the hurt is never repaired. The sexual sin becomes a cause for divorce and the breakup of the home. Children are often pulled back and forth between parents, confused and hurt. A loss of respect for the guilty party results.

Third, one's personal witness is, likewise, sidelined. I think the world enjoys seeing a Christian fall into sexual sin. It feeds Satan's lies into unbelieving hearts. Unconverted people say, "I knew those Christians were a bunch of hypocrites." In the process, our viable witness suffers a black eye.

A Greater Tragedy

While disqualification through sexual immorality is tragic, what causes me even *greater* alarm is the trend today that discounts the seriousness of sexual sin and fails to see it as grounds for disqualification. This tolerant attitude is far more dangerous than sexual immorality itself.

You are surely aware that many highly visible Christian leaders have fallen into—let me call it exactly what it is—gross sexual immorality.

That is painful enough. But compounding insult to injury, many of these spiritual leaders continue to preach from the same pulpit. Some step down for a few token months. But that sounds more like a vacation to me.

The Bible says they are disqualified. They are to be put out of the race. That means they are to be out of the ministry. Let me say it plainly and painfully: They are no longer qualified to lead. Their integrity is shot, and our trust is lost.

If you interviewed a gardener to take care of your lawn and then went past his house and saw that his yard was overgrown and infested with weeds, would you trust him with the care of your lawn? If you went to a dentist to have your teeth checked and saw that he had a mouthful of rotten teeth, would you trust him to work on your teeth? Of course not. It follows, then, that an unholy leader has lost the right to call for holiness in the lives of others. No matter how high his television ratings. Physician, heal yourself.

Personal purity is always the foundational platform for personal ministry. When purity is lost, so is the platform for ministry. Even those with a less visible ministry will suffer a severe disqualification.

The Defense Against Sexual Sin

If sexual sin is this deadly, we had better learn to avoid it. Specifically, how can we discipline our bodily impulses? It is critically important that we know how to deal aggressively with our body lest we be disqualified. How do we bring our sexual drives into submission to Christ's lordship? God Himself has given us our sexual drive. How do we keep it on track so that we honor Him? I want to suggest several steps that all who win must take: We must discipline our eyes, our hearts, our feet, and our flesh, as well as enjoy our own spouse.

Guard Your Eyes

First, we must *guard our eyes*. I want to say a word especially to the men, who are attracted and aroused mostly by sight. Therefore, what we place before our eyes is critically important. It is through our eyes that our heart is so often stimulated. We must purpose to guard our eyes and choose not to gaze upon another woman in a way that would wrongly arouse us and lead us as a pig to the slaughter.

Job said, "I have made a covenant with my eyes; how then could I gaze at a virgin?" (Job 31:1). Now, that is a commitment to purity! We must make an equally serious commitment to God *not* to gaze upon another woman. The word "gaze" is the key here. It means to take a second, lingering look. Perhaps even a third or fourth look. It is a deliberate looking that involves fantasizing with the mind.

The fact is, we live in the real world. Many women package themselves in ways that would make most advertisers green with envy. So we cannot avoid "seeing" an attractive woman. It is the "gazing" that must be controlled.

A wise sage once said, "You cannot keep the birds from flying over your head, but you can keep them from building a nest in your hair." It was allowing a nest to be built in his hair that Job resisted. And so must we.

May I get specific? This means we must control our use of the Internet. We must not linger at the magazine rack. Nor watch films or rent videos that inflame sensual lust. For those of us who travel, our biggest struggle can be with the television set in our hotel room and the lewd movies that are accessible. When no one is watching. "Five minutes free," the sign says. It is a ticking time bomb that should read, "Five minutes to destruction."

For others of us, the magazines we "read" can be our downfall. Even once-reputable publications are now filled with sleazy advertisements and voluptuous swimsuit issues.

Back when Billy Graham did crusades, Cliff Barrows was his much-respected music leader. I like what Cliff did when he checked into a hotel room. He first draped a towel over the television. Then he placed his Bible on top of the towel.

That way, he had to fight through the Holy Bible to get to the trash on the tube. May his tribe increase.

Let me tell you two things we did—and do—around our house.

First, whenever I watch television, I do so with a remote control always in my hand. By hitting one button, I can immediately change channels. This precaution is an absolute necessity when a ball game is on. You cannot watch a sports program these days without being bombarded with nudity, bed-hopping, and adultery via the commercials and movie and program previews. An escape valve called a channel changer is critically important.

Second, back when I subscribed to sports magazines and they were delivered to our house, my wife first "deprogrammed" them by tearing out all the pages that contained smut. And that was no small assignment. One sports magazine that I formerly received weekly since 1960 had an annual swimsuit issue that was totally ripped apart by the time my wife was finished with it.

What about you? Have you made such a covenant with your eyes? Will you guard what you allow to visually come into your heart? Those who win do.

Strengthen Your Heart

Second, we must *strengthen our hearts*. One of the best ways to discipline our bodies is to replace sensual thoughts with wholesome ones. We must occupy our minds and fill our hearts with godly truths from God's Word. We must defend our hearts against lustful thoughts by filling them with Scripture. When our hearts are spiritually strong, we are enabled to resist sexual temptation.

Only the Word of God, dwelling in our hearts through the power of the Holy Spirit, can give us the necessary strength to resist temptation's fleshly desires. You may remember the "Just Say No" advertising campaign that exhorted people to avoid drug abuse. While I wholeheartedly support programs that encourage a drug-free society, the fact is, we cannot say no to temptation until we have first said yes to Jesus Christ. Only in God's supernatural power can carnal temptations be resisted. And His sin-conquering power is transmitted through His Word and His Spirit.

The Bible says, "How can a young man keep his way pure? By keeping it according to Your word…Your word I have treasured in my heart, that I may not sin against You" (Psalm 119:9,11). The Word of God is the greatest restraining force in the world to keep us morally pure.

When Scripture is treasured in our hearts, it shouts, even screams, to our consciences to resist temptation. And it then fortifies our wills to say no.

Likewise, the Holy Spirit does the same within. To be filled with God's Word works the same as being filled with God's Holy Spirit. Take a moment to compare Colossians 3:16 with Ephesians 5:18. It is the power of the Holy Spirit that empowers us to put to death the sinful deeds of our fleshly bodies.

Paul put it this way: "If you are living according to the flesh, you must die; but if by the Spirit you are putting to death the deeds of the body, you will live. For all who are being led by the Spirit of God, these are sons of God" (Romans 8:13-14).

Activate Your Feet

Third, we must *activate our feet*. There are certain places and situations in which we have no business finding ourselves. None whatsoever. An old saying goes, "He who would not fall down ought not to walk in slippery places." So get out of slippery places if you desire not to fall.

God's Word says, "Flee immorality" (1 Corinthians 6:18). That does *not* mean, "Stay and fight it." Instead, wisdom says, "Get out of there. Make tracks. Do not fight it. Leave!" In this instance, it is godly to run away. Only a fool would stay and fight it.

That was Joseph's strategy. Sold into slavery in Egypt, Joseph soon rose to success and served in the house of Potiphar, an officer of Pharaoh (Genesis 39:5-18). Potiphar so trusted Joseph that he left everything in charge of his "handsome" servant.

Potiphar's wife "looked with desire at Joseph." That means, she checked him out from stem to stern and wanted this tall, good-looking guy.

"Lie with me," she whispered seductively.

But Joseph said, "No!"

He flat out refused. He would sooner lie down in a den of vipers.

However, this devil with a blue dress on would not take no for an answer. Like a hungry piranha, she wanted him. Bad. So on another convenient day, she spun her web around her catch. "Lie with me," she smiled as she ran her fingers through his clothing. No doubt, the temperature was getting hot.

What did Joseph do? Did he stay and fight it?

No. He bolted. He ran away so fast that Potiphar's wife was left clutching a handful of his clothes. He fled immorality. He did not stay to give her a Bible lesson on purity and field any follow-up questions. He got out of Dodge, pronto.

You and I will find ourselves in situations that call for a similar response. Quick feet keep a clean heart. You may need to take your coffee break in a different place. You may need to turn and walk another direction in your hotel lobby. You may need to get up and walk out of that movie. Whatever. Just flee immorality.

Enjoy Your Wife

Fourth, we must *enjoy our own wife*. A fulfilling sexual relationship with our wife does marvels to keep our heart pure. When the home fires are burning brightly, wildfire on the prairie is not prone to be a problem.

Solomon, writing under the direction of the Holy Spirit, discreetly recorded this bit of wisdom:

> Drink water from your own cistern and fresh water from your own well. Should your springs be dispersed abroad, streams of water in the streets? Let them be yours alone and not for strangers with you. Let your fountain be blessed, and rejoice in the wife of your youth. As a loving hind and a graceful doe, let her breasts satisfy you at all times; be exhilarated always with her love (Proverbs 5:15-19).

One's sexual capacity is pictured here as a cistern or well full of water. Refreshing, clean, enjoyable. Solomon says to draw water from your own wife's well and share your water with her alone. Be satisfied with her, not with a stranger who contaminates and poisons. The word "exhilarated" means to be drunk, to be under the influence. Victorian prudishness was never called for behind the closed doors of marriage.

"Be drunk with the exhilaration of her breasts," said Solomon. But with no one else.

I will never forget the story I once heard a well-known preacher tell. He was preaching away from home and was put up in a nice hotel. As he got on the elevator to go to his room, two attractive women got on with him. They were dressed to kill.

"Which floor?" Chuck asked courteously, offering to punch the appropriate elevator button.

"I don't know. Which floor are *you* going to?" one said. The innuendo was clear. The offer made.

About that time, the elevator arrived at Swindoll's floor. The doors opened, releasing its prey. Chuck stepped out, turned around to them, and said, "No, thanks. I don't need that cheap stuff. I've got all I need at home."

He then confidently spun on his heels and walked out of the lion's den. Without a scratch.

See what I mean? Keeping the home fires burning brightly helps prevent forest fires.

Resist Your Flesh

Fifth, we must *resist our flesh*. Even as we apply the first four principles above, we will still be met with temptation. That is the nature of the beast within us. We can help subdue it, but it nevertheless is there, like a sleeping bear, and can instantly be aroused, awakened, and brought out of hibernation.

Our sexual drive, like an unexpected earthquake, could hit in a weak moment. Such a seismic jolt could haunt us until the day we die. Therefore, we must actively choose to resist this deadly temptation whenever it comes knocking. We must keep the deadbolt to our heart locked.

With directness and frankness, the Bible does not stutter when it says, "Therefore consider [literally, 'put to death'] the members of your earthly body as dead to immorality, impurity, passion, evil desire" (Colossians 3:5). How do we handle sinful passion? Kill it! Put it to death. Bury it immediately. Crucify it. Do not tolerate it. Not for one second.

This is a matter of our will. We must choose to resist the desires of our flesh. Putting to death immorality, passion, and evil desire is a constant choice that we must make. Paul presupposes here that we will all be faced with this decision. To make no decision is to make the wrong decision. When temptation comes knocking, just say no.

Can I Get Back in the Race?

Maybe you are saying, "It is already too late. I have already fallen into such sin. Is there any hope for me? Can I get back into the race?"

Yes, you can have a new start.

Failure is never final as long as there is the grace of God. Confess your sin. Repent. Turn from it. Humble yourself before God. Seek to do His will. And in time, you can get back into the race.

How long does it take to reenter the race? That varies with each individual situation. Here is a basic principle: The more visible your witness and leadership, the longer it will take to reenter. When trust and credibility are lost through immorality, restoration to ministry is a long, patient process.

Just the mere confession of sin does not immediately restore one back into the place of leadership. Time must be given to regain damaged credibility and to restore lost trust. It takes time for the fruit of repentance to grow and be seen as real. Likewise, the fallen brother needs godly counsel to know if he has regained the needed trust for public ministry.

In the case of a pastor or minister, that restoration is a long, perhaps even impossible, process. For a deacon or elder, such restoration may take years. For a Bible teacher, even more time may be required. Even for a father, respect must be regained over a period of time.

Lost Speed and Effectiveness

Let me give you one more sobering thought. I mention this not to condemn those who have already fallen in sexual sin, but to warn those who have not fallen, to put the fear of God into their hearts. My point is this: After being sidelined through disqualification, do not assume that when you step back into the race, you will run with the same speed and efficiency.

Again, consider Ben Johnson. After a two-year banishment from competitive running, Johnson made his long-awaited return to the world of track at the Hamilton Spectator Games in Canada. A sellout crowd of 17,050 fought a blizzard to get there. A national television audience was tuned in.

The question on everyone's mind was this: Can Ben Johnson still run with his explosive, dazzling speed? In the 1988 Olympics, Johnson totally dominated his last race and crushed the field. As he prepared for his comeback, the twenty-nine-year-old sprinter announced his intention of returning to top running form. But could he?

As Johnson peeled off his warm-ups, he was noticeably less muscular than he once had been. And Johnson's trademark explosive start, which had always been his greatest asset, was no longer what it used to be.

One of his competitors remarked, "Before with Ben, most times you stepped into the blocks it was, 'Who is going to get second?' Now it is, 'Who is in shape, who has worked harder?'"

The Canada race revealed Johnson to be a mere mortal. After two false starts, the field got away evenly. But Johnson did not immediately grab the lead. He was left behind, coming out of the blocks third. Trying to play catch-up, Ben's form was ragged. He ran as though flat-footed.

Johnson made a late charge, good enough to push past all the rest of the field—except for the winner. Johnson finished second by two-tenths of a second. "I am just not race-fit yet," he said, estimating that he needed seven or eight more races to be sharp.

The same is true when it comes to our race of faith. There are definite consequences to our sin. If we are disqualified, sure, we can come back later. All by God's grace. But not without losing something. Credibility. Trust. Influence. Respect. Peace. Power. Joy. Opportunities. Reward.

Trust must be reearned with a spouse. Honor must be reestablished with children. And sometimes it never happens. Lost ground is always difficult to regain. Effective teaching must be reempowered with a life of integrity. The light of your witness must be rekindled. All of which takes precious time.

I say all this to warn you. Resist the sensual lusts of your body. Discipline yourself. Because disqualification brings serious consequences. Benched, booted, disqualified.

Just like Ben Johnson.

The Tragedy of Magic Johnson

The tragic story of another Johnson—Magic Johnson—is yet another example of this truth.

Before a major press conference, Magic Johnson told the world that he had contracted HIV. It was the result of unrestrained immorality. Physically, he was immediately disqualified from playing basketball. He eventually returned to the game, but he was never the same.

Magic Johnson was a key part of Showtime. He won five NBA world championships. He led his college team to the NCAA championship. He received multiple MVP awards for his play during the NBA season, all-star games, and the NBA championships.

But Magic failed to discipline his body. No amount of magic could save him. And his entire life came crashing down. The news media applauded his actions in coming forward and vowing to face the disease and educate the public. The pop culture lionized him, claiming he was heroic to speak up.

But is Magic a hero? God's Word says his actions were immoral, indecent, and self-gratifying. Hardly the virtues of a hero.

Magic's failure to maintain moral purity cost him everything. Surely he would trade his multimillion-dollar salary, all his championship rings, and his days of glory if he could retract those moments of pleasure.

Magic is out of the game.

Benched, booted, disqualified.

Though many will applaud his efforts to tout "safe sex," God's Word remains the same. Outside of marriage, there is no lawful sex. Whatever we sow, we will reap. If we sow to the flesh—that is, if we fail to discipline our bodies—we will reap to the flesh (Galatians 6:7-8).

Sounds like losing to me.

In an open letter to the *Los Angeles Times*, Pamela McGee, a basketball player herself, shared her insight into Magic Johnson. Pam played on two University of Southern California national championship teams. She was named an all-American and also played on the gold-medal US Olympic team in 1984. She wrote,

> As Magic Johnson stood at the podium, the world's superhero still stood 6-feet, 9-inches tall. And he is still standing head and shoulders above the world, having made the hardest announcement he has ever made in his life.
>
> At first, I thought it was a cruel joke. Tears overcame me. He used words such as "HIV Positive" and "the AIDS virus," words that were foreign to my existence, because I am neither gay nor an IV drug user. Magic, the superhero—it would only happen to him.
>
> It hurt even more because Magic is a dear friend. It was Magic who showed me around L.A. the first week I entered USC. I was a then-frightened 17-year-old, a long way from home. Magic made me feel at home. He would pick my sister and me up on weekends and we would all party to the early hours in the morning.
>
> I guess it did not surprise me that Magic has the disease. Knowing his flamboyant life-style, it was bound to happen sooner or later. Magic's closest friends always knew him as a major player and womanizer. He has had one-night stands with what he calls "freaks" across America.
>
> He was always being hounded by women who merely wanted to sleep with the "Magic Man." The reason he probably made it public is to warn the thousands of women he has slept with. So it didn't surprise me that he had the insidious disease called HIV.
>
> Two short months after his marriage to his longtime love

Cookie, it just seemed that Magic had matured and was starting over. It appeared that Magic was committed to one woman finally. It appeared he had his whole life in front of him.

My heart goes out to Magic. I have been on my knees praying constantly for him. The superhero is still my superhero, and a good friend.

Maybe it will take a Magic Johnson to wake us all up.[2]

Magic Johnson learned the hardball reality of the truth of Scripture. Because he failed to discipline his body, he had to leave the game. Unable to finish his career. Unable to play for the gold medal in the 1992 Olympics.

If there is one ounce of godly wisdom rattling around in our brains, we will take seriously Paul's admonition to discipline our body. Play with fire, and you will get burned. Lay down with dogs, and you will wake up with fleas. Magic's tragedy brings home to us the sobering realization that, apart from God's grace, any of us can be benched, booted, and disqualified.

If you are in it to win it—flee immorality.

Even magic cannot make the consequences disappear!

12

For God's Sake, Get in the Race!

We all love to see a comeback. There is something about an against-all-odds, totally impossible comeback that inspires us and gives us hope. Something within us loves to see an underdog come from behind and snatch victory from the sure clutches of defeat.

We all have our favorite comeback stories. Peyton Manning rallying his team to a last-ditch victory. Arnold Palmer charging back from nowhere to beat the field. Joe Montana battling back with no timeouts to put the 49ers in the end zone with only seconds remaining. We all love to see a dramatic comeback.

These all make for good stories, but for me, there is one comeback indelibly etched in my memory more than any other. When you are talking comeback, you are talking the 1986 Masters. In the most improbable comeback in the much-storied history of The Masters, a forty-six-year-old "Golden Bear" named Jack Nicklaus came out of hibernation to beat a pack of flat-bellied young cubs.

Augusta National Golf Club was the stage for this high-drama miniseries, a script even Hollywood would not have dared to write. It was just too fairy-tale. If it were fiction, no one would have believed it.

As a major sporting championship, The Masters is in a special class by itself. As Fuzzy Zoeller so aptly put it, "I have never been to heaven and, as I think back on my life, I probably will not get to go. I guess The Masters is as close as I am going to get to heaven." Having been to The Masters several times, I have often felt that Augusta National is what the earth looked like before the fall.

Augusta National is steeped in rich tradition. Bobby Jones. The Amen Corner. The green jacket. Gene Sarazan's double eagle. Blooming azaleas. Budding dogwoods. Lightning-fast greens. Towering pines. The list of past winners—Hogan, Sneed, Nelson, Palmer, Nicklaus, Player, Watson—reads like a veritable who's who of golfing immortals. Not to mention an international field of players who annually make their pilgrimage across the ocean to golf's mecca. Giants like Norman, Ballesteros, Faldo, and Olazabal.

Entering the final round of the 1986 Masters, Jack Nicklaus was a distant four strokes behind the leader. The final day got off to an inauspicious start for the Golden Bear, who missed makeable putts of twenty, eighteen, five, twenty-two, and ten feet. By the time he reached the ninth green, Jack was running out of time.

As Nicklaus strained to read his ten-foot birdie putt on nine, he asked Jackie, his caddie son, "What do you see?"

"*Left* edge," said the eagle-eyed younger cub.

"How about an inch out to the *right*?" replied the now-nearsighted Bear.

They both laughed.

"I figured he saw something I was missing," said Jack, "so we split the difference." Nicklaus just putted it dead straight. And drained the birdie putt.

"That got me started."

A start is an understatement. Sinking that putt was the spark he needed. The competitive fires were suddenly rekindled in Nicklaus's heart.

As Jack teed off on ten, Ken Venturi, the CBS analyst, uttered his now-immortal words, "The Masters starts on the number ten tee on Sunday afternoon." These words never rang truer than they did on that Sunday.

As a global television audience watched, the golfing world was about to witness the greatest comeback in Masters' history. With only nine holes left and still an insurmountable lead to overcome, Jack mounted his comeback.

First, a birdie at the difficult tenth. Then, entering Amen Corner—the apex of challenge in this "cathedral in the pines"—Nicklaus birdied eleven. An eerie hush began to spread across the course.

"Jack's back" could be heard whispered by the patrons. Other galleries began to stop following their favorites in order to follow Jack. No one wanted to miss being an eyewitness of history. Everyone wanted to view the ensuing spectacle.

But just as momentum was building, the iron door of opportunity seemed to slam shut. Nicklaus bogied the formidable twelfth, a testy par three over Rae's Creek.

With his back pinned against the wall, Nicklaus reached down deep inside. There was no quitting in him. This momentary setback at twelve only served to force him into an all-out assault on the course. Jack would now have to fire at every pin.

The Bear rallied with a birdie at thirteen. Followed by a par at fourteen. But par is not good enough when you are playing to win. Standing in the fairway on fifteen—a par five requiring a long second shot over a pond—a pensive Nicklaus set aim on the distant green. Turning to his son, Jackie, he asked, "What do you think an eagle three would do here?" They both smiled.

With the deadly accuracy of an assassin, Jack pulled the trigger. A high power fade landed stiff on the pin. Twelve feet away from an eagle.

The comeback was happening!

With nerves of steel, and with the delicate touch of a surgeon, the charging Bear hovered over this eagle putt. The gallery was so quiet you could hear a pine needle drop. As the golfing world anxiously watched, Jack stroked the eagle putt. It dropped out of sight, center-cut—eagle three.

The Bear was back in the hunt.

At the sixteenth, a par three over another pond, Jack struck a perfect iron, narrowly missing a hole-in-one by mere inches. From three feet away, Nicklaus drained another birdie putt. The explosion of noise was broadcast throughout the entire course. The great Spaniard Severiano Ballesteros, the steely-eyed Texan Tom Kite, and the "Great White Shark" Australian Greg Norman were being rocked by this comeback.

It had been six long years since Nicklaus's last victory in a major championship. It was widely believed that there would never be another. But Nicklaus would not believe the press reports. Victory was within his grasp.

After pulling his tee shot short on seventeen, a par four requiring a precision tee shot around the famous Eisenhower Tree, Nicklaus nailed a dead-eye short iron to within fifteen feet of the flag. Perplexed, Jack concluded that his putt was impossible to read. So what did he do? He squinted and just banged it dead center. The putt wiggled left, bent back right, then dropped in the center cut of the cup. Birdie—and a tie for the lead!

All that remained was the eighteenth, an uphill par four back to the clubhouse. After a perfect tee shot and safe iron to the green, Jack barely missed a long birdie putt. Amid the bedlam of the gallery, Jack tapped in his par and embraced his son. The pair strode triumphantly off the eighteenth green, arm-in-arm.

There was a new leader in the clubhouse!

Tom Kite, Seve Ballesteros, and Greg Norman all withered under the oppressive heat of this late rally. Seve shanked a four iron into a watery grave on fifteen. Kite and Norman both missed makeable putts on eighteen. And the green jacket was back on Jack.

Nicklaus epitomized the essence of never giving up. A never-say-die attitude. Coming out of nowhere. Battling against impossible odds. Pushing down the backstretch. The Golden Bear would not quit. Even when everyone else had counted him out, Jack staged one of the greatest comebacks ever. No, make that *the* greatest comeback.

It is simply The Comeback.

You Can Make a Comeback!

This scene can be a present reality in your Christian life. In the fashion just described, you too can make a comeback. Perhaps you feel so far behind in the Christian race that you think it is impossible to win. You feel so defeated that you think there is no need to sprint to the finish. Maybe you are looking back at wasted years and want to throw in the towel. Perhaps you are thinking, *What is the use trying?*

I have good news. No matter where you are, you can still stage a comeback. Your Christian life can become one of the greatest comeback stories ever witnessed. Why do I say that? Because your failure need not be final. By God's grace, you can come back.

God's Hall of Fame is filled with many comeback stories of people who looked like life had them down, only to rally and bounce back to win by faith in God. By God's help, we can overcome impossible odds to win the crown.

As long as there is time in the race, as long as there is God's grace, as long as there is the will to win, there is the hope of victory.

This book is all about winning God's race. These pages have called you to be a winner where it really counts. In this closing chapter, I call you again to be a winner with God. No matter how far back in the pack you are, you can still win.

I assume that if you are reading this book, you are already a Christian. You are already running God's race. But perhaps you have slowed down to a jog. Maybe you are shuffling along at a complacent pace. Maybe your spiritual fire and passion are gone. I want you to know— you can *still* come back!

In the upcoming pages, I want to lead you in the steps necessary to reenter God's race. I want to help you return to championship form. I want to point you to refocus your eyes on the prize.

In order to do so, I want us to look at 1 Corinthians 9:24-26. Writing as one intimately familiar with the athletic arena, the apostle Paul wrote,

> Do you not know that those who run in a race all run, but only one receives the prize? Run in such a way that you may win. Everyone who competes in the games exercises self-control in all things. They then do it to receive a perishable wreath, but we an imperishable. Therefore I run in such a way, as not without aim; I box in such a way, as not beating the air.

Here is how to reenter the race.

Recommit to Winning God's Race

First, you must recommit to winning God's race. Make winning this race the sole passion of your life. Maybe it once was, but now you have grown cold. Well, recommit to winning the race.

Paul wrote, "Do you not know that those who run in a race all run, but only one receives the prize? Run in such a way that you may win" (1 Corinthians 9:24).

As long as you are in the race, be in it to win it. Not just to finish the race. But to win it. No one just happens to make a comeback and win. Not when he is far behind. Only with a renewed resolve to win can a comeback be accomplished.

If you find yourself far behind in the race, do not give up. Keep on running. You can still win. Do not quit.

Personally, I find it hard to redouble my effort to finish anything I do not think I can win. Why bother if I cannot win? Listen, the truth about God's race is that you can still win. So, recommit to winning. I do not care how far behind you think you are. You can still come back and win. God would never say to *every* believer "Run to win" if every believer did not have a chance to win.

When Paul said, "Run," he used an imperative—an authoritative command. His words come with binding force upon our lives. This is not a suggestion. Nor optional. It is God speaking directly to us. He is saying, "Run! Do not walk. Do not stop. Do not sit down. Run, because you can still win!"

When the hope of winning is extinguished, the competitive drive is gone. Consider Ben Hogan, a longtime sports hero of mine. As a young boy in Fort Worth, Texas, struggling to hit a one iron, I idolized my hometown hero, the "Texas Hawk."

Regarded as the greatest pure striker the game has ever known, Hogan's swing was the envy of the golfing world. But by age fifty-eight, Hogan felt his game was no longer suitable for public display. Not even lucrative offers and the emergence of the Senior Tour could lure him to play competitively. Sure, Hogan still hit practice balls at his Shady Oaks Country Club in Fort Worth. But why would he no longer play any competitive golf?

"There is no use in playing," replied Hogan poignantly, "if you cannot win."

In other words, the thrill of the crowd was not a strong enough

motive for him to get back into competition. Neither was the enticement of money. Nor the love of the game.

Only one thing could get Hogan back out on the links. That was
the possibility of winning. If that prospect was gone, then so was his
drive to compete. Winning—and only winning—was a strong enough
drive for Hogan to compete.

This drive to win is what so many Christians desperately need to
recapture. The reason so many believers have stopped running is because
they do not think they can still win the prize at the end of the race. They
think, *Why bother? I am so far behind I could never win God's crown.*

But the fact is, they can still win. And so can you.

I want us to consider someone in the Bible who fell behind in the
race but made a remarkable comeback. I want us to look at Simon Peter,
the disciple who suffered from foot-in-mouth disease.

During Jesus' earthly ministry, Peter was sprinting along in God's
race. He was the unquestioned leader of the Twelve. He was quick to
forsake all for Christ. He was ready to defend Christ at a moment's
notice.

Then suddenly Simon Peter tripped and stumbled. On the night
of our Lord's arrest, he fell head first, flat on his face. In the heat of the
moment, Peter out-and-out denied the Lord Jesus before—are you
believing this?—a little slave girl.

When she asked Peter if he was one of Jesus' disciples, he abruptly
chided, "I am not" (John 18:17).

Three times, Peter denied the Lord. Finally, he began to curse and
swear, "I do not know this man you are talking about!" (Mark 14:71).

Talk about falling behind in the race. Peter had crashed and burned.
He was like a race-car driver with a flat tire in the Indy 500. He was
being lapped so quickly he was getting dizzy. It was so bad for Peter that
he left the Lord's work and went back to his fishing business.

If anyone looked helplessly behind in God's race, it was Peter. But
guess what? Peter staged a comeback. He made a recommitment to get
back in the race and win. He determined to go all-out toward the finish line. And I believe he won.

Jesus confronted this burly fisherman who had gone back into the fishing business, probing his heart. The Lord asked, "Simon, son of John, do you love Me more than these?" (John 21:15).

"Yes, Lord; You know that I love You," Peter replied, using a word for "love" with lesser strength.

Three times, Jesus asked Peter this searching question. Perhaps once for each of his three denials. And three times, Peter confessed that his love for Christ, weak as it was, was still there. Three times, Jesus recommissioned Peter, "Tend My lambs…Shepherd My sheep…Tend My sheep." In other words, "Get back in the race and run to win. You can do it."

Now cloaked with new humility, Peter made a recommitment to win God's crown. He drove down a stake and purposed from this point forward, "I am going to run to win again." Did God honor this recommitment? He certainly did! Peter became the great preacher of Pentecost. The pillar of the early church. The author of two New Testament books. I would say that is quite a comeback. He went from being a loser to a winner. From a zero to a hero.

Despite his past failure, a future hope burned brightly in Peter's heart—all the way to the finish line. Toward the end of his race, Peter wrote, "And when the Chief Shepherd appears, you will receive the unfading crown of glory" (1 Peter 5:4). His heart was still set on the crown.

If Peter can make a comeback after denying Christ, so can you and I make a comeback. As long as there is the grace of God, we are not out of it. There is still enough time on the scoreboard to pull out a victory. But it must begin with making a decisive recommitment to getting back in the race and winning it.

As you read these words, where are you in your spiritual life? Have you lost your passion? Has your life gotten off track? Have you not been walking with the Lord? I want to urge you to repent—that is, turn your life around—and get back on track to win.

You can do it! You can still win!

Relinquish Control to God

Second, relinquish the control of your life to God. This is the next step of making a comeback. If you are to win, it takes more than a choice of the will to win again. We must exercise self-control and discipline in this endeavor.

Paul wrote, "Everyone who competes in the games exercises self-control in all things" (1 Corinthians 9:25). Self-control is the key here. A disciplined life, strict training, and rigorous self-denial are the marks of any champion.

What is self-control? The word (Greek, *enkrateia*) means restraining one's fleshly lusts. The idea is that of resisting one's sinful appetites. It is a self-mastery, a curbing of one's sinful impulses. It is an ability to keep one's self in check.

Self-control is a fruit of the Spirit (Galatians 5:23). That means only the Holy Spirit can produce self-control within us. So we must relinquish the control of our life to Christ. We must submit to the Holy Spirit and trust Him to grow self-control within us.

With every step of the race, we must make a conscious decision to run by the Spirit, not compete by the flesh (Galatians 5:16). Our natural tendency is to run according to our own sinful inclinations. This means to run energized by selfish desires. To be focused on selfish pursuits. To be empowered by self. But God's Word says we must run according to the Holy Spirit. This means we must be yielded to the Spirit and live for the glory of God. If we are to be empowered by the Spirit, we must be in hot pursuit of the honor of Christ in all things. Controlled by the Spirit.

The self-control we must exercise is a resistance to the carnal impulses listed as the deeds of the flesh—"immorality, impurity, sensuality, idolatry, sorcery, enmities, strife, jealousy, outbursts of anger, disputes, dissensions, factions, envying, drunkenness, carousing" (Galatians 5:19-21). This is what our self-control must oppose.

Here is the paradox of self-control: It comes as a result of surrendering self-control. As we relinquish control, we gain it. As we relinquish the control of our lives to God, He gives us the control over these vices. We can only experience self-control when we give Him control.

We surrender when we present ourselves to God, like an animal sacrifice placed on the altar to Him. Paul wrote, "I urge you, brethren, by the mercies of God, to present your bodies a living and holy sacrifice, acceptable to God, which is your spiritual service of worship" (Romans 12:1). Just as the animal was to be presented wholly and without blemish—that is, not blind, lame, or diseased—so we must present our lives to God. Wholly. Holy. A living sacrifice to God. Ready to love God, serve God, and glory in God.

General William Booth, founder of the Salvation Army, was asked the secret of his amazing Christian life. Booth answered, "I told the Lord that He could have all that there is of William Booth."

That is what we need to give God. All that there is of us. It does not take much to be a winner. Just all there is of us.

In so doing, we must recognize the difference between involvement and commitment. It is more than just going through the motions. Lou Holtz, the former head football coach of Notre Dame, pointed out the difference: "The Kamikaze pilot who was able to fly 50 missions was involved—but not committed."

In what areas—or what one area—do you still wrestle with giving Christ the control? Recognize there is an internal, spiritual battle raging for territorial rights in your life. You need to surrender it to the Lord. Relinquish the control to Him.

Refocus on the Eternal Crown

Third, refocus on the crown. This is the third step for staging a comeback. Athletes who lose sight of the crown slowly fade to the rear of the pack. If that is true in your spiritual life, you need to refocus on the eternal crown. As you do, you will feel a sudden burst of energy that will move you up in the pack. You will find yourself being propelled to victory.

Knowing the powerful motivation of reward, Paul wrote, "They then do it to receive a perishable wreath, but we an imperishable" (1 Corinthians 9:25). In this verse, the apostle contrasts two crowns—one temporal, one eternal—to show the infinitely superior motivation that we, as Christians, have to run God's race. If the Olympic athlete trains strictly and runs sacrificially, all to win a mere temporal crown and brief acclaim, how much more ought we to be motivated to win the incorruptible crown.

Reward has always been a powerful form of motivation, especially in athletics. Today, professional athletes have incentive clauses written into their contracts to help motivate them to elevate the level of their performance. Added cash bonuses will be theirs if they can reach certain levels of excellence. Such as making the all-star team, leading the league in a particular category, or winning the MVP award.

The hope of winning God's crown was always before Paul. This powerful motivation energized the apostle to run his race with supernatural power, even to the end. From a Roman prison Paul wrote, "I have fought the good fight, I have finished the course, I have kept the faith; in the future there is laid up for me the crown of righteousness, which the Lord, the righteous Judge, will award to me on that day; and not only to me, but also to all who have loved His appearing" (2 Timothy 4:7-8).

Like an athlete looking beyond the pain to the prize, Paul looked to receive his crown from Christ Himself. This crown is prepared by God for those who endure faithful to the end. While in prison, Paul remained focused upon the eternal crown.

The Power of Seeing the Goal

R.C. Slocum, a former head football coach of Texas A&M, knew the power of focusing on the goal. Some years back, his fighting Texas Aggies were in Fort Worth, Texas, preparing to play the TCU Horned Frogs in a key Southwest Conference clash. While A&M was in the midst of their afternoon workout the day before the game, Slocum unexpectedly called the team together at midfield. He announced that they were going to load the bus now and ride somewhere special.

Unknowingly, the Texas A&M team was driven an hour away to Dallas to see their season-long goal—the Cotton Bowl. At that time, the winner of the Southwest Conference was annually invited to play before a capacity crowd and a national television audience in the historic Cotton Bowl game.

It occurred to Slocum that many of his younger players had never even seen the Cotton Bowl. So to heighten their motivation, the coach wanted his team to personally see the goal. If they could gaze upon it, that sight would embolden them to achieve it.

As the team bus arrived, the Aggies got out and walked across the storied turf of the Cotton Bowl. This was the "House that Doak Built." A stage where Doak Walker, Joe Montana, Earl Campbell, Roger Staubach, Bo Jackson, and Jim Brown had starred in Cotton Bowls past.

As Slocum gathered the A&M team around him, he peered into the future and said, "Look around, men. This is our goal. Come January first, this is our destiny." Young Aggie eyes were starstruck as they beheld the stadium.

Inspired to new heights, the Aggies exploded on an unsuspecting TCU team the next day, destroying them 44-7. What brought the best out of them? Most insiders will tell you what raised them to a higher level of play was refocusing on the goal.

It is the same in the Christian life. We must never lose sight of the heavenly crown before us. Keeping our eyes on the prize will empower and elevate our Christian lives. It will energize us to win the race.

Where is the focus of your life? Too often we live focused on temporal goals and earthly records. No wonder we are so spiritually unmotivated.

Perhaps reading this book has convicted you that it is time for you to refocus on winning the incorruptible crown. Maybe it is time for you to take your eyes off this world's riches and become intent upon winning heaven's crown.

The Danger of Losing Sight of the Goal

Her name was Florence Chadwick. She was synonymous with women's championship swimming in the 1950s. Florence was the first woman to swim the English Channel both ways. Her time of thirteen hours and twenty minutes from Cape Gris-Nez, France, to Dover, England, established a single-crossing speed record for women. She conquered the route from England to France three times—each time against the tide.

But one of her distance swims was not so successful. She failed to reach her goal. Why? All because she lost sight of it.

The California coast was shrouded in fog the morning of July 4, 1952. Standing on Santa Catalina Island, Florence Chadwick, age thirty-four, waded into the water and began swimming toward the California mainland, twenty-one miles away.

The water was numbing cold that morning. The fog was so thick that Chadwick could hardly see the surrounding boats in her envoy, there to scare the sharks away.

As the hours ticked off, Florence swam on. Fatigue was never a serious problem. It was the bone-chilling, icy water that was threatening to this champion competitor.

More than fifteen hours later, Florence asked to be taken out of the water. She could not swim another stroke that day. Her mother, in a boat alongside her, urged her to go on. So did her trainer. They both knew the mainland had to be very close. Yet Florence, unexpectedly, quit. She got into the boat, short of her goal.

The boat traveled only a very short distance until—sadly—the coastline could be seen. The finish line was right there—so close, yet so far away. Florence had stopped only a half-mile short of the shore.

"If I could have seen the shore," she blurted out, "I would have made it."

Florence Chadwick was not defeated by the cold. Victory did not elude her by fatigue. Rather, it was the fog that had obscured her goal. Her vision was blinded. So she quit.

In like manner, we must be careful never to lose sight of our final goal. If we are defeated, it will not be because of trials or fatigue. If we lose our reward, it will be that distractions limited or obscured our vision. They caused us to fail to see the Lord Jesus Christ and His incorruptible crown.

I urge you—do not allow anything to blind you. If you have lost sight of the goal, refocus on the incorruptible crown. It is essential to a successful comeback.

Realign Life's Priorities

Finally, you must realign your life's priorities. This is the fourth step to a successful comeback. You must bring everything in your life into alignment with pursuing the glory of God and the advancement of His kingdom. Everything you do must be done with singleness of purpose—to win.

Paul wrote, "I run in such a way, as not without aim; I box in such a way, as not beating the air" (1 Corinthians 9:26). In this verse, the apostle used two metaphors. One from the world of running, one from the world of boxing. These two athletic analogies are parallel and make the same point. They both call for singleness of purpose. They urge us to run with clear direction, not wandering around on the track. Every boxer must throw punches that hit their target. They must not wear themselves out shadowboxing. Nor by throwing wild punches that fail to connect.

Picture a championship boxer competing for the crown against a formidable foe. The bell sounds, and the fight begins. As the competitors meet in the center of the ring, this boxer becomes a windmill of wild punches, jabbing randomly in the air. But he never connects. His opponent keeps his guard up, but he never suffers a hit.

Soon this first boxer begins to wear out. He extends all wasted motion. The more he boxes, the more he tires. He can no longer hold his gloves up. His arms are numb. He is now a sitting duck. Helpless. Defenseless. Totally vulnerable. At the mercy of the other boxer, who moves in for the easy kill.

What was the problem? It was certainly no lack of effort or enthusiasm. Just a lack of direction. There was no real aim. No specific target. As a result, he failed to make his shots count.

Does this picture your life? Do you lack a sense of direction? Sure, the zeal and enthusiasm are there. But you are never striking a blow, never connecting a knockout punch.

A story is told of a concert violinist who played in New York's Carnegie Hall. She was asked how she became so skillful. She replied, "Planned neglect." When asked to explain, she stated that she planned to neglect everything that was not related to her goal. If we are to reach our goal, we must purpose to neglect all else.

All our activities must be directed with Spirit-given purpose. Our efforts must be on target. Wasted motions must be trimmed back.

What do you need to plan to neglect? What in your life needs to be brought into alignment with God's kingdom? The expenditure of your time? The use of your money? The competitive drive to excel? Are you involved in too many projects? Too many ministries?

Too often we frantically run from one Bible study to the next conference, trying to find what is missing in our Christian life. Too often we take on more and more rather than concentrating our few punches on the target. Like a boxer with his shirt pulled up over his eyes, we frantically start throwing more punches, but none of them land.

What most of us really need is to better prioritize our time with the Lord, with family, at the office, in our recreation. Too often we prioritize our schedule when we ought to schedule our priorities.

So here is how to make a comeback. Recommit to win God's race. Relinquish control to God. Refocus on the eternal crown. And realign life's priorities. You can still make a comeback with God; you can still win the prize.

Get into the Race!

For some of you reading this book, a comeback is not what you need. What you need is to get in the race for the first time. Some of you have never entered God's race. You do not need a comeback. You need a conversion.

Perhaps you are realizing that you need to get into the starting blocks for the very first time. If that is the case, I can tell you how to do so. You must surrender your life to Jesus Christ. You must turn away from your life of sin and turn to the Lord Jesus, and receive Him by faith into your life.

I will never forget the Sunday a young businessman named Neal Winstead showed up in our church. Neal had it all going for him—he was successful, strikingly handsome, single, likable, winsome. He had everything a person could want—everything, that is, except God.

I had met Neal once years earlier in a wedding I performed. But he had no time for God then. Yet this time around, something was different. Unexpectedly, Neal came to church one Sunday morning and plopped down in the front pew. He looked weary of the rat race, like someone wanting out. As I preached God's Word, the Holy Spirit was definitely working in Neal's heart that Sunday.

A few days later, Neal called. "Pastor, could I take you to lunch?" It was obvious he was searching, restless, and weary. I said, "Sure."

As we sat down to eat lunch, I asked, "Tell me, where are you with God?"

The emptiness in Neal's voice said it all. He was a ripe blade of grain ready to be harvested by the Lord.

I said, "Salvation is like passing through a narrow gate. That narrow gate is Jesus Himself. He alone is the door that leads to salvation. You enter God's kingdom by taking a decisive step of faith. Neal, have you ever come through that gate?"

A mist fogged his eyes.

I pressed further, "A lot of people respect this gate. They have admired its beauty. They have even acknowledged its existence. They have even seen others go through the gate. They have heard other people talk about their experience. But they have never personally entered the gate. Some people walk up to the gate, are ready to go through it, and then back off. They put their toes right up to that gate, but never go through it.

"Neal, where are you? Inside or outside the gate?" I asked.

As one looking into the depth of his own soul, he choked out, "I keep putting my foot right up to that gate, but then back off. I then step right back up to the gate again. But I always back off. Where am I? I am on the outside of the gate."

"Would you like to come through that gate today?" I pressed. "That gate is wide open. Your toes are pushed right up against it. I urge you to take that step of faith and come on through the gate."

"Yes," he replied. "That is exactly what I want to do."

Neal and I drove back to the church, where my office became a delivery room for the birth of a new spiritual babe. The two of us got on our knees, and my friend prayed and committed his life to Christ. This young man came through the narrow gate into God's kingdom.

He stepped out of the rat race…and into the right race.

He was born again.

Our lives are filled with many decisions. What to wear? What to eat? Where to go? What to do? What to buy? Who to marry? Where to work? Many decisions we make are important; other decisions are less pivotal. But the one single most important decision you will ever make is the one to step through the narrow gate and enter God's race.

Perhaps you find yourself standing at the starting blocks. Will you remain a mere spectator of the race? Or will you get in the race? Will you take that step of faith this moment and come to Christ?

Are you in the race?

Are you in it to win it?

Notes

Chapter 7—Starting Blocks and Stumbling Blocks

1. Michael Green, ed., *Illustrations for Biblical Preachers* (Grand Rapids: Baker, 1989), 289.

2. Green, *Illustrations for Biblical Preachers*, 379.

Chapter 8—You Don't Have to Go to Boston to Run a Marathon

1. Lloyd John Ogilvie, *Your Will, God's Will* (Eugene, OR: Harvest House, 1989), 34.

2. A.W. Tozer, as quoted by John Blanchard, *Gathered Gold* (Phillipsburg, NJ: Evangelical Press, 1985), 203.

3. J.I. Packer, *Hot Tub Religion* (Wheaton, IL: Tyndale, 1988), 114.

4. R.C. Sproul, "God or Chance?" from the sermon series Live from The Falls Church (Falls Church, VA), Ligonier Ministries, 1986.

Chapter 10—Keep Your Eyes on the Prize!

1. Adrian Rogers, "How to Be Filled with the Holy Spirit," sermon preached at Bellevue Baptist Church (Cordova, TN), May 6, 1973.

Chapter 11—Benched, Booted, and Disqualified

1. John MacArthur, *Shepherdology* (Chicago: Moody, 1989), 224.

2. Pamela McGee, letter in *Los Angeles Times* (November 9, 1991), C6.

About the Author

Dr. Steven J. Lawson is the Senior Pastor of Christ Fellowship Baptist Church in Mobile, Alabama. He is the Professor of Preaching at The Master's Seminary, a Teaching Fellow with Ligonier Ministry, and the President of OnePassion Ministries. He is a graduate of Texas Tech University (BBA), Dallas Theological Seminary (ThM), and Reformed Theological Seminary (DMin). A former sportswriter with the Texas Rangers and the Dallas Cowboys, Steve and his wife, Anne, have four grown children.